Chan

A season i

C000193853

Mike Bayly

Blackline|Press

First published in 2010 by Blackline Press
This second edition published 2011 by Blackline Press
Copyright © 2010 Blackline Press
Copyright in text & photographs © 2010 Mike Bayly
FRONT COVER Chippenham Town FC © Matt Smith

ISBN 978-0-9563238-3-5

www.blacklinepress.com
Blackline Press, 15 Lister Road, IPSWICH IP1 5EQ
Info@blacklinepress.com

Changing Ends

A season in non-league football

Mike Bayly

This book is dedicated to the memory of Tony Kempster, who sadly passed away in 2009. Tony was, and still is, regarded as the godfather of non-league statistics and is deeply missed by a community of fans who have come to view his website as the definitive guide to the semi-professional game.

www.tonykempster.co.uk

All author's profits will be donated to Cancer Research

Contents

Foreword

I was born in September 1975. Football was certainly a different game back then. West Ham United were FA Cup holders, Manchester United had just returned to Division 1 after an inglorious season in Division 2. Scotland, not England, were qualifying for international tournaments on a regular basis. Hooliganism was rife, grounds were falling to pieces, star players went drinking with fans, and someone told Coventry City that brown shirts were a good idea for a football kit. This was football a generation ago. It was also, so it transpired, the sport I was to dedicate the rest of my life to.

According to the family photo album (a hymn to child abuse if the hairstyles and clothing choices were anything to go by) I kicked my first football at the age of two though, unlike many children of that age, I wasn't being groomed by a father wanting to live vicariously through his son; not the sporting type, my dad's passion was radio transmitters. To him, football was something played by other people. In fact, looking back, it's a wonder I ever developed an interest in the game at all. No one in the house followed it, I didn't attend a live game until I was eleven years old, and my earliest memory of televised football was a rather nebulous encounter between France and Spain in the 1984 European Championship Final. The first match I actively remember watching (and getting excited about) was the Liverpool v Everton FA Cup Final in 1986, which was the equivalent of taking TV heroin. It was like I had been denied this wonderful all-consuming experience my entire life and, whether it was Ian Rush cracking camera lenses or Jimmy Tarbuck cracking jokes, clearly the day had a profound effect on me. And so it began. Later that year came the Mexico '86 World Cup, during which time I monopolised the television set on empty promises of doing the dishes or tidying my room. Although tolerant of my new found passion, my mum drew the line at me watching Paraguay v Iraq. "Iraq?" she said incredulously, "enough is enough". I am not sure why Iraq were considered the nadir of international football in our household, or if their presence in the tournament was so obscure that compulsive viewing was tantamount to insanity, but I wasn't happy. I could have pointed out that my mother was dismally addicted to Australian soap operas so any attempt to undermine my viewing choice was laughable hypocrisy, but I was eleven years old so I didn't. Instead, I did what all eleven year olds illogically do when trying to prove a point and refused to eat my dinner, going to bed both hungry and furious.

Of course, there were earlier more innocent moments. My earliest recollection of football fandom was scrawling "Liverpool FC" on to a boot shaped pencil case when I was seven years old, having somewhat incongruously crossed out "Carlisle United" in red felt tip pen. Given I was raised in Hatfield, Hertfordshire, a veritable hotbed of Spurs and Arsenal loyalties, it makes both choices somewhat surprising; although Liverpool's dominance domestically and in Europe might explain the former, it will never fully explain a six year old child's interest in (or even awareness of) a team languishing in the old second division at the other end of the country. That said, I do recall having an almost unhealthy fascination with motorways as a child and always remember the M6 not only being the longest high speed road in Britain at the time but also terminating at Carlisle which, possibly, gave this otherwise non-descript provincial town a somewhat ethereal aura. I should add that in the last couple of years, the motorway has undergone a long planned extension to Gretna, should anyone of a pedantic disposition be reading.

In 1984 the family moved to Ludlow, south Shropshire. Accordingly, the first match I ever saw live was Hereford United v Hartlepool in Division 4 during the 1986-87 season. They say your first live match is like losing your virginity, in that you will always cherish it no matter how bad the performance was technically. Hereford won 4-0 but, for me, the game stood out for two slightly more trivial reasons. Firstly, I missed the opening goal whilst going to the toilet. A Hereford fan standing next to me at the urinal found this amusing, advising caustically that I had missed a once in a lifetime experience. The second and most notable aspect of the game was that the Hartlepool goalkeeper looked like Grizzly Adams. Whereas the Hereford 'keeper was a slight, anaemic looking chap, his opposite number was an absolute leviathan, all belly, beard, and monstrous kicks. What was, on the face of it, just a fat bloke in goal assumed Marvel comic proportions to me. A child's first memories of a football match shouldn't be an outsize man in ill-fitting tracksuit bottoms but mine was and the peculiarity of it, not to mention the swearing, cigarette smoke and total football that ripped Hartlepool apart, had set the wheels in motion.

For reasons I genuinely can't remember, the next game I attended was Kidderminster Harriers v Welling United in the 1987-88 GM Vauxhall Conference campaign. Kidderminster had finished the 1985-86 season in third place in the Conference, scoring ninety nine goals, spearheaded by the legendary strike force of Kim Casey (who finished the season on an astonishing 73 goals) and Paul 'Ocker' Davies. Under the management of Graham Allner, they were an attacking flair side, albeit one prone to laughable lapses of concentration which would often cost dear in big games. To be fair, I didn't know any of this at the time. All I did know is Kidderminster were a local side who occasionally appeared on Central TV and whose floodlights could be seen from the Forest Glades leisure centre where we used to go swimming.

My first recollection of Kidderminster's ground, Aggborough, was the obvious step down in size and stature from Hereford's Edgar Street. Given Edgar Street was a mess of corrugated iron and crumbling brickwork it spoke volumes of the architectural prowess of the Worcestershire club's stadium at the time. Although a non league blueprint nowadays, the Aggborough of 20 years ago was a wholly different affair. Aesthetically, it was confusing; apparently someone planned to build a football stadium, got bored halfway through and finished with a motocross track. The main stand had no seats and the affectionately known 'Cowshed' opposite housed embittered Woodbine smoking men whose entire vocabulary consisted of the words "bloody rubbish" spoken in diluted Black Country tones. Of course, these were mere idiosyncrasies. Kidderminster thrashed Welling 5-2, and for whatever reason I was hooked.

Supporting Kidderminster wasn't easy in a school dominated by the Manchester Uniteds and Liverpools of the world; wearing a Harriers' scarf was tantamount to being homosexual. But the truth of the matter is I had no interest in supporting the big sides. I couldn't see them, couldn't feel them and couldn't empathise with them. The more my schoolmates took the piss (and to be honest it was mostly in jest rather than anything malicious) the more it galvanised my support. The late '80s was also an age of limited TV football coverage, which no doubt had a major impact on my choices. Without the subliminal propaganda and blanket coverage of the top flight, I was more likely to see regional highlights of Walsall's League Cup game with Chester City than a clash between Man United and Liverpool. The BBC's *Match of the Day* coverage was sporadic and often limited to FA Cup games, whilst ITV's *The Match*, aside from a few memorable games including Arsenal's astonishing title win at Liverpool, offered games of rather poor quality. Then again it didn't stop my classmates expressing their allegiances to the behemoths of the game; maybe I was just odd.

Whatever the case, football was to shape my life more than I could ever realise. It was to be the pain, the pleasure, the pathos that would steer me like an invisible rudder, drifting on an emotional tide, sometimes running aground, but always setting sail again with an optimistic wind. Football fans are guided by seasons not years. And in these seasons I find the words of A E Housman the most apt, the most poignant, for expressing a love for something that I would constantly return to, and will live on long after I am gone.

And since to look at things in bloom
Fifty springs are little room

There was no escape now: I was in for life.

Introduction

The 18th April 2009 will be recorded as an epiphany in my life; it is the day I fell in love with football again. It was a spring afternoon. I was standing in the forecourt of the Beveree Stadium, home to Hampton and Richmond Borough FC, watching the crowds gather excitedly around the tiny ramshackle ground. People of all ages filtered past, from sparkly eyed pensioners to young families with toddlers called Henry, the whole town seemingly descending on this unassuming part of south west London in an orgy of partisan support. Rival fans draped in flags and scarves exchanged jokes without the officious spectre of authority. Something strange was happening. I was at a football match and I was being swept away by a visceral tide of joy. As I squeezed through the turnstile, the sun smiled and stretched its fingers, caressing the earth with tingling fingertips as if warm with ecstasy; the wind blew a kiss to the trees as their branches danced a soft hula. For the first time in a long time I felt like a football supporter. It was a perfect storm of emotion.

Why I should find myself in south west London on the above date is really the climax to an increasingly familiar story of supporter disillusionment. But it is also one of personal awakening. Kidderminster Harriers were always my first love but, although a keen follower of the club and non league football throughout my formative years, I was not what you might call a dedicated fan. A combination of weekend work, exams and limited finances restricted my attendance somewhat, which meant I had to live out my time on the terraces vicariously, usually by calling the premium rate GM Vauxhall Conference club call line (for which I often got a good hiding) or poring over match reports in the local *Sporting Argus*. By the time I left Ludlow in 1994 to attend university in Sheffield I had, by my own admission, become something of an armchair fan.

It pains me to write this now, but in the years that followed my departure to Sheffield I became very fair-weather. I enrolled as a student member at Sheffield Wednesday with my new found friends and was awestruck by the presence of my all-time hero Chris Waddle, fortnightly visits of teams like Manchester United and Liverpool, and the cavernous, if somewhat infamous, Hillsborough Stadium. In my defence, an eight hour round trip to every home Harriers match combined with a distinct lack of interest from my friends made the prospect of repeat solo visits somewhat unpalatable.

There are people who regularly travel the length and breadth of the country to support teams on their own, and they have my fullest admiration. The truth is I simply didn't have the discipline to do it and, with SKY Sports additionally feeding me live football at every conceivable opportunity, it was a lot easier to sit at home and be sucked into the vortex. Although it sounds a contradiction, my passion for Kidderminster (however one defines that) was still there for all to see, none more so than on Saturday 1st May 2000 when I spent half an hour watching *Soccer Saturday* in the Meadowhall branch of John Lewis waiting to see if the Harriers could clinch promotion to the then Division 3. They did, albeit via a 1-0 defeat to Woking, which sent me into a delirious fist clenched frenzy, no doubt causing the unbeknown bystanders (mostly bored looking men in the cookware section) to view me with an understandable degree of caution and amusement.

I did pop up on the Harriers' radar from time to time but my appearances on the terraces were sporadic to say the least. It was not until April 2006 that I realised just how distanced I had become from the club when my friend Terry got married to his then wife, Rhoda. Breaking with protocol, they wed in a local Kidderminster church before heading to Aggborough to watch the Harriers play Aldershot Town, still resplendent in full wedding attire. The local paper, *The Kidderminster Express and Shuttle*, had a field day, and the pictures even made the populist football programme *Soccer AM* (insofar as I emailed them to the show). It was the first time I had been to watch them play in a long time and I felt like a man returning home to his wife having spent the last few years living a very public affair. The place had changed and sadly so had I. The regulars I knew in my youth who stood on the terraces were gone, the current batch of players looked totally apathetic and disinterested, and the 0-4 score line at half time, and the subsequent indifference I felt towards it, only compounded my growing belief that I was no longer part of this club. They had even had a whole new stand built which I knew nothing about. I felt sad and I felt fraudulent. So I did what I had done for the last ten years; I went to the pub and watched *Soccer Saturday* on SKY.

Looking back I wonder if my feelings at the Kidderminster game were symptomatic of a general malaise I was developing toward the game, or at least certain aspects of it. I still followed the Harriers through increasing media streams available to the tech-savvy football fan and still spent hours reading, and re-reading, national and regional football results in the Sunday papers. But I had spent the last decade graduating from live fan to armchair fan to Sunday session in the pub fan and, in retrospect, realise the camaraderie of those days probably outweighed the actual football content. Given my slightly esoteric team choice as a youngster, I was denied the opportunity of going to the match with 'the lads' so any chance to watch 'live' football with my friends was welcomed with open arms. Football for me now was ostensibly the Premiership, or whatever output SKY dictated. The problem was, when I started watching these live games in isolation, away from the machismo of the public house, I realised that I was really rather bored by it all.

In 2005 I moved to London, which gave me the chance to watch a host of top flight teams, often on a complimentary basis through a contact at work. Yet the experience was increasingly alienating and uncomfortable. As far back as 2003 I had first started to question the motives behind those running top flight clubs during a visit to Stamford Bridge. Chelsea were playing Leeds United and during the halftime break the big screen in the corner was advertising a host of corporate facilities available at the ground. After reeling off the virtues of their "enviable location" and "fantastic conferencing facilities" or even their "world class hotel and leisure complex" it ended by saying Stamford Bridge was "also home to the famous Chelsea Football Club" as if it were merely an afterthought. I was watching the match surrounded by men wearing long Armani overcoats with briefcases wedged between their legs. They clapped politely when Chelsea scored. There was something very unnerving about the whole experience.

As it transpired, this experience would signal the decline of my long running affair with the beautiful game. I stopped watching increasingly protracted and dull televised matches in favour of *Rick Stein's Food Heroes*. I read with increasing disquiet the manner in which clubs would throw vulgar sums of money at mercenary self-important players in an attempt to buy trophies, and then try to recoup money by inflating ticket prices. I cringed when managers fielded reserve teams in cup competitions or talked about promotion in purely financial terms. I started to hate the pomposity and the arrogance of the Premiership and hyperbolic endorsement of its virtues by a sycophantic mass media. Propaganda became the name of the day; football started in 1992; the Premiership was the holy grail of football. Money was infiltrating the game like a cancer, removing the element of competition and conventional ethics, dictating kick off times, pricing fans out, turning players into celebrity millionaires and causing those entrusted with the well-being of our clubs to mortgage decades of social history in the quest for personal gain. The fundamental demographic of the game was shifting like a rogue ice shelf where changing crowds sat inside out of town stadiums amidst talk of revenue streams and product loyalty. The sport was turning into a soap opera of *Dallas* style proportions where millionaire speculators reduced the worth of clubs to crude business parlance. I just didn't recognise top flight football anymore as the same game I grew up with. My memories, my fondest memories of the sport I loved and cherished, were of people standing on terraces exchanging jokes inside archaic yet beautiful grounds, where fans and players were separated solely on ability and not lifestyle and in many cases knew each other by name. The spectre of hooliganism and caged terracing may have gone but I took no solace in the laundered virtue of corporate white wash. I decided the only way to reconcile all this was to go back to my roots. I needed to feel something for football again and replace the emptiness I had inside.

3rd March 2009. Kidderminster was playing away at Woking, which from the perspective of someone living in London represented one of the easier chances to see them play. Despite my last visit to Aggborough to watch them play being a rather depressing affair, the chance to watch the club away from home in new surroundings gave the match greater meaning. On arrival at Woking's ground the weather, which was already fairly horrendous, became even worse[1]. The away fans' section is usually an exposed area of terracing (or at least it was now - there is a fair chance the wind on the night could have blown the roof off before I arrived) to the far side of the ground, but the stewards had mercifully granted all away fans accommodation under the stand behind the goal, which provided the amusing site of seeing 100 or so diehard (or maybe foolhardy) Harriers' fans stood next to the most vocal element of the Woking support. The somewhat claustrophobic environment created some excellent exchanges of banter without the merest hint of aggression. Amongst the other fans on the terraces was an AFC Wimbledon follower who was "checking out next season's opposition" and the Woking website editor who stood there, rain from his forehead dripping into a drink masquerading as coffee, ruminating on how football makes people endure the most torrid of conditions for just a few minutes of pleasure.

---

[1] http://www.youtube.com/watch?v=2sIbBOFDT5U

By the time the game kicked off, the pitch was virtually unplayable. The crowd kept their spirits up despite the game being a complete farce, with the ball sticking in puddles and players sliding and falling over the pitch like new born calves. Almost inevitably, the referee called a halt to proceedings shortly into the second half. The decision met with considerable vitriol but there was really little choice in the matter. The most vocal and perturbed component of the crowd was the Wimbledon fan, who I ended up sharing a taxi back to the station with.

Aside from the rain, the force ten gales, and the fact we weren't refunded our admission money for a match that bore more resemblance to *It's a Knock Out*, the trip had been a complete success. It felt different to last time; I suddenly felt part of something again, like I had membership to a small and exclusive club that only a few people knew about. The clutch of fans huddled together under a corrugated roof in this desolate windswept saturated ground only added to the sense of camaraderie. There was no glory here, no pretence, just two sets of fans standing on the terraces supporting their teams in the most adverse of conditions. I wanted more, but this time somewhere completely different, somewhere where I could see if my enjoyment of this match wasn't merely blinded by a dubious allegiance.

I had been keeping a close eye on the Conference South and Conference North tables throughout the 2008-09 campaign as any promoted teams would offer opposition for Kidderminster the following season. Scouring the remaining fixtures for the leading clubs one game stood out in the Southern section as being an absolute belter, namely the match between second place Hampton & Richmond Borough and table toppers AFC Wimbledon. To add an extra element of spice, the clash was a local derby (in geography if nothing else) with the winner almost certain to gain promotion to the Conference National.

The match was to be played on 18th April 2009. I had been offered free club level tickets for Chelsea v Everton the same day but had been so disenchanted with my last trip there (the VIP tickets cost nearly £9,000 a season and it was like watching a game in the clubhouse of a Masonic Lodge) that I made a choice - in retrospect a rather spontaneous one - to watch a match that might be a little more down to earth.

Given the huge support AFC Wimbledon were likely to bring, the game was declared all ticket so I eagerly phoned the Hampton box office (box being the operative word) where a very enthusiastic member of staff advised me I had obtained one of the last spaces available. I thought at first this was just a ruse to generate interest but the next day the club website indicated the game was a 3,500 sell out. I was genuinely excited. For a club averaging 600 fans at home these were unparalleled times and the match offered everything I could have wished; vociferous support, full blooded commitment, a controversial last minute equaliser, and a pitch invasion. AFC Wimbledon continued their march through the non league divisions and for Hampton it was the lottery of the play offs. I wish I could articulate my feelings of the day to give shape to the joy it gave me, but I fear such literary talent is beyond my grasp. I have always been one touched by the smallest of sentiments and it was the little things that made this day so memorable; the friendly and approachable staff outside the ground, two elderly ladies selling raffle tickets, the sense of community togetherness, the fact you could stand and move freely around the ground, the loudspeaker plea asking for people to join the supporters' committee, the programme notes advertising for volunteer match day staff to keep the club running. Even the woman in the refreshment kiosk looked like Jane Seymour. I suspect these scenes resemble many up and down the country and that this regalement comes across as slightly gushing, but if felt like the club actually wanted me there, that, if I chose to, I could become an important and valued member of this small suburban outfit, rather than an anonymous spectator or a quantifiable accounts statistic. The whole experience obviously had a profound effect on me; I even wrote to the club the next day thanking them for such a good day out.

A few weeks later, with the season over and no international tournament to keep me stimulated, I started re-reading David Conn's brilliant book *The Beautiful Game: searching for the soul of football*. One chapter on Glossop North End, who currently play in the North West Counties League, really moved me. In a tome that paints a fairly depressing picture of our national game, the Glossop essay stood out because it focused on a set of volunteer staff who keep a small yet famous club going against all the financial odds. Books on the perilous state of our game are being turned out with worrying alacrity with many commentators, such as Conn and John Samuels (*The Beautiful Game is Over*), providing persuasive argument that the game is teetering on the brink of oblivion. Given my recent experiences at the Woking and Hampton match, from a man who is openly critical about many aspects of the modern game, it struck me this may not be the case. The question as I saw it, was what do people mean when they refer to "the beautiful game" in this country?

The mass media tends to view football, or at least a barometer of the football climate, solely in terms of the professional game and, more often than not, the Premiership. This is all well and good, but it rather ignores the semi-professional and amateur organisations that have existed in this country since the game first took root. The FA estimates there are nearly 7,000 registered clubs in the English Football League System, a structured pyramid with the Premiership at the top, stretching down 21 levels to amateur park football at the bottom. In theory, any club in the pyramid can seek promotion through the leagues assuming the correct finances and facilities are in place. At levels 5-11 of the Football League System sits the National League System, which incorporates the first seven 'Steps' below the Football League. The National League System incorporates over 1,500 clubs and 91 league competitions (see diagram on page 20) and its members are eligible for entry to national competitions such as the FA Cup, FA Trophy and FA Vase, assuming certain criteria is met. In light of these statistics, it could be argued that viewing the national game in terms of a handful of professional clubs is somewhat folly. Granted, the teams in the Premiership and Football League account for the vast amount of supporter allegiance in this country, but even conservative estimates would place around 250,000 fans who regularly watch non league football, week in, week out. Is it really possible to make such sweeping generalisations about our national sport when it is so far reaching and so deliciously varied? Maybe it was time somebody tried to find out.

When I told my mate Will I was writing a book on the non league game he asked why, and for a while I struggled to give a definitive answer. Certainly non league football has never known better coverage. There is a national Sunday paper, *The Non League Paper*, a non league podcast on the BBC Website[1], a host of professional non league websites with up to the minute news and match reports as well as an infinite amount of blogs and fan sites dedicated to the semi-professional game. The evolution of the internet means that anyone with a basic aptitude for IT and an opinion can

---

[1] http://www.bbc.co.uk/podcasts/series/nonleague/

masquerade as a writer or journalist, so where exactly did this proposed book fit into the grand scheme of things?

In order to give the work integrity, I realised the best option was to be totally transparent. I do not have an encyclopaedic knowledge on non league football, and I am not a diehard on the terraces. I am someone who grew up supporting a non league team, flirted with the professional game, spent years being an armchair fan, became utterly disillusioned with the sport and then found salvation back where I started. I am hardly a model fan, at times I am even a raging hypocrite, but after my visits to Woking and Hampton, coupled with all the negativity that is engulfing our national game, I felt compelled, almost obliged, to dig beneath the surface and see if football - from recreation park and beyond - really was in the sorry state that so many commentators would have us believe.

First and foremost this is an account of the non league game from a man going back to his (grass) roots after a long time away. Beyond that, it is the journey of a fan looking to see what else the game has to offer beyond the Premiership and Football League. There are no hypotheses to prove or agendas to fill, though it is highly likely that the more pertinent aspects of the wider game will be discussed as I travel round the country. Yes, I might be biased, and, yes, there is a Road to Damascus element inherent, but there is a world of football out there that I, and many others, still know very little about. This may sound disingenuous but twelve months ago I had never even heard of the National League System, never mind the dozens of leagues and teams which create it. If I wrote this as a hardcore non league fan the book may lack a frame of reference, so in many ways my layman approach can be seen as a bonus not a hindrance.

In terms of approach, the *modus operandi* includes attending a match, documenting the sights, sounds, feelings and experiences of those involved, and then bringing in wider issues such as supporter owned clubs, the role of football clubs in smaller communities and how the non league game survives in a country dominated by a powerful few. In terms of which teams to feature this is a bit trickier and I readily concede that with so many options available will be as much about personal bias as anything else. In order to delineate the sample pool, the book will focus on teams within the National League System and will include at least one club at every step, across most of the major non league competitions. In terms of actual clubs, there are certain issues I want to explore but as much as anything it will be about how

I feel nearer the time, where the book is taking me, and who is actually available to speak to.

As a fan I am excited, as a first time author I am trepidatious. To anyone reading this, I hope we both enjoy it.

The National League System 2009-2010

Reproduced with kind permission of the Football Association

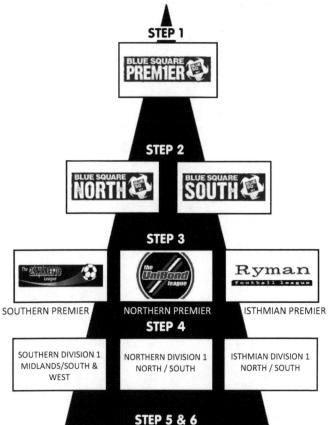

STEP 1

BLUE SQUARE PREM1ER

STEP 2

BLUE SQUARE NORTH   BLUE SQUARE SOUTH

STEP 3

SOUTHERN PREMIER   NORTHERN PREMIER   ISTHMIAN PREMIER

STEP 4

SOUTHERN DIVISION 1 MIDLANDS/SOUTH & WEST	NORTHERN DIVISION 1 NORTH / SOUTH	ISTHMIAN DIVISION 1 NORTH / SOUTH

STEP 5 & 6

Combined Counties,East Midlands Counties, Eastern Counties, Spartan South Midlands , Sussex County Essex Senior, Hellenic, Kent, Wessex, West Midlands, Midland Combination, Midland Football Alliance, North West Counties, United Counties, Northern Counties East, Northern League, South West Penisular,Western.

STEP 7

Anglian Combination, Bedford & District, Cambridgeshire County, Central Midlands, Cheshire Alliance, Dorset Premier, Essex & Suffolk Border, Essex Olympian, Gloucestershire County, Hampshire, Herts Senior County, Kent County, Leicestershire, Liverpool Combination, Manchester, North Berkshire, Northamptonshire Combination, Northern Alliance, Oxfordshire Senior, Peterborough & District, Reading, Somerset County, Staffordshire, Suffolk & Ipswich, Surrey Elite Intermediate, Wearside.

Ebbsfleet United v Kidderminster Harriers

Conference National – Step 1
Saturday 15th August 2009

Final Score: 0-0
Attendance: 865

I've never been one who believes in fate, just occasional coincidence. Fate suggests predetermined governance of our lives and as an atheist I would have to question who is pulling the strings. If there are external forces at work, I subscribe to the Durkheimian school of puppetry rather than any notion of a celestial being playing Geppetto in the sky. So, it was with striking coincidence that the first match I planned to cover for this odyssey involved Kidderminster Harriers. It was a nice coincidence, but nothing more. I had wanted to review Ebbsfleet United after they became the first ever sports club to be run by an online internet community. In this respect, Ebbsfleet were the main chat show highlight and Kidderminster the provincial guest asked to stay behind and bask in the A-list aura.

My brother Richard, a fellow Kidderminster fan, had joined me for the first match of the new season. On pulling into Northfleet station, he voiced serious doubts we were actually in the right place. Although my younger sibling attended a more cynical finishing school, I placed good faith in the directions on the club website, even though stepping off the train at Northfleet feels part of some elaborate practical joke, to the point where you expect Jeremy Beadle (or his spiritual incarnation) to magically appear dressed as a ticket inspector *avec* comedy beard. There is, to put it bluntly, just nothing there. In the distance stood Ebbsfleet International, a grand sounding terminus on the newly constructed cross-channel line, which cut a space age slash through the Kent countryside. It was hot, dry and there was no noise.

Given it was only midday, the first logical step was to find a pub, ideally one in close proximity to Ebbsfleet's ground that showed live sport. Chelsea were playing Hull City at midday on SKY, which gave Rich and I a chance to share in our mutual apathy toward Richard Keys, the king of subjugated hyperbole. The first public house we happened upon, the boarded up and angry looking Coopers Arms, could hardly have offered a less ingratiating welcome to the town and gave the entire place a distinctly *Westworld* feel.

There was another pub, The Rose, about a hundred yards away with a SKY Sports banner flapping boorishly across its brickwork, but I have always been wary of drinking establishments that look like someone has set up a bar in their front room. Devoid of inspiration, we ventured into the local newsagents, partly for light refreshment, partly for direction, and partly for the comforting assurance of seeing another human being.

Descending the hill from the station, the floodlights of Ebbsfleet's Stonebridge Road soon came into view. I have always been enchanted by floodlights. They are by definition suggestive of a ground and, therefore, a football club. There is a rush of excitement, like emotional Viagra, on seeing their grand structures emerge, even when they transpire to be a well illuminated railway siding. For me, floodlights are like urban lighthouses, symbolic of life and spirit and a totemic monument to so many endearing passions. Unfortunately modern stadia design has all but done away with them, the preference being well organised rows of spotlights embedded in the stand perimeters. There is something very sad about this seemingly insignificant transition, like a part of our football identity and culture is being eroded, and lower and non league teams seem to represent the last outpost of these historical stadium pieces. For whatever reason, football grounds seem more like football grounds with floodlights; without them they lack an identity and slip into the pool of generic entertainment arena.

Of course, this is all a slightly rose tinted viewpoint. To view anything at a distance or through a flash frame in a passenger seat allows a degree of artistic interpretation and imagery. The close up reality can be somewhat more stoical. Arriving at a locked ground three hours before kick-off is an unsettling experience. Non league grounds can be quiet at the best of times and seeing them dormant, still and void of life, is like seeing someone you care for in a coma. Football grounds, especially those of a more 'rustic' persuasion, need people in and around them, not just to make them alive, but to also detract from their more obvious lack of aesthetics.

Ebbsfleet's ground stands on the corner of a roundabout and over the years has been enshrouded by industrial buildings and flats for young professionals, no doubt sold on the notion it will whisk them to the bright lights of London in a matter of minutes and away from the artificial satellite environment that property economics create. Next to the ground was that most ubiquitous of establishments, the pub with SKY Sports, which most fans gravitate towards for a pre- or post-match pint. We had arrived almost comically early and, in keeping with the day so far, The Plough public house bore no sign of life. Prepared to sit on the benches outside and wait for opening time in the guise of one desperate for some alcoholic relief, we wandered over, only to be greeted by an amiable and weathered looking gentleman in paint splattered clothes who allowed us inside and took an order of drinks. I couldn't quite establish if he was a punter, a workman, both or neither, but the fact the place was closing for redecoration suggested he was a labourer of some description. I wasn't going to enquire any further anyway; I am always wary of anyone who has more tattoos than teeth.

I had arranged to meet local journalist and club Vice President Charles Webster at around 1pm, via a very helpful young lady who had responded to my request for an interview. I left my apoplectic brother watching Hull beating Chelsea ("I should have got Stephen Hunt for my fantasy league team": repeat reactionary and irrational early season self-doubt *ad infinitum*) and made my way to the ground, which was now showing signs of life.

Charles is an Ebbsfleet stalwart and lifelong fan of the club, having first watched them with his father over fifty years ago, almost as long as the club has been in existence. For the most part of their history, at least until recently, success has been relatively limited and their presence in non league football largely innocuous. The club started out life as Gravesend & Northfleet FC, following a merger between Gravesend United and Northfleet United in 1946. They moved to Gravesend's Stonebridge Road ground, which remains their home today, with their first ever home game against Hereford United where they ran out 3-0 winners in front of over 5,000 fans. Despite full time investment and an ambitious board, it wasn't until 1957-58 that the club experienced league success, with manager Lionel Smith's cavalier side claiming the Southern League title and scoring over 130 league and cup goals along the way. Like many embryonic sides, success was fleeting, and the 1960s proved a turbulent time for fans of the club, despite achieving a 4th round FA Cup replay at Sunderland. In 1967 the entire board resigned *en masse*, leaving a legacy of considerable debts and a ground in need of improvement.

The 1970s picked up slightly, with a Southern League title win in 1974-75. Their improved standing in the league meant they qualified as founder members of the newly formed Alliance Premier League (later Vauxhall

Conference and now Blue Square Premier) in 1979-80, finishing a creditable 5th in its first season. Unfortunately the cycle of history was to repeat itself. The club was relegated in 1981 and again in 1985-86, putting the existence of the side in severe doubt. A new group of directors under Chairman Lionel Blair stepped in to save the club and promotion to the Premier Division followed in 1988-89, along with a best ever FA Trophy run.

Relegation followed again in the early '90s, reinforcing the team's reputation as something of a yo-yo side, although there was a highlight in the 1995-96 season when the club reached the FA Cup 3rd round proper only to lose 3-0 to Aston Villa at Villa Park. In May 1997 the club transferred to the Ryman League in an attempt to cut costs and, after a few non-descript seasons in mid-table, landed the Ryman League Championship in 2001-02, following an enthralling battle with Canvey Island. Local legend has it that a crunch match between the two sides in April 2002 was watched by over 6,000 fans, some 2,000 more than the official attendance suggested.

As well as being match day announcer, fanzine writer and Vice President, Charles writes for local publication *The Kentish Times* and reports for Radio Kent. I met him in his usual gantry position, located high up in the main stand with a Zeus-like demeanour. This was the first time I had interviewed anybody about football since I was eleven years old, which spoke volumes of my own journalistic credentials. On that occasion it was recording the thoughts of my classmate Michael Woodcock, who had scored a couple of tremendous goals against the local senior school. History will record I had toe-poked a third in a 3-0 win. The tape recorded interview was sent to the *Ludlow Advertiser* in an optimistic attempt to put the story into print. It never came to fruition. My then teacher, Mrs Finney, tried to console me by saying "you still write very good poetry" but it was no use. I turned my back on sports reporting indefinitely. Telling a failed football writer he is good at haikus is like telling a failed Man United trialist he could always get a job in the club shop.

We spoke at length about the recent name change of the club (in May 2007 a name change of Ebbsfleet United was announced, presumably to cash in on the massive regeneration of the area spearheaded by the new Ebbsfleet International station on the Eurostar line) and the realistic ambitions of the club given that crowds hovered around the 1,000 mark every season.
"The ambition has to be the Football League, though we would need bigger gates which would no doubt come if we got there. The club is important to

the community; I have no doubt of that. We took over 25,000 fans to Wembley for the trophy win against Torquay, so we know the support is there. Also, the club is famous worldwide now because of the internet based takeover."

My first dabbling with the internet was in 1994 at Sheffield Hallam University. From recollection it had two main purposes; to send email to your mates saying "twat" or to search for pictures of Liz Hurley. ISP transmission speeds have come a long way since then. Now you can download entire movies in the time it takes to fetch a coronary inducing outsize tub of popcorn. At Totley campus, we used to plan afternoon laundry sessions around the time it took to conjure up a single JPEG: It was primitive (and frustrating) stuff. Back then, the internet was a crude and amusing plaything. Now it is like a vital organ, a virtual friend, which allows us to communicate with more people than ever before without having to rely on the hideously dated art of conversation. Life without it would be inconceivable, especially if you are crap at chatting up women.

It was a commercial *fait accompli* that a football club would eventually be made available for public purchase via the click of a mouse. On 13th November 2007 it was announced that the website MyFootballClub had entered a deal in principle to take over Ebbsfleet United.[1] Around 27,000 MyFootballClub members each paid £35 to provide an approximate £700,000 takeover fund and all own an equal share in the club but make no profit nor receive a dividend. Members have a vote on transfers as well as player selection and all major decisions. The idea was eventually ratified in February 2008.

On paper, the scheme sounds progressively utopian, a real life fantasy football for the working man, run by the fans for the fans. It gives shareholders the opportunity to believe they are in some way individually autonomous, that they have a very tangible role in the club's affairs, from picking the team to ruminating on the annual budget.

This paradigm might work if the shareholders/fans (delete as applicable) had access to inside information or proximity to training sessions, but the truth is they don't. Given the obvious distance between keyboard and

---

[1] www.myfootballclub.co.uk

training pitch, the average punter is simply too detached to make any informed judgement of team selection, let alone important long term decisions. Handing delegation to individuals with such varied and capricious opinions on the game also presents a selection headache way beyond anything a Premiership manager will ever have to deal with. It is one thing having a stadium full of fans offering their views on a manager's team selection; it's another when these views have a legitimate ratified voice. Could a scenario where a manager picks a player but is subsequently forced to drop him after an internet vote ever really work? Almost certainly not. But then, in practise, it was never more than a headline grabbing stunt anyway. Even the most delusional fan would need to accept that the final selection decision needs to rest with the manager, particularly on key match day decisions. Sitting pitch side with a laptop waiting for substitution votes to come in like a tracksuit wearing Simon Cowell is a notion bordering on insanity.

As covered in *When Saturday Comes*[1], there are better examples of where My Football Club's (MFC) policy seems to be working. The proposed sales of Michael Gash and Darius Charles (Charles subsequently stayed with the club but would later move to Stevenage) for a joint fee of £80K was voted for by over 75% of MFC members after earlier smaller bids were rejected. This sale also coincided with MFC giving Ebbsfleet manager Liam Daish a greater say in transfer dealings, meaning Daish can now reject transfer offers before they go to members. Reasons for this are speculative, but around two thirds of subscribers failed to renew their MFC membership in February 2009, meaning a subsequent reduction in the playing budget. In light of this, attempts to block the sale of players, rightly or wrongly, can have a huge impact on the club's attempts to reconcile finances. Although the decision to empower Daish was no doubt done with the best of intentions for the club, it does question how much self-government MFC shareholders actually have and whether the system is retaining its egalitarian principles.

The fans, specifically those who regularly attend matches, seem divided over the issue. Those in favour see it as an essential source of funding, allowing fans to have a say in the running of their club at a very granular level and acting as a conduit to raise their profile around the world. Those against see it as a fanciful scheme for impersonal cyber space speculators which has robbed the club of credibility and placed decision making in a

---

[1] www.wsc.co.uk/content/view/3555/38/

farcical context. My housemate at the time was a shareholder and very proud of the fact too, in a conversational context. This pride didn't extend to actually watching a game. When I told him I was off to watch Ebbsfleet and asked if he wanted to come, he replied "you must be joking."

After I bid Charles goodbye and wished his team as much luck as an opposition fan could, I reviewed my slightly alcohol induced hand written notes and realised I couldn't understand a single relaxed vowel, as if the words themselves had consumed quantities of strong lager and decided to slouch against each other in the afternoon sun. I cursed the delayed delivery of my voice recorder; this book was going to be considerably harder to write armed only with a jotter and a bounty of choreographed questions.

I met my brother on the open terrace behind the goal known as the Swanscombe End, where away supporters congregate. There were probably 100 or so Harriers fans that had made the trip down from the West Midlands. On paper this sounds relatively impressive but, in reality, the vast stepped area made the travelling support look distinctly thin on the ground, particular as some insisted on standing on their own away from the main huddle, which was either an open display of agoraphobia or an over sensitivity to the musty cologne of processed meat, gassy beer and bodily odours excited out by the August sun.

A lifetime of supporting Kidderminster means expectations of glory are somewhat capped. Aside from a brief flirtation with the Football League, the odd heroic FA Cup run and a few Wembley appearances in the FA Trophy (where we have never won) life has been a series of ifs, maybes and philosophical retrospect. Blind optimism is the preserve of most football fans. Aside from a handful of clubs, the season will be littered with let-down, bitterness and mediocrity, punctuated with the occasional semblance of glory. I used to work with a Brighton and Hove Albion fan who once said that the unswerving devotion of football support was the most illogical thing known to mankind It is probably the truest thing I have ever heard.

These brief moments of glory are what keep fans coming back though. Hope binds us to our clubs like rope lashed to a mast. Season 2008-09 was Kidderminster's best since our relegation back to the Conference National and only a last day home defeat to Kettering prevented us entering the lottery of the play offs. Unfortunately, the well-crafted side Mark Yates had assembled was scattered to the winds pre-season by the gods of downsizing, leaving only a handful of recognisable faces from the previous campaign. Like so many seasons before, the Harriers kicked off in hope rather than expectation.

The game started superbly for the away side. McPhee, Smikle and Barnes-Homer all tested the excellent 'Fleet 'keeper Cronin inside the first ten minutes but, despite registering double figures in shots on goal and having 70% of the possession, the score, inexplicably, remained 0-0 at half time. I sensed impending doom. Bereft of anything else to do, and hungry from the day's earlier drinking, I sought out half time refreshment. According to the website www.conferencegrounds.co.uk the culinary delights at Ebbsfleet include Chicken Curry, Chilli Con Carne and baked potatoes. Clearly the author had been on a different day to me. All I managed to find was a trailer staffed by two angry looking men selling burgers and hot dogs; I was almost scared into buying something.

Back on the terrace, and chewing mechanically on my patty, I looked around me. It was a familiar scene. Two lads next to us were listening intently for the Villa score line; another was eagerly scouring the internet on his *IPhone* looking for fantasy league assists. Behind me a group had apparently smuggled a bottle of vodka in and were refreshing themselves, prostrate in the afternoon heat like a dish poaching in liquor. I took a minute to survey the grand historic ground. It had a charming antiquated feel, though in parts looked like it was kept alive via life support. Foliage sprouted through the concrete beneath my feet. Cigarette butts smoked their last breath and rolled lazily on the breeze in front of me. Polystyrene cups crunched underfoot. Men gazed blankly into the distance. Children swung on the crash barriers. I was in a ground I had never been before, surrounded by people I didn't know the names of, yet felt as close to home as I ever could.

The second half continued in the same vein. Barnes-Homer hit the bar. Cronin defied physics in the Ebbsfleet goal. The 750 or so home fans in the ground reacquainted themselves with the word *blitzkrieg*. Then, as is often the case, particularly if you have a selective memory, Kidderminster conjured up a moment of farce and almost gave the game away. Gavin Caines' back pass to the Harriers' 'keeper was woefully short and Ishmael Welsh forced the stopper into an excellent save. Ebbsfleet clearly found solace in this moment of madness and mounted their only sustained pressure of the game. The home fans finally found their voice, as much through relief as anything else. I couldn't work out what they were actually singing. They were drowned out by a series of expletives next to me which usually follow in close proximity to your team's name when defeat is being snatched from the jaws of victory.

The pressure was a blip in an otherwise consistent afternoon. Harriers finished the game as they started, with Cronin sealing his man of the match performance, blocking McPhee at point blank range from a by-line pullback and then seeing Barnes-Homer's follow up deflected wide. It was agonising, breathless stuff. Fans slumped head in hands lamenting missed opportunities. The final whistle brought collective groans from the away contingent and cheers from the home support. A 'keeper being named man of the match tells its own story, and in this case one with a highly unsatisfying ending. As we left the ground and walked back to the station, a group of Ebbsfleet fans were waiting at a bus stop. One looked at me, shook his head, smiled and said "that was fucking awful", as if we were in some alliance of the damned.

It was good to be back.

Enfield Town v Potter Bar Town

Isthmian League Division One North – Step 4
Saturday 5th September 2009

Final Score: 1-1
Attendance: 208

There's "too much information", sang *Duran Duran* on their self-titled 1993 album, a relative hiatus after their 1980s peak during which there was almost certainly too much hair. Sixteen years later and the concept is more pertinent than ever, even if the ageing rockers aren't. The commercial genesis and subsequent explosion of the internet - manifested in particular by the socio-cyber sprawl of Facebook and personal blogging - has meant that information, both historical and real time, has never been more readily available. Gone are the days of trawling to the library and painstakingly tracking down relevant quotes to substantiate research essays; now anyone with a keyboard and a laymen knowledge of search engines can be instantly guided to infinite vaults of literary wisdom. Or at least so the theory goes. The major problem with internet based reference material is the unchecked and often unsolicited nature of its content. More often than not search engines will redirect the end user to material that is at best unsubstantiated, and at worst plain libellous. Moreover, even those sources which purport to be of a more official nature can still be glaringly inaccurate. Opinion blurs with fact like a child painting the truth with watercolours. Taking source material from a ratified book or university paper is one thing; going on the musings of a fan forum or unofficial history site is another.

Given the loquacious nature of the web, and the universal popularity of football, the internet provides an extraordinary amount of information on the game, some valid, some not. It also offers a world of personal thoughts and observations of which some are unsubstantiated rants and some are invaluable sources of unfettered historical commentary. What makes a good website is of course hugely arbitrary, but those that are free from corporate dogma, political agenda and irrational thought are usually a good start. Those that see football in terms of the wider national game - not just the commercial leviathans of this world - are even better. For some time now, there has been a rather splendid website called www.twohundredpercent.net which has been reporting on the less glamorous aspects of our beloved game, a million miles away from the sanitised gloss of Satellite TV or official club offerings. One article, entitled "The 20 'most important' Football Clubs in the world", offers an arbitrary look at the real diamonds in football's crown, not simply the biggest or the wealthiest. There are, of course, some obvious inclusions, such as Real Madrid and Ajax, as well as some fairly obvious not so obvious inclusions such as Sheffield FC, the world's oldest club. In twentieth place, nestling behind Olympique de Marseille, sits Enfield Town. It's a fair bet most people who follow the game in this country, certainly those without an interest in non league football, would struggle to point out Enfield on a map, never mind admit to knowing they had a team. That they occupy a list bereft of Manchester United, Liverpool and AC Milan would initially suggest insanity. On closer inspection, and in the context of a website which casual observers might dismiss as merely querulous blogging, it is a list, and an entry, which reflects the changing times - and concerns - of our game.

So who are Enfield Town? And more to the point, why are they so important? In laymen terms they "are the grandfathers of the movement that uses supporters' trusts for fans to create their own destinies and break free of the madness of some football clubs".[1] Before AFC Wimbledon, before FC United, Enfield Town were trailblazing a way as the first supporters' owned club - in this case as a response to a situation deemed untenable by the fans. In a decade of increasing financial uncertainty engulfing many clubs, often at the mercy of overzealous speculators and money men, their *modus operandi* has become the benchmark for fans looking to regain control of their team before they become another liquidation statistic.

Enfield Town formed in 2001, a breakaway supporters' team from the original Enfield FC, who in turn were founded by John Skinner in 1893 as Enfield Spartans. The club moved to the North Middlesex League in 1896 and shortly afterwards dropped the 'Spartans' from its name, as well as moving to a new ground at Cherry Orchard Lane. This move, whether coincidental or not, was a prosperous time for the club, winning back to back titles in the 1901-02 and 1902-03 seasons, and so attaining 'senior' status. As a result of their title winning exploits, 1903 saw the club join the London League Division Two, winning the title in 1911 and so gaining promotion to the Premier Division. In 1912 the club was invited to become a founder member of the Athenian League and two years later won the

[1] www.twohundredpercent.net/?p=1219

Middlesex Cup for the first time. After the First World War, Enfield disbanded. Rather than let the club die completely, members of local side Grange Park FC met with a view to progressing to senior football and taking over the reins of Enfield FC, in doing so entering the club in the Middlesex and London Leagues before returning to the Athenian League in 1921, where it remained until 1963 (save for a brief spell in the Herts and Middlesex League during the intervention of the Second World War).

The club moved to a new ground in Southbury Road in 1936, but it wasn't until 1962 that the Athenian League title was finally won, and in some style, with every home game won. This impressive feat was bettered the following season when the league was retained by a winning margin of seven points and a record 130 goals scored. This success led to promotion to the Isthmian League, where the club stayed for 18 years, finishing champions seven times, with the pinnacle being the 1977-78 season during which Enfield won thirty five of their forty two league games.

The club continued its rise up the non league ladder and joined the Alliance Premier League (which became the Conference and now the Blue Square Premier) in 1981. They finished runners up in 1982, won the title in dramatic last day fashion in 1983 and won the title again in 1986 with a team generally considered one of the finest to ever grace the non league game. The club also complemented their dominant league form with two FA Trophy wins in 1982 and 1988 respectively. It was therefore hugely unfortunate for Enfield FC that it wasn't until the 1986-87 season that the Football League replaced the reflectively unfair 'election' system with automatic promotion and relegation between its own league and the Conference.[1] Bobby Robson once observed that 'if' was the biggest word in football and nowhere is this more applicable than Enfield. Scarborough and Wycombe, promoted from the Conference in the 1987 and 1988 respectively, more than held their own in the professional game and if Enfield had been granted promotion to the Football League with the squad they had, one can only guess at what they might have achieved. As it stood, the club started to move in the opposite direction. Despite maintaining a strong presence in the Conference, the club was relegated to the Isthmian League in 1990. A perennial contender in the Isthmian League, the club were eventually

[1] It was mooted that the FA did sound the old Enfield Town out about taking on Division 4 fixtures when Wolves were on the brink of being wound up during the mid 1980s

crowned champions in 1995 but were denied promotion as the Football Conference had major concerns over the club's financial position. Ironically, this came at a time when Conference sides (namely Kidderminster Harriers and Stevenage Borough) were being denied promotion to the Football League over concerns their grounds were not of suitable standard. The outrage expressed by the Conference at these draconian regulations were seen in some quarters as rather hypocritical given the Conference were wielding the same arbitrary rulings over clubs seeking promotion to their league.

Enfield FC continued to push for promotion to the Conference but earlier concerns of finances may have proved prophetic. In 1999, the club sold its Southbury Road Stadium, eventually deciding on a long term ground share with Boreham Wood FC some ten miles down the road. Concerned that the club was no longer in the borough and would struggle to attract crowds, a group of fans set up a supporters' trust with a view to help in running the club and returning it to the borough of Enfield. Their attempts were thwarted somewhat by then Chairman Tony Lazarou, who stalled on a deal to transfer control of the club to the trust and then, after legal action, seized the £750K which had been placed into an escrow account after the Southbury Road ground was sold. This proved the breaking point for supporters of the club who, clearly disillusioned with proceedings, formed a supporters' trust club in 2001 called Enfield Town FC to keep football alive in the borough of Enfield. Enfield FC reformed a few years later as Enfield 1893 in order to remove the debts created by the previous chairman and now play in the Essex Senior League (the feeder to Enfield Town's current league) at Broxbourne Borough's ground.

Enfield Town's inaugural season was the 2001-02 Essex Senior League Campaign, playing their games at Brimsdown Rovers' ground, which at least brought a semblance of locality back to proceedings. The following season the club won the league but was refused admission to the Isthmian League as Brimsdown's ground did not meet the necessary requirements. Promotion was soon to follow in the 2004-05 season when, with ground improvements in place, the club were promoted to what was then the Southern League Division One East, meaning that during the 2005-06 season they would be playing the old Enfield FC. The two matches between the clubs clearly showed the depth of feeling and interest present, with 802 at Enfield Town and 522 at Enfield FC. After restructuring, the club now find themselves in the Ryman League (Isthmian depending on your lexical loyalties) Division 1 North.

Enfield Town has attracted a lot of praise for their pioneering work as a supporters' trust club, and has been cited as an "inspiration" to their respective counterparts at AFC Wimbledon and FC United, as well as gaining praise from the hugely important Supporters Direct Organisation. Supporters Direct was set up ten years ago to provide assistance to fans and supporters' trusts who wish to gain greater representation and accountability within their football club, be it a stake hold or, as in Enfield Town's case, full and democratic ownership. It was created as a by-product of a late 1990s report which highlighted clear problems with the way football had been developing, specifically that fans were putting a lot into clubs and getting very little back. The organisation is not government funded but has the patronage of the main political parties, receiving money instead from the Stadium Improvement Fund.

I arranged to meet Kevin Rye, Communications Manager and case worker for Supporters Direct, to gain a personal insight into an organisation that is a response to - or a reflection of - modern football business practice. Their opulent offices nestle in affluent Bloomsbury Square and my immediate reaction was to draw penthouse and pavement Dickensian images of deluded supporters going cap in hand to the palaces of the mighty for benevolent aid. For some reason, I expected the organisation to be operating out of a grubby nicotine stained office situated over a fast food outlet, as if to preserve their modesty and virtue in bricks and mortar.

Kevin reminded me of a young Will Self and certainly talked as eloquently. His role as case worker allows him the opportunity to assist trusts on campaigns and crisis strategies; on how to present a case to the council where a ground is concerned or how to deal with the financial regulations authority. The role, as Kevin argues, is about helping fans "who seek to gain influence in a club through a legal binding relationship", often in circumstances where the club they love is teetering on the blink of oblivion. Unsurprisingly, he is cynical of the way football has engineered itself to become the bloated unregulated behemoth it is today.

"I am intensely suspicious of any club who has a wealthy benefactor as you have to ask yourself why they are doing it. Money? Ego? History has continuously shown people coming in to football with a supposedly open cheque book, only to leave a club in a far worse state than when they arrived. Then again, the problem isn't with benefactors *per se*, more the structure of football that allows you to spin a yarn about what ownership is achieving. Look behind the facade and you often see speculators with little interest in football, such as the individual who sails into town, sells the club ground, builds a bunker on the outskirts of the city and then absconds with a nice profit. These people are not good for football."

Unfortunately, benefactors, speculators, whatever you want to call them, are ubiquitous in the modern game. Moreover, it would seem some clubs simply cannot operate without them, particularly those who need new or improved stadia. This very real problem befell Chesterfield's trust who was forced to sell a majority stake hold in the club to ex-Sheffield Wednesday Chairman Dave Allen in an attempt fund their new stadium. So how can supporter owned clubs compete with both rival teams and pragmatic finances when faced with such adversity?

"I could point to Exeter and Wimbledon as an example of trust run clubs who are doing very well without large cash injections. But the question isn't about supporter run clubs keeping up with their big spending counterparts but about how current regulation allows the actions of bad clubs to have a very big effect on what good clubs can do. A lot of clubs propelled through divisions usually have something sinister behind them. Winning trophies on borrowed money that can never be paid back is nothing short of cheating when you think about it. Again, it comes down to a problem of regulation. We can do all we can to support democratically owned clubs and to improve circumstances and methods, but if you are faced with the fact that being decent means you constantly lose then people - the fans - start becoming disillusioned."

This problem becomes even more magnified in an era where success is everything and the word 'crisis' is used to describe any team that loses two games in a row. Chairmen lured by the promise of increased TV revenue now see the higher echelons of the league as something financially tangible, dismissing the historical meritocratic of sporting competition and glory in favour of a more calculated business minded dogma.

"Supporters' trusts are not exempt from bad decision making either, nor are they exempt from wanting a quick fix at an irrevocable long term cost.

Supporter ownership is about being frugal as much as anything; supporter ownership does not mean you are exempt from poor management. Ultimately - and I always try to bring people back to this point - everything is affected by the ability for football clubs regardless of who runs them to act in their own self-interest with few checks and balances. Until there are proper controls like a licensing system or similar, then supporters' trust ownership will not be a panacea that solves all these problems in one fell swoop - of that we've always been certain and have consistently said so publicly."

It was fortunate for me that a club of Enfield Town's stature should be within such easily commutable distance of my home in Finsbury Park, given I had been out celebrating my birthday the night before on (thankfully not in) the Thames and was slightly worse for wear. As the train pulled into Brimsdown station, I soon realised I was a million miles from the ostentation of the West End or the chaos of the high rise inner city. There was an almost eerie nothingness to the place, like the Langoliers were about to descend.

Finding the ground proved to be slightly more difficult than first imagined. There were no signposts, or at least ones that gave me any indication a football club were in the vicinity, and, as most non league fans will testify, asking locals where provincial sports grounds are often draws blank expressions. Thankfully the local populous were fairly knowledgeable and after stopping in a local pub to clarify my route, which makes it sound like I was pursuing the Inca Trail rather than crossing a main road, I soon found myself heading down a *cul de sac* towards Brimsdown Sports and Social Club, Goldsdown Road, where Enfield Town play their home matches.

I am not sure quite what I was expecting to find but years of supporting Conference football had probably given me a distorted image of the game at this level. First impressions were of how small the ground was; a small seated stand sat on the halfway line with a covered standing area opposite. Behind the goal to the left was another covered area and opposite that a railed area of grass. There were sheds and trailers dotted around the ground near the turnstile doubling as souvenir stalls and a temporary office. As David Baukham notes on his excellent Pyramid Passion website[1], many clubs, for a variety of reasons, unwittingly shed their history and character

---

[1] www.pyramidpassion.co.uk

when moving to a purpose built flat pack stadium on the edge of town and clubs whose very roots are in the local community, especially those with historical or intriguing stadia, are a joy for the non league aficionado. Needless to say, I loved it.

I had arranged to meet Town Chairman Paul Millington who had kindly and enthusiastically agreed to talk to me before the game. I was told to meet Paul in the 'boardroom' which from recollection looked like the kind of prefabricated unit which "troubled" kids went to at our school and never seemed to emerge from. Standing pitch side while the players warmed up, I asked Paul, first and foremost, why he was involved with the club.

"It's a labour of love," he confessed, almost slightly embarrassed. "I travel up from Brighton for home games and usually stand over there," pointing to a modest structure on the other side of the pitch. Although it was a pleasant summer's day, the English weather is notoriously fickle and I found the idea refreshingly incongruous that a chairman could be found standing on the terraces with other fans exposed to the elements. "I have offered to hand over the reins to someone else but they don't seem to want to get rid of me."

"Are you expecting a big crowd today?" I asked expectantly, given Potters Bar represented one of the more local of local derbies in the division.

"We might get 300," responded Paul optimistically, "turn out has been good so far this season." Three hundred fans may not seem much but Enfield Town had the highest average attendance in the league last season with 218, which represented a (disappointing) drop on the previous season's 255. This is also higher than some teams in the Ryman Premier, though one would suspect that in order to progress through the leagues and attract players they would need to at least double this, certainly if they were to reach as far as the Conference South, which Paul indicated would be a realistic ambition for a club still in its embryonic stage. Quite how feasible this would be remains a disputable point. Even during their 1980s heyday, Enfield FC were never the best supported of teams. Their average gate during the Conference Championship winning side of 1985/86 was rarely over 1,000 and Enfield 1893, the effective incarnation of that club, struggle to attract crowds over 100.

"We do struggle for support - but we are a new club, and you have to remember that while we are ground sharing this will impact on attendances." This brought him to the new stadium. In October 2008 Enfield

Council announced a deal to allow the club to relocate to the Queen Elizabeth Stadium, near to Enfield FC's old Southbury Road ground. The proposed move should see the club kick off there for the 2010/11 season, a move which Paul has described on record as "Momentous". Speaking to the *North London Press*, Paul revealed "I am confident Enfield Town can show what a supporters' run club can achieve by producing a first class stadium for the benefit of the whole community." I looked wistfully around the current ground. Although Enfield's temporary home, it was obvious there was a fondness and graciousness for it and a real sense of appreciation of the debt of gratitude owed to Brimsdown Rovers for providing the opportunity to play at Goldsdown Road. Paul advised that one matter high on the agenda is to agree what mutually beneficial opportunities exist for ETFC to continue to make use of the facilities there.

The sense of community is prominent in everything the club does, indeed, it was their *raison d'être* for forming in the first place. Paul talked confidently of the move back to Enfield, specifically that it would be a better measure of the popularity of the club. Although the day was about Enfield Town, I couldn't help but ask about Enfield 1893. I was curious to learn what the relationship was like with them, especially as there had been talk of them moving to the QE Stadium instead. To cut to the chase, I asked why he felt there was a need for two clubs.

"You'd have to ask their players and staff that - personally I don't really know if it's in everyone's best interests," he mused. This was consistent talk. In June 2007 Paul released a statement via the official website, following the liquidation of the original Enfield FC, inviting the two clubs to pool resources in an attempt to galvanise the community and create a team to challenge for major honours again. The proposal was rejected out of hand and Enfield 1893 was born instead.
"Is there any animosity between the two teams?" I enquired.
"I wouldn't say so, no. I think both sets of fans understand why they did what they did, but that's not to say there isn't a competitive rivalry. There will always be a few people who are bitter about things but we did what we thought was in the best interest of the community at the time. We are also very proud of what we have achieved."
The community theme kept cropping up. In May 2009 Enfield Town became part of a Programme for Academic and Sporting Excellence (PASE) but, unlike most schemes which tie a single club to a single college, this scheme

involves the club directly and has already been set up in Boreham Wood and Oaklands College. Speaking to the ETFC website, Paul announced, "Led by Boreham Wood FC and Oaklands College, Enfield Town FC will work collaboratively alongside not only Enfield College, but CONEL and the BeauSandVer consortium of schools, to ensure the youngsters on the scheme will receive not just a football education but a programme of study leading to academic or vocational qualifications that should help them to get off on the right foot when they enter the world of work."

There are many clubs doing good deeds out there, some big, some small, some publicised, some not. The fact that a team as hugely important as ETFC is carrying out this kind of work is truly admirable. Admittedly, the club has a vested interest in producing quality players for their own use, though it shouldn't detract from a model that is grassroots in its concept and focused on assisting the local people. 'For the fans by the fans' is a powerful ethos and one which resonates at many levels of football. Although nearly all teams talk of their 'role in the community', some are guiltier than others of merely paying lip service to it. Additionally, it would seem ETFC want to adopt a strict model of (sporting) behaviour. Unlike rugby, football is often seen as the poor relation of discipline and constraint and it is a concern the FA have tried to address via a number of much maligned projects, notably the Respect for Referees programme which seems to have had little or no impact. Paul advised that the club had certain codes of conduct regarding visiting teams, namely that they were to be made welcome and encouraged to interact with fans and opposition before and after the match. One suspects that these moral codes are easier to administer when the club in question has such an interdependent relationship with its fans but it was incredibly heartening to hear and, later, to see, especially if the same moral backbone is being installed into junior players at a young and impressionable age.

By now the match was about to kick off, which meant Paul had to take his place in the stand. "If you want a fan's perspective, I need to introduce you to Dave," he smiled, leading me into the club shop and the avuncular presence of a solid smiling man behind the counter. Dave was clearly popular. He knew by name almost every person who came in the shop and seemed to be the hub of all activity ranging from programme selling through to raffle tickets and away travel. I started talking to him about Enfield Town and his experiences, role and motivations. Like everyone else at the club, his position was purely voluntary. I asked Dave why he followed Enfield Town in an area so dominated by Tottenham Hotspur.

"I always have; they're my local team," came the frank response. "There are people here who openly support Spurs (I noted this personally from the array of shirts behind the goal) and some who only see Enfield play when Spurs are away from home, but to be honest any support is good support. Spurs are a big side and Enfield will never compete with them at a playing or fan level but the more we can get involved with the area the more people will know who we are." We talked about the role of the club in the local community. Playing devil's advocate somewhat, I pointed out that a fan base of 250 in a borough with a population of several hundred thousand represents a fairly small cross section. I asked Dave a blunt question; what would happen if the club ceased to exist? Who would actually care?

"Well - it would be a disaster. But we are a supporters' club and if we closed down we would just reform again." It was a pragmatic response from a dedicated fan and to be honest I felt slightly awkward pressing the matter further given I was surrounded by people who gave up vast amounts of their free time to keep the club running. By the time I had exhausted Dave with my amateur journalism it was half time, at which point I realised I hadn't seen a single kick of the match. It's a regular conversation amongst football fans that the match itself can play second fiddle to the match day experience as a whole; watching your team slug it out for ninety minutes is not the be all and end all. Personally, I just love being at a ground and meeting new people, reading old programmes or taking in the atmosphere. This was very much the case at Enfield, though admittedly my circumstances were slightly different to the average paying spectator, in that I was hoping to document the quirks and idiosyncrasies of the day; anyone can read a match report in a paper - and probably in a better style than I could hope to achieve.

Half time at non league grounds often gives fans the freedom and interaction you are seldom granted at many league grounds, where there are sometimes very strict policies of where you can and cannot go. A lot of people were wandering around the ground, catching up with friends and staff and popping into the club shop for a complimentary slice of cake (I can only assume it was someone's birthday rather than standard practise to double as a patisserie on match days, but I may be wrong). Although it is hard to quantify - though I am sure somebody somewhere has - the demographic at non league games seems somewhat different to top flight football. However, this might be down to the fact that the protagonists stand out more. Al Needham sums this up perfectly in his *When Saturday Comes* 2004 Match report of Mansfield Town v Kidderminster Harriers by referring to a "row of chip pan-headed youths with Obligatory Bored Girl Who May Be Going out with One of Them" standing behind the goal, which

I can joyfully confirm is a common and amusing sight at lower league level.[1] Although this crowd seemed relatively chip pan-headed youth free, there were one or two observational points of note amongst the largely middle aged crowd, particularly the presence of fidgety pre-pubescent children who, presumably disenchanted with events on the pitch, took to using the ground and its license to roam as a makeshift Gulliver's Kingdom, be it scrambling over unused pallets, kicking a football against the portakabins or using the club shop railings as uneven gymnastic bars.

I decided it might actually be an idea to watch the second half and took my place next to a gentleman with a speaker who it transpired was the ground's PA system. Enfield were leading 1-0 at half time thanks to the exotically named Fabio Valenti (who, to bring proceedings back down to earth, started his career at Slough) and after Potters Bar's Joe O'Brien was somewhat dubiously sent off, it probably should have killed the game as a spectacle. Credit to Potters Bar though, who played some good football on the floor and were eventually rewarded when Ellis Remy beat Enfield 'keeper Rob Blackburne (one of three brothers in the squad) with a neat finish to make it 1-1. Although there were the inevitable cheers of celebration, I was struggling to see if any of it had come from an away support, creating a sort of non league version of *Where's Wally*. There were two teenage youths who seemed vaguely excited behind the 'away' goal but that might be because they had found some loose change or been texted details of a cider binge down the shopping precinct - you just don't know. Enfield, helped by the extra man advantage, laid siege to the Potters Bar goal with some incisive attacking play but against a team who were now playing for the draw and content to hoof the ball into the crowd at every given opportunity that killer slide rule pass was never forthcoming. When the game was a contest rather than a salvation mission the standard of football was pretty decent. You suspect that people unfamiliar with this level of the game expect a collection of well-built hungover blokes who are more likely to suck on a Rothman than an orange at half time but this blatantly isn't the case.

[1] www.wsc.co.uk/content/view/1953/29/

A lot of players at this level are ex-league academy players who didn't quite make the grade and in the case of Enfield midfielder Andy Jones, the ex-Wrexham Academy player, has also appeared in *Hollyoaks* and *Emmerdale* as an aspiring actor. Football and celebrity spotting in one package: not bad for a seven pound entrance fee.

I had every intention of leaving the ground after the game had finished but this meant walking past the strategically placed social club to do so. Given I was on a fact finding mission and the England v Slovakia friendly was on, I felt obliged to wander in for a quick pint. My experience of social clubs to date was synonymous with battered stacking chairs, plates of sandwiches, tattooed forearms and overdressed women and thankfully the Brimsdown Sports and Social Club was no exception. It might be a little naive to assume it was always this busy but either way the place was very lively. Of particular note was seeing both sets of players come in for a post-match drink and buffet, which had a charming bygone innocence about it. There is something of a self-fulfilling prophecy surrounding top flight players nowadays that they are somehow too important to involve themselves with fans, as if in some way their lifestyle, indeed their very existence, is in some way too highbrow for the fans who pay to watch them. If this myth is allowed to perpetuate itself we will have a generation of people growing up who think footballers are beyond approach, whereas in actual fact they are just men, specifically young working class ones much like the fans. Whether the players actually believe their own hype or whether they would be happy to socialise with fans were it not for security men in dark glasses bundling them on to coaches is debatable. Stories emanate from all over the British Isles about players who are happy to chat with fans in bars as well as those whose status has clearly gone to their head. Clearly, there is a vast difference between someone who earns a non league and a Premier League wage, in both their lifestyle choices and geographical loyalties. Many players at Enfield Town's level will have been born and raised in the area and hold down a full time job with a local company. Consequently they may know the fans, have ties with the area and perhaps, most crucially, still see football as a game they love playing rather than a means to fame and fortune. This isn't to say any of them wouldn't be tempted by untold riches were they suddenly given the opportunity: they invariably would. The difference is these players are still very much just 'one of the lads' and, quite literally, someone you can have a pint and a chat with after the match. It might be naïve to assume the likes of Jermaine Defoe and Robbie Keane would pop in for a pint and a sausage roll if Enfield ever drew Spurs in the cup but, as a football fan, you always live in hope; I am sure Paul will still insist on it regardless.

About twenty minutes into the England match, I was introduced to two thoroughbreds of Enfield Town's fan club, Phil and Mark. Mark in particular had the air of a non league underworld figure. When I mentioned I was writing a book both would give knowing looks and Mark would scroll through his phone reading out names and numbers of people I "might like to talk to". It became clear that I was in the presence of people who really knew their stuff. Every team I mentioned taking in on my odyssey, they had been there and had a story about it, but in a sincere rather than sanctimonious way. It suddenly dawned on me that I really knew very little about non league football, at least compared to these guys, but in some ways this wasn't a bad thing. I am the first to admit that this was a relative journey into the unknown on my part and these were exactly the kind of people I was hoping to meet.

As it transpired, the pair was more than just mere fans. Mark is reserve team secretary whilst Phil operates as webmaster and unofficial club photographer. I asked them the question I was duty bound to ask on this ceremonious occasion: what got you involved with Enfield Town? As Phil was at the bar facilitating my future hangover, Mark replied first:
"After the painful experiences for supporters associated with the demise of Enfield FC, I think most of the founding membership were determined to be involved with a club that wouldn't put its fan base in that position again. That in turn led to the creation of a club that has a set of visions and values that were, and probably remain, unique. My take on it is that these remain sufficiently powerful to make individuals proud to support ETFC and probably explains why people are regularly prepared to go that extra mile for the club. Finally, I believe that the structure requires the board to treat supporters etc. as individuals, rather than as objects in the way that I suspect happens elsewhere." I sensed I had hit the jackpot. After a furtive check that my voice recorder was working, Phil returned with supplies and a passionate defence of his own allegiance.

"My reason for supporting Enfield Town is that I supported Enfield FC and at the time of the split, decided the new club was going to be more like the old one had been in the past than the old one was going to be once supporters started going to the new club. A huge reason for it is the social aspect. After all, I don't deny I could see better football by going to a

Premier League club. I actually started watching Enfield because my postman talked me into it and because my school got one of the Enfield players as a games teacher, who handed out junior season tickets. When I couldn't use mine any more I just carried on going along. The reason I have stuck with the new club is, as Mark probably pointed out, we are treated as people by the members of the board. The directors are well aware that we are, in effect, a captive audience and the source of most of the club's funding but they somehow manage to get detached from that way of thinking and don't just look at us as a cash cow. Also, whatever happens, we know that each member of the Trust has the same vote as any other and if you want to change things, or to support a particular point of view, you can talk to the directors and, if necessary, apply to join the board. It is a much more inclusive system than you get at clubs with a single benefactor, even where that club also has a Trust and even then where that Trust has a presence on the board, because their Trust is always one step further away from being able to make a difference than we are."

It wasn't the first time I had heard fans talk of wanting recognition from the club they support, to be treated as supporters and not figures on a balance sheet. Nearly every team in the country has a supporters' club or trust organisation but just what influence these factions have, and how seriously football club authorities take them, is debatable. To have a club who not only values your support but encourages you to be part of a democratic decision making process is quite something. With this in mind, I asked what their hopes and expectations were for the years ahead. "I think you'd probably need to speak to the Chairman for the exact line, but I would sum it up in two ways" said Mark. "Firstly, to be playing in the borough at a ground of our own and, secondly, to be playing at the highest level the club can sustain. This means remaining solvent and not throwing money at the team in order to try and push things along too quickly." So would they sell out to a benefactor given the right circumstances?

Mark shook his head. "That would be out with the terms of the Trust's constitution and the past experiences of Enfield FC would inevitably make members extremely circumspect about the club being owned in the conventional way. Equally, if adequate safeguards were in place and the needs of the club were to be better served by such an arrangement, I don't think supporters would rule it out. But the important thing is that any such change would be determined by the Trust's membership democratically."

"A couple of years ago," Phil added, "some of our supporters actually suggested this but the majority appeared to be anti so it never even got as far as a formal vote or anything like that."

"Besides," continued Mark, "you don't necessarily need a wealthy benefactor. It should be perfectly possible for the economics to be sustainable by ongoing success bringing in more support, sponsorship, etc. and raising the revenue required to balance the books; and even to borrow collectively to speculate. Personally I think I am a little more sceptical and suspect that there is a glass ceiling. Intuitively the domination of the traditional ownership model must tell you something. In reality, I suspect it's too early to tell for sure."

"It should be pointed out Barcelona are a supporters' owned club - and they're pretty good," finished Phil, adding a boy's own dream aura to proceedings.

I decided to call it a day around 9.30pm. As I walked somewhat refreshed into the eerie twilight calm of Brimsdown railway station I reflected on my day out. The standard of football may not have been the best and the facilities somewhat basic but the experience was a triumph because of the people, their passion and sheer devotion to the cause. If there was a concern, it was how long the integrity of the clubs' principles can last in a world where fans increasingly demand instant success. As a mutuality, particularly one that has already run the gauntlet of ground loss in a past life, you would hope that history provides a cautionary tale. From talking to the fans, you suspect they want to keep things just the way they are. Anyone with a vested interested in the people's game returning to the people would be wise not to disagree.

Colwyn Bay v Garforth Town

Northern Premier League Division One North – Step 4
Saturday 19th September 2009

Final Score: 3-1
Attendance: 302

Colwyn Bay holds many warm childhood memories for me. We used to go there regularly on family holidays and even now I can still recall the smell of Nant-y-Glyn Hall, the never ending beaches, and my dad's amusement at being served by a local waitress called Gaynor Pigeon. The problem with childhood memories is they are often best left in the past; like school reunions or vain attempts to continue youthful pursuits into middle age, you realise that it's the zeitgeist not necessarily the people that made these times great. As a returning adult it concerned me that I might see Colwyn Bay as just another destitute seaside town - glorious in black and white and dubious in colour.

The town also has a football team playing in the Unibond League Division One North. It would be a fairly shallow premise to focus on a club simply to indulge a trip down memory lane and if this were the protocol for the book it would be as much a testament to the enduring spirit of British seaside holidays as anything else. Perhaps of more relevance is that Colwyn Bay FC are a Welsh club playing in the English Non League System which, aside from being a curious rarity, is even more remarkable given they were once banned from playing in their own country by the Welsh FA. And you thought administration and a ten point penalty was harsh.

On arriving at Colwyn Bay station, I decided to reacquaint myself with the place and see if it stirred any forgotten memories. The station is right on the sea front, although there isn't much to see in September other than the all too familiar imagery of a tired looking pier and an overcast horizon. There was also not a trace of beach to be seen. I distinctly remember there being a beach; I can still hear my brother's hollow screams when he fell head first into a dead fish during a beachside frolic here many years ago. Slightly disappointed, I headed back to town, which in all honesty was totally unrecognisable from the selective recollections I had of it; hardly surprising given my last visit was over 25 years ago. Although its location will always attract tourists or day-trippers, the modern day Colwyn Bay appears to be more a town by the sea than a 'seaside town'. There was the odd gruesome reminder of a long declining tourism scene in the local bingo arcade and the slightly scary looking Wings social club, but for the most part it was a run of the mill market town centre populated by people with Welsh afflicted Merseyside accents. In fact, one or two exceptions aside, I struggled to hear anything with even a vague semblance of 'Welsh' about it.

Colwyn Bay (*Bae Colwyn* in its native Welsh) has a population of around 30,000 split into five communities. The club itself is situated in Old Colwyn, a beautiful historical setting with grand Victorian buildings and picture postcard backdrops. Speaking to a couple of locals, the town has inherited a degree of spillover from Liverpool and the Wirral, and with it something of a drug problem, which has blighted what was a relatively prosperous and aesthetic coastal dwelling, as gloriously documented in Roberts and Morley's *The Spirit of Colwyn Bay*. Presumably this problem, such that it may be, has filtered through to the nearby town of Abergele and Pensarn. Sprayed in large letters as you pull into the station are the words "smoke weed everyday" which is either an advert for the Cannabis Liberation Movement or a pre-emptive warning that the prefabricated environment you are passing through can only be tolerated in an altered state of mind.
After grabbing a sandwich and feeding the gulls (one or two I can deal with - a whole flock has Hitchcock style overtones) I headed back to the station to meet one of Colwyn Bay FC's directors, Mark Williams. After a few minutes, a man in his 40s wearing casual sports dress approached me and introduced himself as the man I had been emailing for the past few weeks. Directors of clubs are generally synonymous with club ties and sharp suits but Mark looked more like a bloke on the terrace which was pleasantly reassuring.

Mark has been involved with the club for about 15 years now and is involved with many operational aspects. As we drove to Old Colwyn, he talked me through his role there with obvious enthusiasm and spoke fondly of both the club and the local area. Our route took us past Eirias Park which used to house several life size plastic dinosaurs and was a kind of British forerunner to Jurassic Park. In fact there is a picture of me aged about six years old in the family photo album casually leaning against the leg of a Tyrannosaurus Rex, like a young Carl Denham. The arrogant swagger is somewhat undermined by the red velvet shorts I was wearing, which immediately put to bed any big game hunting credibility.

Both the dinosaurs and the football club are now gone from there. Colwyn Bay used to play their home games at Eirias Park, until they moved to their current Llanelian Road ground in 1984. There has been talk of a move back to the original location at a stadium to be shared with the local rugby club, but Mark voiced doubts over the feasibility of this for a variety of reasons. "If you look at ground shares with rugby clubs they can cause problems. Newcastle Blue Star shared with the Newcastle Falcons and their pitch was compromised by this. Also, we own the clubhouse at the current ground which has functions on most nights, which for a club of our stature brings in important revenue. Any move away to a leased stadium would see us lose that income. Besides, we have done a lot to improve the ground. When we first moved there it was just a field. Now it is a grade C stadium; grade B satisfies entrance to the Conference North."

As we approached the ground I was struck by how idyllic it was, nestling in a valley dominated by hills to the grandstand side and grazing fields to the rest. Of all the grounds I have visited, it is probably only rivaled by Stalybridge Celtic's Bower Fold for aesthetic qualities and, above anything else, is a quintessential example of a setting that should only be sacrificed to a non-descript new stadium elsewhere if it was absolutely the last resort. With this in mind, I asked Mark what the realistic ambitions of the club were and how these could be fulfilled. "The club will expand as they go rather than overspend to achieve instant success. Our realistic ambition is to get back in the Conference North, but this will be done with consideration and care. We are more than capable of getting out of this current league, but it is very hard to do so. All it takes is one team to have a lot of money thrown at them each season and they run away with it. This season it's hard to see beyond FC Halifax Town (the old Halifax Town before they were wound up) who are really a Conference National outfit in support if nothing else."

Although Colwyn Bay has a five year plan - including proposals for a new 500 seat stand with sports facilities and directors' boxes - they are still very much reliant on a volunteer work force and people coming through the turnstiles. Most people in the area follow Premiership sides but even local nuances, such as school holidays or seemingly insignificant rival sporting events such as Crown Green Bowls, can affect attendance at this level. At the time of writing, the club have been averaging around 300 fans for home games but towards the play off push last season this figure was almost doubled.

"One advantage we do have over other teams in this division is we are not bang on the doorstep of bigger sides and this is something we need to tap into in the context of being a local, cheaper alternative. That said, I have friends who follow Curzon Ashton and Warrington Town who pay £6 to watch a game of football and can't work out why people still fork out £50 to watch a local Premiership side, especially as we are in the middle of a recession. I think sometimes that some clubs can't win whatever they do. Cammell Laird have had a meteoric rise through the pyramid yet still struggle to get crowds above 50 people, meaning they are unlikely to progress beyond their current status, which means people won't go and watch them. It's your classic catch 22."

Historically, Colwyn Bay has been a well-supported team. Pre League of Wales debacle, they often commanded crowds of 1,500 plus and Mark was confident that for each divisional rise the average attendance would increase by a few hundred. "Part of the problem we have now is a legacy of our exile in England. We have lost a generation of supporters who missed out on having a club play in the town for two seasons." It probably didn't help the club's case that around that time the Premiership launched, bringing with it televised top flight football on a scale never previously seen. Devoid of a local team to watch it is very easy to turn attention elsewhere, especially for those fans that were new to the non league scene and had limited time to forge any real bond with the club. SKY, with its televised pomp, must have seemed a very easy option, especially as it meant a new terrace culture could be forged in the pubs and the clubs for the price of a round of drinks.

The exodus from Wales in 1992 came at a time when Colwyn Bay FC were on a roll and the momentum behind the club was such that plans were being put in place to deal with the demands of Conference National football. The Welsh FA had revealed the formation of a new national league and stated somewhat dictatorially that the English based non league clubs would have to join. Then Bay Chairman Glynne Owens argued that his club were not against the league in principle but were angry at the apparent change of heart by the Welsh FA (FAW) which would "undo years of hard work to step into the unknown." An independent panel turned down the appeal of seven of the clubs protesting but curiously allowed Merthyr Tydfil to continue in the Vauxhall Conference. The battle between club and association became increasingly hostile, making national news and allowing angry supporters the right to voice their frustrations at a club being halted at the peak of its powers. Naturally, these background disruptions tampered what should have been a memorable promotion to the Northern Premier League (two Steps from the Football League).

Tim Shannon, a journalist from the Wirral who now covers Colwyn Bay for the local paper, told me that the club couldn't see a future in the League of Wales (LOW), especially after experiencing so much success prior to its inception. Whilst other clubs took the battle to the LOW they slowly caved in when they realised it could have serious repercussions. Colwyn Bay took the decision to fight the Welsh FA as it would have undone everything the club had worked for had they quit the English pyramid.

The decision to stand their corner came at a price. The club's supporters eventually gave their backing to a CBFC committee to continue playing in the English League system, even though this would mean playing some sixty miles away at Northwich Victoria's Drill Field. Despite stepping up a division and playing in new surroundings, the club finished a respectable 12th in their first season. The following season, and now playing at Ellesmere Port, the team finished an incredible 6th. Concerns were mounting at just how sustainable this scenario could be though; the cost of playing in exile as well as the loss of income put the club in an unfavourable position. Left with little option, CBFC, along with the remaining exiled clubs, Newport AFC and Caernarfon Town, took the fight to the WFA and in July 1994 secured an interim injunction on the grounds of restraint of trade, which would effectively allow them to play in Wales again.

The first game back at Llanelian Road on Tuesday 20th August 1994 attracted a crowd of 1,679, a then record for a league match at the ground. Celebrations abound but the move had come at yet another cost, specifically the £20,000 in legal fees to fight the case. Although back at their ground it was only considered 'half time' in the fight to overturn the ruling. The funds were eventually raised by contributions from supporters all over the country, as well as the local council, and led to the creation of a dedicated club fanzine and enhanced supporters' club who eventually helped finance concrete terracing at the ground on what used to be a grass bank.

In spring 1995 Judge Justice Blackburne ruled that the FAW had exercised "unreasonable restraint of trade" against the clubs, allowing the club to move home permanently without fear of any legal respite. Unfortunately, the turbulent events off the pitch had left a lasting legacy, as attempts to progress up the league were hampered by the financial strain playing outside of Wales had taken on the club. Towards the end of the millennium long-time Chairman Glynne Owen retired, bringing about the end of a 30 year era, coupled with an impending financial crisis which was temporarily staved off by contributions from local supporters. By November 2003 things had taken a dire turn for the worse and, faced with potential extinction, a new group of directors made up of supporters took over running the club and set about restructuring the club's operations.

I spoke to Darren Cartwright, current Managing Director and Chairman, to try and gain a better understanding of how the club operated now. Darren, unsurprisingly, was weaned on non league football. He used to watch Runcorn FC with his granddad and, as a member of a local family with a successful business, responded to a request from the club for financial support. Recognising there could be a lot of potential in the area, their proposal to the shareholders was accepted, albeit with certain hard-line changes being made along the way.

"It's critical that the club doesn't rely solely on volunteers or a single benefactor. We want to put a structure in place for financial stability because money is a problem at all levels of football. There are just as many clubs struggling in the Premiership as there are down here, only they have more noughts at the end of their debt. We don't have a big support, so we need to be realistic about our ambitions. Fortunately, those fans who do turn out are very loyal, which is good for attracting future generations. It is critical we attract local kids at an impressionable age, whilst realising that we are both a football club and a business; ultimately you are still offering a 'product' and therefore you have to ensure what you are selling is worth paying for. You can't simply say 'its local therefore you are obliged to go and watch it.' Unfortunately football just doesn't operate like this anymore." There has been an inevitable paradigm shift over the last fifty years with regards football demographics and choices. The advent of increased mobility and live television means fans are no longer tied to their local club for a football fix. Brand globalisation means that any fan can latch on to a particular football club, irrespective of local or cultural ties; Manchester United now estimate they have over 75 million fans worldwide, with an astonishing one million in England alone. Of course, how one would define a 'fan' is a moot point; following your team home and away every season is one thing. Buying a replica shirt and watching the odd match on Satellite

TV is another. From a local club perspective these factors impact massively. Given this, I was curious as to what Darren thought about the position of the club as a community stronghold, especially given their recent community football initiative, 'CIC', which allows the staff involved to bid for grant aid only available to non-profit making organisations.[1]

"We are a big part of the community and do a lot of work here. The town wouldn't allow there to be no team. I can guarantee that. The truth is crowds here are not always a true representation of popularity. Many fans in the area, who admittedly support Premiership sides, see us as their 'second club' and can generate very partisan feelings; people like and need a local identity and this can be expressed through football."

There is no doubt a lot of truth in this. The people of Colwyn Bay have a lot to be proud of here; the lush surroundings of the stadium, the award winning pitch, the volunteers who turn out even in bad health and, of course, the team itself, riding high in the league. It's just a shame the rows of empty seats didn't do justice to the club's endeavours.

To gain a fan's perspective, I had a quick pre-match coffee with Arthur Holden, a key contributor to *Come on the Bay* an official anniversary history book of Colwyn Bay Football Club. Arthur also started the "Raise The Roof" campaign which aims to collect £5,000 to offer covered standing areas on the main side terrace, particularly useful on a fine frosty February evening when the drizzle is soaking you into the latter stages of shivering hypothermia. To put this into context, at the time of writing Manchester City striker Emmanuel Adebayor had just been fined £25,000 by the FA for winding up a lot of angry Arsenal fans with itchy pie throwing fingers; you'd hope the money is spent wisely.

We made our way to a portakabin, a hymn to tea stains and allotment chic, for a spot of pre-match sanctity. Arthur was born in Bolton, Lancashire, but his family moved to Colwyn Bay when he was three so effectively The Seagulls are his hometown club. He went to his first game as a child, a heady recollection of cut grass and ale fumes, and never looked back. Like so many though, Arthur is a man estranged from an increasingly changing game.

---

[1] www.northernpremierleague/leaguenetwork.co.uk/news/details.php?news_id=237

"I look at the Premiership and don't understand it any more. What have I got in common with 22 millionaires? Football is more distant in the top flight now from the average man on the street than it ever has been: the players' life experiences are more like rock stars. At least in the days of George Best and the Charltons you could empathise, as they probably earned the equivalent of a good middle class wage: they were economically aspirational. As such, I can't see where the next level of pundits and analysts, commentators or journalists will come from. On the flip side, you may find people down the leagues who are motivated to take on management positions."

All this said, Arthur was gracious enough to accept a degree of fate in his choice of football team. Like me, an early childhood move had inevitable consequences on the team we ended up supporting.

"My first live match could have been Man United and things could have been very different. As it was, myself and a few lads from the estate went to watch Colwyn Bay. It just shows how important it is to get kids in early and let them enjoy the experience as much as they can, to offer then something more tangible than images on a TV screen."

Inevitably this led to a wider discussion about football, namely what motivates someone who professes to love football to sit at home and ignore their local side whilst claiming to support a club at the other end of the country who they never see play.

"To me, it's almost symptomatic of people's desperation to be attached to what they see as success. I remember when people in Colwyn Bay were wearing Blackburn shirts around the time they won the Premier League. The fact is, if you follow a non league club 90% of it is laced with misery, particularly midwinter trips to some god awful Yorkshire town, stood on an uncovered terrace getting soaking wet. There's no glamour in that. But since the inception of the Premier League, I haven't been to a single game because I just haven't wanted to go. The game at that level has changed. There is also a massive culture of watching it in the pub now, as if the terraces are recreated in the pub to a degree, which is a little strange. It's almost like 'retail park' football where you get everything - your drinks, camaraderie, live match and warmth - under one roof. At some point you need to make a conscious decision whether you want to be part of that world or not. To me it's a world of celebrity entertainment and, the way it's going, there will soon be two versions of football in this country; the game like we are watching today and a detached and corporate soap opera being played out on SKY. To me it's not the real world."

I glanced round at the humble surroundings the interview was taking place in. This was certainly the real world alright but a world which offered opportunity to feel part of a club rather than simply part of a revolving door of ticket holders who merely turn up and go home. Arthur's view seemed to corroborate this.

"I enjoy the fact you can talk to the directors, players and the referee after the game. I am not sure I would enjoy going somewhere that is too authoritarian, where I am told where I can and can't go, where I am charged five pounds for a pie, five pounds for a programme. The crowds are changing at bigger grounds; less atmosphere, more corporate packages, more middle class families on day trips who offer little to the match day experience. I have nothing against this as long as it doesn't stop the ordinary fan from attending, but I think it probably does. We need to be careful we aren't alienating a generation of fans."

I had effectively held Arthur captive for an hour by this point and the game was about to kick off. Today's opponents, Garforth Town from West Yorkshire, have flirted with notoriety over the last few years by virtue of being associated with some of football's greatest legends. In 2003, Simon Clifford - whose good looks might forge him an alternate career pointing into the distance in a Kays' Catalogue - purchased the club and with it strong connections to football, specifically via his ICFDS (International Confederation of Futebol de Salão) footballing academies which encourage a *Futsal* type game, only with a size 2 ball to put an emphasis on touch and passing. Clifford now manages the club too, with some aptitude, and has guided them to two recent promotions, casually assisted on occasion by ageing samba stars such as Socrates and Careca, albeit now in the same shape as the fans who stand on the terraces and no doubt with the same penchant for post-match drinks and cigars. Very few clubs at this level would have the audacity to chant "it's just like watching Brazil" but, in their *Canarinhos* style yellow and blue kit, Garforth fans have more reason than most.

Ex Manchester United poster boy Lee Sharpe also had a brief spell with the club. I can only assume the suspiciously random inclusion of Sharpe's autobiography *My idea of fun* in the Colwyn Bay club shop was a desperate attempt to cash in on this short lived association. One thing is for sure; given his limited amount of appearances, you can pretty much guarantee Lee's idea of fun wasn't being kicked up in the air by uncompromising semi-professional centre backs looking to make a name for themselves in the bar afterwards.

After reading some programme notes in the clubhouse (which for some unfathomable reason chose to play unnecessarily loud Euro house music, much to the amusement of four middle aged Garforth fans sat drinking pints of bitter in front of me), I headed to the main terracing where most of the home fans congregate for the match. As the players readied themselves for kick off with various motivational expletives, the stadium announcer sent out a stern warning to everyone in the seated area not to stand up, just in case the handful of fans scattered across that side of the pitch had any plans on ruining the view of the people not sat behind them. There are many facets of English football which thankfully haven't percolated down to the non league game, so it puzzled me why something so bureaucratic (and given the size of the crowd, quite pointless) was deemed necessary. Imitation may be the greatest form of flattery but fans need a little bit of credibility; it's a sad day if you're told to sit down and behave when the person sat nearest to you is only just within shouting distance.

The game itself got off to a slow start. Bay centre back Dave Challinor, the ex-Tranmere defender once famed for having the longest throw in English football, showed he had played at a higher level with his positional sense and distribution but was woefully exposed for pace by the Garforth front line, particularly the lively Darren Thornton and Mark Piper, the latter who looked like he needed a few years to grow into his kit.

The great thing about sparsely populated grounds is you get to hear everything the fans and players say, something you are singularly denied when there are larger crowds present. The usual shouts of 'man on', 'easy ball', 'get a name on it' are par for the course, but it's the otherwise hidden gems that are so satisfying, such as Garforth's football purist central midfielder berating his teammates for not playing it on the deck and then hoofing the ball into the car park a few seconds later with a self-righteous thwack. Simon Clifford made for interesting viewing as well. Clearly incensed at the distinctly non Brazilian hit and hope long ball game he was watching, the would-be Mario Zagallo took to kicking the dugout in frustration. It didn't help his cause that a Bay fan picked up on this and started mimicking him, like an infuriating toddler adept with testing the patience of an elder.

Commentators often say how awful it must be for players to be barracked by fans, though I sometimes wonder if 40,000 Mackems chanting "Alan Shearer, what a wanker" is more pre-emptive theatre. Personally, I would be a lot more perturbed if I was singled out for abuse by a gruff vociferous protagonist with a vendetta. There can be few things more disquieting than standing two yards from the crowd on a barren and breezy afternoon and hearing a lone voice shatter the autumnal calm with a random and unjustifiable "number seven - you cunt."

As the half wore on, Colwyn Bay started to make their superior league position tell. Apparently bored of trying to hit livestock in the adjacent field, players started knocking the ball to feet and Bay right winger Ian Sheridan, who looked like an extra from the indie group *Cast*, was particularly impressive. The passages of play were occasionally broken up by 'proper' tackles, so proper they would have Premier League insurance underwriters reaching for the Valium. "It's typical Unibond blood and thunder this," commented Arthur, who was stood next to me, arms folded, with a barely camouflaged smile. Fans like to see commitment at any level, in any part of the country and there was 'commitment' in abundance here. It's probably why I have never been able to reconcile with that well-trodden stereotype of "they like a trier in these parts", as if certain geographical areas have the monopoly on effort and endeavour.

The second half started in much the same bone smashing vein but saw first blood (other than that already pouring from gashed leg wounds) fall to Garforth, with 'Dazza' Thornton tapping in from a Tom Greaves cross to send the handful of travelling Garforth fans into a state of yellow ecstasy. Colwyn Bay manager Neil Young decided to take 'affirmative action' to this obvious affront and brought on two substitutes, partly as a response to the crowd's growing displeasure with one or two lacklustre players who were "standing there admiring the fucking view", although I could hardly blame them, given my eyes wandered to the lush and pleasant landscape behind the ground during the more soporific patches of the game. It wasn't long before one of those subs, Tom McGill, was pulled down in the area in a move that hasn't been seen on these shores since *World of Sport* featured prime time wrestling. Steve Aspinall scored from the spot and for the first time the Bay fans found their voice, albeit a repetitive chant of "Colwyn Bay! Colwyn Bay!" A few minutes later Rob Hopley scored with a neat finish and, just to infuriate the Garforth manager, who by now was on the verge of a seizure, Lee Davey wrapped the game up with the best goal of the game to seal a fine, if somewhat laboured, win. The fans clearly appreciated the effort put in by both teams and several gathered by the players' tunnel to clap off both the home and away side, which I thought was a nice touch. The referee still got called a cheating bastard though; no matter what level you watch at, they remain the scourge of the beer drinking masses.

Like Enfield Town beforehand, the players from both sides gathered in the social club afterwards for light refreshment. I had a chance to chat to one of the Bay players, Alex Hay, about his experiences of football at this level. Alex had tasted League football with Tranmere Rovers and also spent time with Rushden and Altrincham in the Conference National. "It's a good standard," he advised. "Some of the players could definitely play at a higher division - but a lot depends on personal circumstances. I'm a teacher in Liverpool and work round that. In fact nearly all the lads are from Liverpool. The pay is pretty good too."

Before I left, I joined the huddle around Mark's laptop as he logged on to the Non League 24 website's live vidiprinter[1] which updates Step 1 to Step 4 matches on a goal by goal basis (much like SKY's *Soccer Saturday* results service). There was much fist pumping when Curzon Ashton's result came in - a 3-1 defeat to Warrington Town - meaning this afternoon's win had taken on even greater significance. I flirted with images of Alex Ferguson watching *Final Score* in the Man United clubhouse after another injury time extravaganza, fist pumping and ruddy cheeked after seeing his closest rivals come a cropper. Whilst I cannot pretend the town of Colwyn Bay was at all how I remembered it, the club was all I could have wanted it to be. I only hope that when, and not if, I return they are still playing at Llanelian Road; what you may sometimes lose on the pitch, you gain with the view.

Notes

I would heartily recommend Daniel Fletcher's amusing yet highly partisan match reports on the official Garforth Town website www.garforthtown.com.

---

[1] www.nln24.com

South Shields v Newcastle Benfield

Northern League – Step 5
Saturday 10th October 2009

Final Score: 1-6
Attendance: 228

The North East of England is a place I have lived vicariously through but actually know very little about: Kevin Keegan, the works of Harry Pearson, documentaries on the mining strike, the Likely Lads, Byker Grove, Ant and Dec. My only previous visit to this part of the world (aside from a university jolly up on the Bigg Market which hardly qualifies) was during a brief stay in Peterlee, a new town in County Durham. In a former life I was an IT contractor, before IT contractors were sussed by the taxman and fixing computers became too much for a modest wage, or sanity, to justify. Sold the prospect of a well-paid job "near Durham" I asked my mate's mum what she thought of Peterlee. Given Gill was, like so many natives of the region, a walking tourist board for the North East, I should have taken more heed to her reply "it's not that nice", which in less flattering translation would read as "bloody awful". I won't go into detail - partly for fear of stirring repressed trauma - but suffice to say I lasted less than one day. It wasn't the people, who were actually very accommodating, but the wrist slashing, post pit town landscape. When John Ruskin coined the phrase "pathetic fallacy" to talk of inanimate objects having feelings, he must have stayed here: 'the thoroughly depressed flat roofed housing estate' would be one example that springs to mind.

One common denominator about this part of England, familiar to it or not, is the supposed passion for the local football teams. Now we should probably clarify something here. I have never, and will never, subscribe to any platitudes about certain teams having the most passionate fans, not least because it is a wholly unquantifiable concept. There is a lot of nonsense spoken about Newcastle United, for example, having the "best" fans in Britain, though how this was ever concluded is beyond me. A quick check through the attendance archives shows some fairly poor turnouts at St James Park during the 1980s, including a meagre 7,134 against Wrexham in the old second division during the 1978-79 season. This is not to say the Geordie fan base isn't loyal or don't love their team, because they invariably do. But as a per capita comparative they are a well-supported side and little more. Some media departments may be drawn to images of half-naked fans cavorting around in the snow to the backdrop of Blaydon Races, but a more salient barometer of fandom are the frequent sub 40,000 crowds they are now achieving in the Championship, which means somewhere along the line 8,000 fans have melted away (if such a term is possible given the arctic conditions prevalent here throughout the year). Moreover, as a Geordie friend of mine recently observed "there were just as many wankers with scarves appearing on the terraces when they got in the Premiership as any other club."

Tyne and Wear is dominated by another huge club, Newcastle's bitter rivals Sunderland AFC. Almost exclusively, everyone I have ever spoken to or read about from the area has supported either of these sides with a manic passion, with loyalties generally split depending on which side of the Tyne you are born on. Given the monopolisation of the fan base here, I was curious to know how the smaller teams in the area fared, particularly those in the much heralded Northern League.

The Northern League was founded in 1889 and remains the oldest surviving league in the country after the Football League. In informed circles, the Northern League is considered the most prestigious of all non league and amateur enclaves, providing a string of FA Amateur Cup winners and, in West Auckland, the champions of the world's first international football competition, the Sir Thomas Lipton Trophy. It may seems incredulous given their status today but West Auckland actually won the cup twice. Firstly in 1909 against FC Winterthur and then in 1911, hammering Juventus (yes, that Juventus) 6-1. Nowadays this kind of result is reserved for would be protegees on Championship Manager, but it gives an indication of the kind of quality the Northern League was producing at the time.[1]

Historically an amateur league, the Northern League was forced to find a place in the football pyramid when amateur status was abandoned by the FA in 1974. Unlike its equivalents, the Northern League opted out of invitations to become a feeder league to the Alliance Premier League (later the Conference National) when it was created in 1979. The Northern League

---

[1] For more details see
www.westaucklandtownfc.co.uk/index.php?Option=com_content&view=article&id=273&Ite mis=91

remained out of the pyramid until 1991, during which time the status of the competition declined as leading clubs defected to other leagues which gave a chance of upward promotion. When the league was finally forced into the pyramid it was not as a feeder to the conference but as a feeder to the lower divisions of the Northern Premier League, as indeed it remains today. Clubs in the Northern League are not eligible to enter the FA Trophy, but rather participate in the FA Vase, generally regarded as the superseded competition of the FA Amateur Cup, in which their clubs had so much success. The trials and tribulations of the Northern League are documented in the quite superb "Northern Ventures - Northern Gains" fanzine which is one of the most lovingly partisan publications I have ever read. At 30p - the price it cost me to purchase a number of back issues - you feel almost embarrassed paying so little for such a glorious publication. One member team in particular that stood out was South Shields FC, who in the 1926-27 season recorded an astonishing crowd of 24,348 for an FA Cup Quarter Final match. Regular home crowds of 10,000 in this era weren't uncommon. Last season they averaged 188. Maybe the catering has gone downhill?

To the foreign traveller, South Shield's ground is a nightmare to find, unless of course the foreign traveller has a map which usually makes things considerably easier. The whole of Tyne and Wear is served by a localised train network called 'the Metro', a sort of updated version of the London Tube without the impending sense of doom and delay. The nearest stop to the ground was a Station called 'Bede'. Aside from the football club, the stop seems to exist purely for anyone wanting to spend the day shopping on an industrial estate. The main road running through the site is called Shaftesbury Avenue, though instead of theatres and hotels stood a Tesco and the potentially *Viz* tinged Biffa waste services. There was also a fitted kitchen shop with a selection of optimistically priced units; I am not sure granite work tops are a big seller in an area where tracksuits and flat caps are *de rigueur* clothing items.

These soulless industrial environments, which even Bill Bryson would struggle to eulogise on, are of course exactly the kind of place many football clubs are now moving to. They offer cheap alternatives to traditional city centre locations, though at an inevitable aesthetic and social cost; anyone who has visited Derby County's Pride Park will know that no amount of Harvester pubs or Frankie & Bennie's outlets will replace the warm elixir of piss stained Victorian back to backs and the smell of rancid chip fat. Besides which, I can't buy into the idea I am suddenly transported into a 1950s Italian American diner when the waitress serving me has a strong East Midlands accent and, more notably, is Asian.

South Shields' ground is well hidden. Even the locals of whom we asked directions struggled to direct us; we would have had more joy asking David Cameron if he could point us to the nearest Netto. This is due in part to the modest size of the place. Three sides of the ground are simply fenced off, with the grandstand side housing a small seating area, as well as players' dressing room, club shop and club house. The club only moved to the ground in 1992, following years of ground sharing, relocations and false dawns. In fact the history of South Shields FC is rather complex and nebulous, and can be documented through various incarnations. Local paper archives make reference to a 'South Shields Association Football' team's first official result as a 2-1 win in September 1889 against Gateshead Albion, despite mention of three other games the season prior. To further muddy the water, a South Shields Athletic club formed in 1897 to play in the Northern Alliance but folded in 1902.

South Shields Adelaide was formed in 1899 and joined the Northern Alliance, before moving to the North Eastern League in 1908-09. Adelaide was dropped from the name in 1905 and in 1913 the club applied to the Football League but were blackballed polling no votes. Unperturbed, Shields eventually joined the extended Football League Division Two in 1919-20. The first game was a 1-0 defeat at Fulham watched by 20,000 spectators. To put this figure into context, Newcastle United was averaging around 30,000 a game during this period and Sunderland around 25,000. Despite the support for the team, relegation came the following season, and after two Division Three (North) seasons, the club folded in 1930 despite a respectable 7th place finish and were taken over by Gateshead. Franchising, it would seem, was alive and well long before MK Dons rode into town.

The team re-formed in 1936 and entered the North Eastern League, enjoying immediate success in both the league and Durham Challenge Cup before war broke out. Gates often exceeded 10,000 during this period, with the record at Simonside Hall (the club's home from 1951) thought to be 18,000 for the 1957-58 FA Cup tie with York City. The club then entered a nomadic period of their history, as enforced moves resulted from the folding of the North Eastern League in 1957-58, the Midland League in 1959-60, the Northern Counties League in 1961-62, the re-formed North Eastern League in 1963-64 and the North Regional League in 1967-68. The Northern Premier

League was the next stop and though the League didn't fold the club did, again, in 1974. By this time crowds had dwindled down to a few thousand spectators.

The club in its present form was born that year (after another defection to Gateshead) under Chairman Martin Ford and were based at the council's Jack Clark Park after the sale of Simonside Hall. After two title wins in the Northern Alliance, and a quarter final appearance in the FA Vase, Shields joined the Wearside League. It eventually fell to chairman John Rundle and his family to provide a long awaited home at Filtrona Park, which was extensively re-developed and first used by the club in 1992. I was to meet John later in the day.

The turnstile was manned by Phillip Reay who I had previously spoken to by phone. There is something about a North East accent which transports me back in time to the 1950s, as if the entire vernacular represents a culture untroubled by modern times; it is probably why I expected everyone watching the game to look like Alf Common. Phillip doubled up (or trebled up to be precise) as club secretary, turnstile operator and general South Shields philanthropist. We took advantage of our early arrival and had a chat with the bloke who ran the club shop. Of course, I say 'club shop' through habit. This was more a desk with souvenirs.

"Are you researching then?" he asked in an accent thicker than a welder's forearm.
"Sort of - I'm writing a book."
"He's come up from London," added Steve, in the guise of one trapped between awe and bafflement.
"Well you should speak to that man there," pointing to a slight middle aged chap near the stairs. "He's ran the club for 25 years." There was a light hearted exchange of North East humour. I didn't recognise a single word.
"Are you a Shield's fan?" I asked the club shop man.
"They're my home town team, so yes I am. I used to be a Sunderland fan until 1984." His voice drifted off. "Then I gave up and started coming here." I am no Sunderland FC historian but 1984 must have been a traumatic time at Roker Park.

I bought a pen and a pin badge and headed upstairs to the bar. It was quite an expansive setup, with the main drinking area affording a view over the pitch, which gave the feel of being in a very large directors' box, albeit one that sold Monster Munch. We were the only ones in the bar which allowed time to talk to the aforementioned John Rundle, who had been the owner and Chairman of the club for 25 years before staying on as landlord while a new consortium took over. John talked about football with a sense of weariness; a lifetime in the non league game no doubt does that to a man. He seemed somewhat disillusioned about both South Shields FC and the game in general. When he talked, you listened, not least because he looked quite animated when he spoke and stared at you in the manner of one who had just had his pint spilt. A friend of mine opined about North East folk after a trip to watch Arsenal play Newcastle United, that "they're all hard as nails up there" so who was I to fly in the face of sweeping generalisations?

John Rundle is a controversial club figure if documented history is anything to go by. Despite funding the current ground and giving the club a home, he publically threatened to fold the side if relegation followed from the Northern League First Division in the 1999-2000 season. Despite relegation the Chairman had a change of heart. However, problems resurfaced again in 2006 when Rundle again announced the club was to fold. Incensed at the prospect of South Shields FC ceasing to exist, a group of local people held talks and agreed to take the club on. Vice Chairman Gary Crutwell, Secretary Phillip Reay, Assistant Secretary Dick Bailey and Brinley Griffiths now run the club.

"We used to get three or four times this when I was first here," John commented, as he gazed onto the crowd below with a dishcloth in one hand and empty pint glasses in the other. I peered over the roof of the stand from my lofty perch. It was a sea of caps and bald heads, the wind tugging flocculent white hairs like tissue paper caught on barbed wire. To be fair, the elevation offered a slight reprieve from the blandness of the ground level view. Rather than a series of corrugated buildings I could see the odd field, subtly hinting back to the natural glories of the pre-industrial splash wave. It reminded me of a less attractive version of Telford Retail Park. Anyone who knows Telford Retail Park can read much into that statement.

"Why don't you get the same crowds anymore?" I enquired. John stared out of the window for a long time.
"Football isn't the same round here anymore. The Northern League used to have some of the best players in the North East on its books. The standard is nowhere near what it was twenty or thirty years ago. There are less youth

leagues in the area now meaning kids stop playing once they leave school. This has a knock on effect to local sides. If the standard here isn't as good, the people won't pay to watch it. I don't know; the game has just changed."

Like so many stories that circulate in pubs, clubs and terraced backstreets, quite whose opinion you side with depends on the prevalence of facts available. No doubt, to many at the club John is *persona non grata*. From speaking to John personally, I sensed a stubbornly principled man, a football purist who saw things in black and white, who was prepared to help out the local club but only if certain caveats were in place, not least that the team on show be worthy of funding. Of course, this is just my opinion. What is obvious is John feels he has poured his heart into the club and built it from nothing without possibly receiving the recognition he deserves. Pride is a strange thing and not something I want to postulate too long over on these pages, particularly when I am not privy to all the facts.

An important point of note, which may in part account for limited attendance figures or a sense that the club is not progressing as it might, is the club's reluctance to apply for Step 4 football, which would almost certainly be the NPL Division 1 North. When I asked John about this, he indicated that the funds and the infrastructure weren't there to deal with the additional travel requirements promotion would bring. Although on the surface this may seem a trivial matter, many Step 5 clubs often cite travel costs as a reason not to seek promotion and it is rare for more than a handful of clubs to actively seek promotion from this level each season. Furthermore, Step 5 leagues are almost exclusively localised; most teams in the Northern League are within 20 to 30 miles of each other. Put another way, in the 2008-09 season South Shields had to travel a total of 498 miles for all their away games. The similarly placed Newcastle Blue Star, in the league above, had to travel 2,659 miles on the road to complete their fixtures, which is an enormous jump. This added cost, although on the surface quite superficial, can eat into club budgets, particularly when potential stopovers need to be considered. Likewise, the logistical problems of travelling far afield can mean certain players are no longer available, particularly if they work shifts or have tight schedules to maintain.

It could be argued that this reluctance to progress is a catch 22. If a club gets promoted, the chances are their gates will go up and revenue will increase, but for teams out on a geographical limb, the lack of local derbies as teams progress higher up the pyramid can see crowds plateau and in some cases drop. The Northern League particularly is quite close knit and a good away support is par for the course. Whether an increased home support can sufficiently subsidise this potential loss is educated guess work. At this point, a decision to press on and climb the league structure is as much about sound investment and calculated risk as hope and ambition. Many clubs have taken the step up at all levels of the pyramid and suffered as a result, particularly if the local support just isn't there to justify it.

For many fans, particularly those who have grown up supporting teams where promotion and relegation is the norm, football needs to be aspirational. The concept of supporting a team which has no means of upward progression is almost anathema. It could be argued that glory or achievement is therefore highly relative. It wasn't until 1987 that promotion from non league to the Football League became automatic, but this didn't mean each preceding season in the non league pyramid was totally meaningless. Manchester United, if viewed in the same manner, are simply trying to win the league they are in and be crowned champions, albeit champions of England, but there is nowhere for them to go after that, no higher plane to ascend to. If we take the Northern League as a microcosm of English football, the glory of winning that competition is relative. To fans of the club, this is what turning up week in week out is all about; local pride, the odd cup run, the emergence of a local player who goes on to big things. Many non league fans I have spoken to don't actually want their team to aspire to higher divisions, certainly not if it means being whipping boys and coming straight back down, and certainly not if it means being subject to a lot of formalities higher level football brings. I recall speaking to a Kidderminster fan one bitterly cold afternoon in Southport, who gazed wistfully round the away team clubhouse and said "you can forget doing this if we get promoted (i.e. mixing with away fans before the game) - we'll just be a shit team with no fans in a big league. Nobody will know who we are. At least now we command a bit of respect." It would be disingenuous to say fans might not want a sugar daddy at somewhere like South Shields but I doubt they would want to sacrifice certain traditions and principles, like fielding a community team full of local lads at a reasonable admission price.

Whatever the case may be, South Shields FC is a shadow of the team they used to be in terms of support. Of all the teams reviewed so far (and certainly of those I intend to spend time with) few could document such a fall in stature. The explanation could lie in a number of factors, not least the collapse and subsequent rebirth of the side on more than one occasion, coupled with a long period of homelessness that may have ostracised a generation of fans. Perhaps of more important note is the socio-historical context of changing support patterns that have affected all sides over the last hundred years, particular ones which drew a fan base from vociferous and polarised working class communities.

In the 1920s, when South Shields were recording attendance of five figures for every home game, the country was a very different place. If you lived in a town or village and wanted to watch a game of football your options were pretty much limited to your local side. Travel networks were sparse and deemed an unnecessary cost to communities on limited incomes. There were no games to be seen on TV (in fact there were no TVs) no matches to be listened to on the radio and, as crucially, no other major forms of entertainment for a working man to indulge in of a weekend - certainly nothing that offered the community based camaraderie football could. Fast forward through the decades and the world has become a lot smaller and a lot more competitive. A young fan growing up nowadays has the luxury of cheap travel, blanket coverage of every major team, and access to online communities of fans which can substitute the bricks and mortar of their home town.

Of course, this is a thoroughly simplistic and (dare I say) biased view, which one could easily dedicate an entire book to. Irrespective of motivations or aspirations, the 200 or so fans that had gathered for the game were looking forward to a top of the table (of sorts) clash against local side Newcastle Benfield. Newcastle Benfield won the league last season but were not eligible (or like many in this division, did not apply) for promotion. With an average home gate of 73 they are one of the least supported sides in the league, hardly surprising given they are on the doorstep of Newcastle United. Although only founded in 1988, the club has already had more names than Elizabeth Taylor, including Brunswick Village Football Club, Heaton Corner House Football Club and, the rather awful, Newcastle Benfield Bay Plastics.

If the surroundings were somewhat drab, the kits that emerged from the tunnel certainly livened up proceedings, with Benfield's orange number clashing marvellously with Shield purple and maroon offering. If I hadn't been watching the match from behind reinforced glass I am fairly sure I would have had to squint or at least wear polarised glasses, irrespective of the sun hiding in a sulking manner behind the gathering cloud.

Benfield had beaten South Shields 4-1 at Filtrona Park earlier in the season in an FA Cup extra preliminary round game and when the away side took an early lead it looked like recent history could repeat itself. The standard of pass and move football by both sides was quite outstanding - easily the best I had witnessed so far on my travels - which suggested should either side ever move through the leagues, they could more than hold their own. Then again, it was quite conceivable that the precise reason the teams were so good was solely down to the retention of Step 5 status. There are an inevitable pool of players in the area who could play at a higher level but simply don't have the time to devote to the logistics that go with it, which creates an artificially high level of football at this level; It can be no coincidence that the most successful sides in the FA Vase and FA Amateur Cup have constantly hailed from the North East.

At half time, we were joined in the clubhouse by a number of fans for a half time pint and analysis. All football fans are genius tacticians by the way. A lifetime of watching football and shouting "fuck off" at every refereeing decision qualifies us to hold court with the likes of Rinus Michels or Brian Clough and, on frequent occasion, tell them where they are going wrong. Of the growing throng in the building, two characters particularly took my eye. Firstly, the club announcer who, like all lower league disc jockeys, seemed convinced that paying punters want to hear Britney Spears during the halftime interval. The PA system did his strong accent no favours; I would have had more joy deciphering the concepts of A Brief History of Time. In Arabic. The second chap was the walking exception that proves the theorem wrong; a Sunderland native who supported Manchester United.

To say this came out of leftfield would be like saying waking up in hospital to find myself circumcised was a bit of a shock. A North East accent with an allegiance to the Red Devils just didn't compute. I looked at my mate Steve, a Sunderland fan. They say a picture paints a thousand words. If I had a camera right there and then it would have painted three: away and shite. As it transpired, he was a fundraiser for South Shields and held a raffle on home games presumably to cover the trauma counselling for any bewildered locals who learnt his terrible secret. Leaving my own prejudices aside, he was a thoroughly likeable guy and made no bones about his support for Shields, as well as his involvement in youth football in

Sunderland. South Shields has a large Sunderland fan base and there were a number of them in the bar taking advantage of the international break and indulging in a spot of local football. It was particularly nice to see a group of teenage lads in the corner that had clearly come down for the first time and were obviously enjoying the day out, but this may have been in part due to the glut of goals that were now going in, unfortunately into the South Shields net.

The final score was a 6-1 trouncing. To their credit, the Shields players still came into the clubhouse after the game; no doubt the temptation of chips outweighed the wrath of a few angry pensioners pointing accusing walking sticks. One of the more impressive performers on the day was Shields striker David Graham, who refers to himself on the clubs official website as "the ultimate male". Interestingly, under "most desirable lady" David responds "any hole's a goal". Chelsea's John Terry is said to be a fan.

We left the ground shortly after the final whistle and took the brief walk back to Bede Metro stop. The place was deserted. You would certainly never have known there had been a match on round the corner, featuring a team that used to command crowds bigger than Sunderland, the team now playing in one of the most sophisticated grounds in the country in front of sell out 50,000 crowds. Football is a fickle business.

A few days later I posted a message on the South Shields fans forum asking for views on the game. I only got one reply, which read:
"Here's a question back - couldn't you have picked a better display to watch Shields?"

Four games in and already I was feeling like a gypsy's curse.

Wealdstone v Rotherham United

FA Cup – 1st Round
Sunday 8th November 2009

Final Score: 2-3
Attendance: 1,638

Ah, the magic of the FA Cup: the Mortensen Final, Jim Montgomery's saves, Ronnie Radford's piledriver, Keith Houchen's diving header, white horses prancing amongst a monochrome of flat caps and rattles; The greatest cup competition on earth, the envy of every other national association, a day when mere mortals can leave their emasculating jobs behind and spend 90 minutes living the dream in the gaze of the national spotlight.

Of course, like most shibboleths of modern football, the truth paints a more sobering picture. Historical imagery is easy on the manipulated eye but recent attendances, team selections and prevailing attitudes suggest if there is any romance left in the Cup it can be bought more easily than Demi Moore in *Indecent Proposal*. I remember back in 1990 when Hereford United drew Manchester United in the FA Cup 4th round. Half of the region started queuing for tickets at 2am, some seven hours before they were due on sale. I was one of the unfortunates left clinging to hope and a thermos flask who failed to get a ticket that day. In fact I still remember the stonewashed Wrangler wearing twat who gleefully shouted "tickets have run out" as he drove off in his Sierra Ghia some six hours later past a queue of defeated looking also-rans. The Sierra Ghia was proof, if ever it were actually needed, that the British public are a sucker for a marketing scam. Putting 'Ghia' after something as socially graceless as a Sierra is like putting 'Turbo' after a Betamax video recorder.

The anticipation at Edgar street was not only of a glamorous cup tie but of Man United fielding a side full of seasoned internationals, which they duly obliged with. Hereford eventually lost the match 1-0 thanks to a Clayton Blackmore tap in. The game was also noteworthy for a fan in the Hereford end smuggling a whistle into the ground and blowing it every time Jim Leighton had the ball. This caused much confusion in the United defence, which Colin Robinson, the laughably poor Hereford striker, who played with the air of one astounded he is making a living as a professional footballer, singularly failed to capitalise on. Although a fairly unspectacular story in itself, it marked a time when big clubs still took the cup seriously or at least had the integrity to field their strongest side even against lesser opposition. Fast forward to Exeter City's fairytale tie at Manchester united in 2005 and the travelling Grecian fans must have been mildly annoyed to see Sir Alex, who had already preceded over his club boycotting the competition completely a few years earlier in favour of an arse kicking tournament in Brazil, fielding what effectively amounted to a reserve side.

The story has been similar across the country and, as a general rule, the larger the side the less interested both the management and the fans appear to be in taking it seriously. Weakened sides playing out dull and protracted games in half empty stadiums has become a worrying benchmark, particularly in the 3rd round of the cup, which historically was the trump card of the competition. Granted, the increasingly stoic nature of the competition is occasionally punctuated with unpredictable delights, like Havant and Waterlooville's extraordinary run in 2007-08, but for the most part you get the impression that for too many clubs, even those in the Conference National, the cup is now an unwelcome distraction. Kidderminster Harriers boss Mark Yates, along with several players, saw their cup run last season, which culminated in a 2-0 defeat at Coventry City in round three, as the main reason for not reaching the Blue Square play offs. The sense of barely concealed bitterness was there for all to see. Almost invariably, Harriers Chairman Barry Norgrove took a more pragmatic view, describing the increased revenue as "a godsend" that helped keep the club afloat.

If the attitude to the FA Cup is, to put it mildly, somewhat ambivalent, what do the players make of it all? The answer, certainly if you prod about in the higher stratosphere of the game, is not a lot. Dave Kitson, the flame headed Reading striker, who forms part of a rare groups of players versed in language of two syllables or more, crystallised the current apathy towards cup competitions with this sacrilegious outburst in January 2008:

"We are not going to win the FA Cup and I do not give two shits about it, to be honest. I care about staying in the Premier League, as does everybody at this club. Our Premier League status is not protected by winning the FA Cup and it is as simple as that."

Whether one views Kitson's words with scorn or sympathy, he is probably only articulating what others are afraid to say yet happy to do, but it would be almost unthinkable to imagine a player of Kitson's ilk uttering these same blasphemous words only a generation ago. Then again, a generation ago, it would be almost unthinkable to imagine someone of Kitson's ilk a earning in a week what most fans earn in a year. Whatever way you look at it, the FA and SKY are suffering a *foile a deux* if they honestly believe the FA Cup can pull rank on viewing figures any more. In reality, there are only a handful of ties that truly engage the public conscious these days, namely clashes between the big four and anything involving plucky part timers taking on the behemoths of the English pyramid. Of course, the public conscience is an abstract notion, as it inevitably gauges the opinion of those following league sides with more important agendas. For non league sides, or at least non league sides who live hand to mouth in a regionalised bubble, the FA Cup, or at least the chance to experience a brief moment in the sun by virtue of pulling a League side out of the hat, is too good to be missed. There are few scenarios where playing Accrington or Rochdale at home would have the Chairman of the host club doing war whoops round the clubhouse but the FA Cup 1st round offers just that kind of unparalleled elation. Hoping to tap in to this well of euphoria, and in blind belief that the FA Cup was still an important part of our national game if you looked hard enough, I set off to Hillingdon to watch Wealdstone FC take on Rotherham United in the FA Cup 1st round proper.

The first point of note about Wealdstone is they don't actually play in Wealdstone but Ruislip. In fact this once all conquering non league club, who were Conference and FA Trophy double winners in 1985 shortly before automatic promotion to the Football League came in, have led a somewhat nomadic existence ever since they left their Lower Mead Stadium in 1991, when then Chairman Alan Clifton, sold the land to Tesco, with the club receiving very little by way of recompense, leaving them homeless for the next seventeen years and teetering on the edge of oblivion. For the record, Tesco reported annual profits of £3.1 billion pounds in April 2009.

There are some on the more virulent non league forums who point to the fact that Wealdstone's new ground at Grosvenor Vale was only obtained at the expense of Ruislip Manor FC, who were forced to move, thus making the acquisition slightly dubious and even hypocritical. Further investigation suggests the leaseholders of Grosvenor Vale, home to Ruislip Manor FC, desperately needed financial investment and approached Wealdstone with an offer. A consortium soon purchased a majority shareholding in the site, finally giving Wealdstone FC a home. There is a strong possibility that Ruislip Manor, who were surviving on threadbare support, would have folded anyway and, if anything, were being subsidised by their new landlords. Others take a more cynical view. In an attempt to try and clarify the matter - which is fairly important given the context of Wealdstone's recent history - I spoke to Stones' chairman Howard Krais for a more official take on events. "This is something that has been raised more than once before," he began. "Ruislip Manor Sports and Social Club Limited are the leaseholders of the ground and before we came in they had allowed Ruislip Manor FC to play on the site rent free for many years. We signed a groundshare agreement for our reserves to play at Ruislip for season 2007-08 and through that became aware of the many problems that existed on site, which all emanated through a complete lack of investment in either football stadium or social club facilities for many years. This was evidenced through the football ground being closed down for over a month due to the dangerous nature of the pitch, which impacted our reserves as well. Added to the fact that there were relatively new freeholders who had demanded considerable work and raised the rent it was no surprise that the people running both the football club and the social club wanted out.

We began to talk about taking over and a consortium of Wealdstone people bought the shares in Ruislip Sports and Social Club Limited around New Year 2008. One of the first things we had to do was to shore up Ruislip Manor FC to ensure they were able to complete their fixtures and we helped them find a new manager and worked with them to ensure their survival. We also started talking to them about the following season. It was clear that everyone involved on site, including the juniors and RMFC and Wealdstone FC, would have to contribute to make the site a workable proposition. It was because people were not paying their way that the site was in such a state of disrepair.

We offered RMFC a ground share agreement at about 50% of what we had paid at Northwood the previous three seasons. We believed this a good deal. The guy who took RMFC over, however, decided to take them nearer his home base and instead moved them into the old Viking sports ground in Greenford under a new name. Wealdstone FC has always strongly refuted the very few people who claimed we were in any way responsible for RMFC's demise. In fact this was something that a few journalists kept going and no one else. Had RMFC continued they would have gone bust - no question."

With an issue as emotive as football, it is inevitable that the respective officials and supporters of the clubs concerned will have differing views on major events such as these; there is rarely an 'official line' that everyone subscribes to. In reality, it is the job of the individual to listen to all sides of the story and draw their own conclusions. What is certain is Ruislip Manor now exist under the name Tokyngton Manor FC and, as Howard pointed out, play at Greenford in the borough of Ealing. They have an unenviable record of recording an official attendance of 1 (one for vidiprinter aficionados) during a game against Buckingham Athletic in the 2008-09 Spartan South Midland League.

The fact Wealdstone were even able to stage the game today was something of a minor miracle and testament to the loyal and dedicated work force that have kept the club going during the last two decades. During their darkest hour, supporters "unwittingly adopted their *bête noire*'s 'Every little helps' slogan" and pitched in with a variety of fundraising activities, from sponsored walks through to bucket collections. These benevolent acts continued after the move to the new stadium, with supporters working round the clock getting the ground up to Isthmian League standards; in short, the club almost certainly wouldn't be here were it not for the efforts of its volunteer fans. As director Paul Rumens notes in the excellent match day programme:

"We do not have sugar daddies and wealthy backers to compete with richer clubs at our level but we do have a brotherhood and sisterhood that is virtually unbreakable and is just getting stronger and stronger. Maybe we have won nothing yet on the pitch, but we are certainly winning over new hearts and minds be it local Ruislip people or disenchanted ex-Premier League fans and the like who can see the honesty and purity that clubs like us bring to the table."

Recognising the overwhelming help that has come from voluntary sources and the importance of engaging local people, Krais remains pragmatic. Speaking to *The Guardian* in 2008, he observed "There are too many clubs in this area, all at a relatively similar level and all swimming against the tide. Only the healthiest clubs will survive those that have financial investment and are well-run as football clubs and community organisations."

It would be easy to be carried away in a tide of sentimental slush when commentating on these triumph-in-the-face-of-adversity stories. And it isn't just non league teams who are subsidised by volunteers and well-wishers, as many supporters of Football League clubs will no doubt testify to. But for a club whose average attendance is less than four figures, it shows testament to the good will of people in wanting their community to have a club, irrespective of its chances of winning trophies. Given Wealdstone took 500 fans to Aylesbury in the 4th qualifying round and now take their place in the FA Cup first round proper for the first time in 23 years one could argue this is exactly the kind of glory that can't be quantified by a trophy cabinet. Despite asking at least four people where the ground was ("dunno - in Wealdstone I imagine, mate") I spent the first half an hour in Ruislip in an oblivious haze until, like Robert Newman's predatory lothario *Jarvis*, I finally locked onto a young man wearing a blue and white scarf who eventually pointed me in the right direction. Being a football fan, especially one who seeks thrills in the less chartered areas of our country's backwaters, can make you feel like Blanche Dubois at times, eternally dependent on the kindness of strangers.

Wealdstone's stadium sits in the middle of a housing estate about ten minutes' walk from Ruislip underground. Despite the endeavour of the supporters' groups, the ground is still very modest even by Isthmian League standards, though funds are available for slow and progressive development if and when promotion dictates. Today was not really a day for aesthetic musings though. Given Wealdstone's average attendance has been around the 450 mark this season, the potential of a 2,000 sell-out crowd not only offered a financial windfall but also a chance for the club to really celebrate the end of their exile to a national audience. Once inside the ground, it felt more like a Sunday fête. There were food stalls, programme kiosks, pin badge displays, face painting and a general feeling of a community day out. The term 'carnival atmosphere' is often thrown around on days like this, usually prompted by the presence of anyone waving a flag. This metaphor inevitably depends on what one would define as a 'carnival'; there is a world of difference between, say, the Winterbourne Down Village Carnival near Bristol and the Notting Hill Carnival in west London. Given the recent security alerts surrounding the latter event, anyone who has been pickpocketed or threatened with actual bodily harm by roaming feral gangs can justifiably say they have experienced a carnival atmosphere; whether this is a positive thing is a moot point.

Today's opponents, Rotherham United, are no strangers to the vagaries of financial crisis. Always a modest outfit with modest resources, and relatively dwarfed by nearby neighbours United and Wednesday in Sheffield, problems mounted in 2006 when it was revealed the club faced financial ruin unless a funding gap of £140K a month could be met. Administration was not a viable option as the club had already sold its ground to clear previous debts, leaving them with no obvious assets. This led to the creation of the "Save our Millers" campaign, aiming to raise the £1m needed to complete the season. Although saved from oblivion by a late consortium takeover, the club fell into administration and started the 2006-07 season in administration. Relegation followed and, despite spending most of the following season in a play off place, the club fell back into administration again and consequently trailed away to mid-table. The 2008-09 campaign proved even worse. Shortly before the start of the season, the Football League threatened to ban Rotherham from playing in League 2 as the club had failed to exit administration or transfer ownership. This resulted in a 17 point deduction and Rotherham being forced to leave Millmoor, its home of 100 years, and move to the nearby Don Valley Stadium in Sheffield, after disputes with the landlord. The Football League has further complicated the issue by demanding a £750K bond from the club for playing outside of the town's boundaries. Rotherham has four years to move back to the town or face serious ramifications from the Football League.

It could be said that today's clash was symbolic of the problems affecting the modern game. Whether you choose to take a righteous or romantic view depends on your personal viewpoint, but the one common denominator when clubs hit the wall or leap from one disaster to another is that the fans pick up the emotional bill. The day was cold but the sun shone brightly - a worthy metaphor if one were needed.

The teams entered from the players' tunnel to a fanfare of noise and expectation, orchestrated by an assortment of fans with their faces daubed in the club colours. I can forgive this for anyone aged under ten, but I have always found the idea of grown men walking around football grounds looking like Young Kenny from *Phoenix Nights* somewhat disquieting. Given Wealdstone play in a striking azure kit also meant that a group of painted middle aged men stood next to me looked like the Blue Man Group if they really let themselves go.

Wealdstone started in true underdog fashion by throwing themselves into every challenge, much to the approval of the 1,500 or so home fans in the stadium. Unfortunately, endeavour and spirit can only carry a team so far and Rotherham slowly started to exercise their superiority, with the skilful Adam Le Fondre looking particularly impressive. Stones striker Charlie Mpi, who despite his pace was as raw as an Astroturf burn on an elbow, caused the Millers' defence problems, particularly on one tumbling fore in the box which saw most of the home fans clambering for a penalty kick. I say most; some remained tight lipped. "He went down a bit easy," rumbled one observer in a Chelsea drill coat, "he was looking for that". Given the tirade of causticity aimed at both teams, it was hard to establish who his allegiances were actually with, though you got the impression he was doing the club a big favour by being here today, especially as he continually asked his chain smoking mate if there was any news from Stamford Bridge where Chelsea were playing Man United. I've never been a big fan of fans turning up to lower league grounds in Premiership attire and treating the game like a side show. Granted, a lot of people have a 'second' team they follow occasionally, but personally I find it a bit disrespectful to march into a ground wearing another team's shirt: the subtext is almost "well, they're so bad, who will care?"

Rotherham continued to press (I have really slipped into football-journo cliché mode here) and, aside from a speculative shot from Stones' brilliantly named Mark E'Beyer, the game started to resemble a training session for the League Two side. When the pressure paid off and the first goal came, it flattened the crowd completely. Sean Thomas, who had played admirably in the Wealdstone net, fluffed his lines on clearing an innocuous back pass and slammed the ball into the backside of the onrushing La Fondre, sending the ball ricocheting into the net. Most football fans are gracious enough to accept when they have been beaten by a piece of toe-heel magic or one touching passing genius, but to go a goal down scored by someone's arse puts a depressing hue on proceedings. When Kevin Ellison scored a 20 yard piledriver a few minutes later to make it 2-0 an eerie silence fell over the ground. In the space of half an hour the Wealdstone faithful had gone through the bi-polar extremes of emotion. The huddled masses were no longer singing, the balloons had floated away into the grey sky over the nearby rooftops and the fifty year old men with blue faces stood shivering with a look of comic book hypothermia. All, it would seem, was lost.

With fifteen minutes to kill, and the wind biting my neck like a teenager drunk on alcopops, I joined the queue for a slice of gastronomic Russian roulette. Most *bon viveurs* would blanch at the fare offered by football caterers; unless you like chips, burgers, or tomato soup with more sediment than the Thames Estuary you are pretty much buggered. There are notable exceptions - some of the West Midlands venues I have frequented pull off Balti pies with varying degrees of success - but they are few and far between. Half time food is ritualistic at football matches and its universally renowned crapness is proof that the British are never really happy unless things are just a bit shit. I don't want some culinary necromancer trying to reinvent the wheel when it comes to a half time pie and Bovril. Haute cuisine and terrace culture don't mix. Besides, no terrace chant ever got off the ground that rang "who ate all the pan fried bream?"

By the time I had purchased my burger, the Rotherham players were back on the pitch. Rotherham's 'keeper Andy Warrington, whose grey hair and avuncular appearance belied his relatively tender years, attracted a small crowd of hecklers to my right. Small is the operative word here; they looked like Statler and Waldorf's grandchildren. Given their youthful stature, the level of banter was fairly innocent: "where's your letter from the queen?" was relatively amusing, although "your surname's a small town near Manchester" was the most informative catcall I have heard in a while. They were certainly a lot more innocent than the token gruff-bloke-behind-you who shouted out "Warrington, you grey haired twat" whilst simultaneously spitting boiled onions over everyone in a fifteen metre radius.

Wealdstone started the second half in positive fashion but their strikers were well marshalled by the hirsute Millers centre back Ian Sharps. It wasn't until Stones Danny Spendlove came on with around 25 minutes left that the game really turned, with his speed and close control causing their opponents' back line problems. It was he who set up Ryan Ashe on 62 minutes to score a fantastic volley past a stranded 'keeper and the same player who put E'Beyer through to wastefully put wide a few minutes later. Of course, as any smart arse will tell you, maverick football can leave you short at the back and a rash challenge from a Rotherham breakaway led to a Drewe Broughton goal from the resulting free kick. Wealdstone, to their credit didn't give up and retained a degree of self-belief which embodies the whole club, not least their loyal fans. Ryan Ashe added a brilliant second with only minutes left on the clock before a melee in the penalty error resulted in the ball scuffing the post, the ball going out for a goal kick and Wealdstone going out of the cup. The final whistle brought a dramatic game to a close, with players and fans slumped in symbiotic exhaustion. Twenty two men left the field to a standing ovation. The overwhelming impression from the applauding masses was of humility and pride. The team had done their club proud, irrespective of the result, and that is all any fan can ever ask. I daresay the whole experience was somewhat cathartic; a happy crescendo to years of struggle. Walking out of the ground through the mud, chip trays and crushed plastic pint glasses into the half-light of the dimly lit street filled with footsteps and sharp fogs of breath I felt privileged to have been here.

Maybe the FA Cup had some magic left after all.

Truro City v Halesowen Town

Southern League Premier Division – Step 3
Saturday 14th November 2009

Final Score: 1-2
Attendance: 429

Cornwall is not exactly synonymous with football. The county has never had a League side and until recently has never even threatened to. Given the county has a population of over 500,000, and a fiercely partisan one at that with both its own flag and own language (albeit somewhat redundant), it seems surprising that football hasn't been able to tap into these favourable factors and produce a team of any note.

The game is played here of course, like everywhere else in the country. The county has a presence in the National League System (NLS) with a number of clubs playing in the South West Peninsular League at Step 6. There are also a number of smaller county leagues, outside the NLS, such as the Cornwall Combination at level 12, and the Mining League directly below it, which offer the chance for progression through the pyramid providing certain criteria are satisfied. Such progression, though, remains static; quite why this is remains open to debate.

The first obvious problem facing any team in Cornwall is a logistical one. Sitting at the tip of the peninsular of South West Britain, it is a somewhat geographically isolated area. If promotion to the Western League at Step 5 were to be considered, sufficient time and funding would be needed to take on the enormous amount of travelling this would involve. Given the scarcity of established non league teams in both Cornwall and Devon, clubs wishing to progress are lumped under a "South West" regional umbrella which in certain cases can mean travelling as far afield as Wiltshire, some 150 miles away from the county border. For clubs this far down the pyramid, it presents an almost unworkable conundrum, particularly as the average gate for the South West Peninsular League in season 2008-09 was just 97: the maths just don't add up.

The second issue concerns the established status of Rugby Union in the area which is arguably the dominant sport culturally and in terms of attendance figures. The Camborne based Cornish Pirates average around 3,000 spectators a match, which may seem relatively modest but dwarfs local attendance for football. To put it into context, Penzance FC, who were South West Peninsula Division 1 West (Step 7) champions in 2009, only averaged 159 fans.

The final problem is one of history. Anyone looking for a big team to cheer on was never going to find it in Cornwall. Many of the county's fans therefore gravitated to nearby Plymouth Argyle or simply opted to follow one of the giants of the game and pledge their allegiance to Manchester United or Liverpool. Many Cornish fans would argue that when you live so far from any League side, following Plymouth Argyle some 80 miles is as arbitrary as following Spurs or Arsenal. 'Local' is a very relative term in this part of the world. As with all football families, loyalties tend to be passed down by generation. Of the non league sides in Cornwall, such that they are, few have any discernable history of success and can number their hardcore supporters in less than three figures. Football it seems was just never meant to thrive in Cornwall. Then, in 2004, a man called Kevin Heaney turned up at Truro City FC and all that changed.

At the time of his arrival, Truro City were playing at Step 7 of the NLS in the now defunct South Western League and were in severe financial difficulty. They had been members of the League since 1951 and had won it five times, which ostensibly represented a degree of success, but since their formation in 1889 as founding members of the Cornwall County FA the club had never ventured beyond local league football, presumably for financial or operational reasons. The first thing Heaney did was to wipe out the club's crippling debts and resolved to invest sufficient funds to get the club moving up the football pyramid, which had previously been something of a glass ceiling. Heaney, a successful business man and property developer saw Truro, the county town of Cornwall, as an untapped well of support and a fitting place to start his project. Although home to a modest population of just over 20,000, it was his belief that Cornwall was capable of sustaining a Football League team, based on catchment areas, local passion and investment in the club. The last factor cannot be understated. Money talks at any level of the game and Truro's new found wealth allowed them to attract players from higher leagues, particularly ones on the fringes of established 'local' clubs such as Plymouth, Torquay and Exeter, which in turn started to propel the club through the Regional League System.

Their meteoric rise started in 2005-06 when the club finished runners up in the South Western League which took them into the Western League Division One. The 2006-07 campaign which followed proved to be nothing short of astonishing. Not only did the club win the league at the first attempt, they did so with a record amount of points (115) and a record amount of goals (185). To bring the curtain down on a truly spectacular season, Truro then reached the FA Vase Final and beat AFC Totton 3-1, thus becoming the first Cornish team to win a national trophy.

Of course, success often comes at a price. For many clubs and fans in the region, Truro were simply a small team buying their way out of the leagues. Whilst some might argue it is simple envy, others pointed to the lack of fair play abound, as the team steamrollered the opposition week in week out with a squad that wouldn't have looked out of place several divisions up. In 2007-08 Truro won the Western League Premier Division which took them into the Southern League Division 1 South and West (Step 4) alongside such luminaries as ex-Conference National side Slough Town. Many non league fans argue that once a club hits this level the football ceases to become 'regional' and the 550 mile round trip to the likes of AFC Hayes bore testament to that. Incredibly, Truro won the league again, at something of a canter, sending them into the newly named Zamaretto Southern League, two leagues below the Conference National. Their most recent promotion also meant that Truro had now equalled the record for successive promotions through the League System. The good times just keep on rolling in this picturesque part of the country. Or do they?

The concern for many Truro fans is that the success of the club is built on a house of cards. Although Kevin Heaney wants to make them self-sufficient, this could prove difficult when the club has an average gate of around 650 and huge overheads in terms of wages and travel. Moreover, Heaney only has finite resources to throw at the club and the uncertainty of the housing market, culminating in the liquidation of his Cornish Homes company to a reported personal cost of £2m, has questioned just how much longer he can keep funding this rising team. Heaney has been quick to distance himself from any talk of pulling out of the club but history has shown the dangers of relying on a single benefactor. Perhaps the most high profile example of this trend was in 2005 when Hornchurch FC, dubbed "the Chelsea of the non league", was liquidated when their major investor Carthium Ltd went bust. What made Hornchurch's collapse even more bizarre was the arbitrary decision to invest so heavily in a club that was within spitting distance of West Ham United and other Football League sides and had kicked around in the lower reaches of the Isthmian League in front of three figure crowds for most of its innocuous existence. A similar fate has also befallen Northern Premier League outfit Burscough, after its wealthy owner Chris Lloyd quit the club and froze funding. Burscough were FA Trophy winners in 2003. At the time of writing they had an estimated six weeks before being wound up, although a press release on the official website in April 2010 indicates the ground will now be sold off to manage debts.[1]

I asked Truro City Secretary Ian Anear how he saw things developing in light of their rapid rise to prominence. Ian had spent most of his life supporting and working for the club, which obviously gave him a broad perspective on which to comment.

"In two to three years the club are moving to the other side of the city to a purpose built development. There will be a new 4,000 seat stadium, three additional pitches, covered tennis courts and some 5-a-side courts. The planners are all in favour - we are just waiting for the results of the environmental impact study which will take nine months before go-ahead is given." Clearly these are plans built on estimated progression. Truro's average attendance this season has been around 650, up from 490 the season before and 300 in the 2006-07 season. The stadium, on paper, appears overkill, though it will resolve issues that surround the current Treyew Road ground which is currently a D grade and requires upgrading to C grade by the end of March 2010 if the club wish to remain in the Southern Premier. So would the fans turn out if Truro made the Conference South or National in their new ground given their relatively humble background?

"We've always been a big team in Cornwall," Ian checked, "and we are gaining fans all the time. There are external factors; the weather, the Rugby, whether or not Plymouth Argyle are playing at home, but we are optimistic we can get the 2,000 fans needed if we made it to the Conference National. Who knows, we may even get some Plymouth fans come down here if they drop through the leagues!"
Obviously to reach these fans will require a combination of good marketing and good results. You would fear for the side if they planned for a future on a speculative attendance figure that was totally unobtainable. 2,000 fans

---

[1] www.burscoughfc.co.uk/news/archives/41/

may not sound much but the town only has a population of 20,000. As Ian pointed out, Truro has a fairly central county location so the business plan assumes that the club will become a beacon for all Cornish football fans, rather than just those in Truro. Given there are few, if any, deep seated rivalries that would keep fans away, it may be a realistic target. Although not directly comparable, the much maligned MK Dons have shown that with the correct application on and off the pitch, fans with no prior attachment to a club will turn out and watch. Since forming in 2004-05, their average attendance has more than doubled, boosted in part by the move to a state of the art stadium. It would be reasonable to assume that as the Dons grows roots in the local community and progress up the League, this fan base will continue to grow.

Truro have taken steps to promote the club in and beyond the town limits by outsourcing their marketing to a company called FS Media Solutions, an offshoot of local solicitors Follett Stock. Chris Lingard, part of FS media solutions, stated their intentions on www.southwestbusiness.co.uk as well as providing a cautionary note of the club's current setup:

"We are delighted that one of our first clients is Truro City Football Club. During the next few months people will see a big change in the way the off pitch business is conducted. It is essential that the club becomes financially self-supporting. It is unhealthy for any club to rely on one benefactor however generous he may be. In my view the benefactor should be there to buy the extra things in life and not be relied upon for the everyday items. We shall be working closely with the fantastic supporters of the club and the community as a whole which we hope will throw itself behind the team's push for a record breaking fifth promotion by offering us even greater support. We shall be trying to attract as wide a fan base as we can and intend to have a family zone available together with a zero tolerance on foul and abusive language."

Whilst these comments are very noble, you hope it isn't another corporate statement paying lip service to a potentially flawed business model. Ian admits himself that as long as Truro is reliant on Heaney's handouts they are operating from a dangerous position. Whilst there may be no doubt of the Chairman's good intentions nobody has the ability to predict the future, least of all the financial whiz kids who brought about the current recession by grossly overestimating the ability of people on limited resources to operate above their means.

On the plus side, the club are making positive strides to obtain financial independence. It was refreshing, for example, to see club merchandise for sale in an independent sports shop in town. Coupled with a venture to let Tiger Commercial use the club's name and its facilities at the ground to generate income and interest, there is clearly a degree of optimism that the club can continue and compete as a self-funded sporting outfit for the good of the local community.

Truro's recent good fortunes lay in stark contrast to today's visitors Halesowen Town. Non league football has many charming and wholesome facets that may be missing at the very top of the English game but it seems there is still a level of financial skulduggery, mismanagement and corruption going on which would put a South American politician to shame. At the time of writing, Halesowen find themselves in administration and wholly uncertain about what the future holds, despite optimistic noises coming from the Yeltz Trust that the club will fall back into the hands of the supporters.[1] Local press reports suggest the problems are largely attributed to the tenure of ex-Halesowen chairman Morell Maison. Despite arriving at the club in 2007 with high hopes and ambitions, the last six months have been a PR disaster, involving administration, a fans' boycott, expulsion from the FA Cup and Trophy, an attempt by a former employee to wind the club up, and the involvement of the West Midlands Police's Economic Crime Unit.[2] One ray of light is that the ground is owned by "The Grove Trust", an independent trust set up by James Grove, the founder of the button factory next door, to keep the ground for the sporting benefit of the people of Halesowen, which is then leased back to the football club. Quite whether the current team (or indeed a future supporters' club) continue to play there is another matter.

Despite their troubles, Halesowen had brought a healthy number of fans on the long journey down from the West Midlands, giving the splendid Truro

---

[1] No one exactly knows why Halesowen Town are called the Yeltz. For further details, see http://www.yeltzland.net/contents.asp which offers, in their own words, a boring pseudo-historical explanation, as well as a much more likely one.

[2] Details of the boycott can be found at http://www.theyeltztrust.co.uk/sitefiles/trustadmin/141509/why%20are%20we%20protesting.pdf

clubhouse a distinct *Crossroads* quality. I had a chat with a couple of ladies bedecked in club colours to get a fan's perspective on the recent turmoil at the club. The general consensus seemed to be that despite the last year being something of a nightmare, things were unlikely to get any worse. They were clearly proud of their club and were keen to point out the profound effect the recent troubles had had on the entire town and not just the immediate supporters. As the oldest club in the West Midlands, there is a legacy to protect and it was interesting to hear that supporters of nearby giants West Bromwich Albion had pledged an allegiance to the cause.

Not content with pestering the female element of the travelling Halesowen fans, I moved on to a group of unsuspecting males near the bar. The stand out interviewee was a bald chap with a huge goatee beard, (who as it later transpired was Yeltz Trust Chairman Gary Willetts) who would have looked more at home on *Pimp my Ride* or *WWE Smackdown* than a Zamaretto Premier League match. I asked him why he supported Halesowen and followed them round the country.

"Now that's a good question. The main reasons are days like today. You can have a pint in the clubhouse, talk to the home fans, abuse them for 90 minutes during the game and then chat with them afterwards and no one had a bad word to say, whatever the score line." It transpired my new friend was on the board of the Yeltz Trust and also co-ordinated the away travel for the club, which often numbered 50 to 70 on a good day. Of particular interest was a recent fans' survey which suggested 60% of home supporters didn't live in Halesowen. Quite why this is wasn't explained, though suggestions went from ex-pats staying loyal through to Halesowen having gained kudos due to its historical status in West Midlands' football.

Halesowen remain a club cast in perpetual shadow by near neighbours West Bromwich Albion and, like many smaller clubs in large urban conurbations, face competition from a high concentration of rival teams. Within a fifteen mile journey of their ground there are five Football League clubs, a Conference Premier club, two Conference North clubs and two Zamaretto League clubs, which gives an indication of the contest for support, in stark contrast to the situation at Truro. Albion's ground, The Hawthorns, is only seven miles from The Grove and generally mops up support in the area like a naan bread mops up one of the region's famous Baltis. Some of the supporters I spoke to today openly admitted they had strong Baggies tendencies but stressed that the two teams offered different things.

"A day out at the Hawthorns would cost you £50" one commented "At Halesowen you can get entrance to the ground, a few pints, a pie and a programme for under £20. Plus, you can go on your own and are guaranteed to see people there you know. It's more like a social club for the community and its fans."

I liked the idea of a club being a place for people to go and meet friends or just to feel part of something. Sociologists have continually debated the role of football in providing meaning to people's lives in both an individual and collective sense and you sense this role is magnified where it's indulged by people in such a highly focused and parochial way. Not surprisingly, the Yeltz supporters' trust has already prepared should the worst ever happen; it is an increasing trend that teams with an asterisk after their name one season has AFC before it the next.

The clock now read 2.55pm. I had bored people long enough and stepped outside to watch the teams take to the field. Truro's Treyew Road ground is a gorgeous slice of Cornish countryside, magnificently isolated on the outskirts of the city and a short walk from a tumbling basin that overlooks the 19th century cathedral skyline. Unfortunately the aesthetic qualities of the ground are a little more stunted. Progress on the pitch has vastly outstripped progress off it, leaving the club with a distinctly local league looking stadium for Step 3 football. The areas behind both goals were simply grass separated from the pitch by advertising boards and the only covered area was a small terrace to the left of the clubhouse. The opposite side had an ostensibly impressive looking seated area for some 1,200 fans, but on closer inspection looked like the kind of temporarily erected seating you see at a bad pop concert. One could imagine Chris De Burgh hammering out *Lady in Red* on the centre circle after the game, only to fewer people than the exposed handful sat hunched playing chicken with the capricious weather.

Thankfully there was no rain today. At the first drop you imagined everyone scurrying for cover under the small sheltered area, like cockroaches running under the fridge when the kitchen light goes on. Mind you, these were Cornishmen we were talking about. Being exposed to the elements (literally in the case of the Tin Mining industry) is practically a way of life down here. For a man who bores both clients and himself with talk of virtualised IT solutions, and flirts nervously with the idea of manicures, I just can't compete in the macho stakes. If it rains I tend to hide, less I smear my fake tan.

Most home fans gather at the clubhouse end before kick-off but those who stick to true non league traditions tend to migrate to whichever end the home side are kicking towards. Depending on the age of the supporters, indicated by a useful flat cap barometer, this could mean reaching the other end of the ground just as the referee blows for half time. For years this was always the norm at Kidderminster. There were exceptions, such as when big sides came to play, or crap sides came to play and brought inexplicably large numbers of fans. When Harriers were promoted to the Football League, this tradition was rather watered down, not least because some non league fans (and indeed the local police) seemed to view their league counterparts as potential hooligans. This view is partly born out of stereotype and partly out of statistical inevitability. One major difference between League and non league fixtures are the number of away fans that come to games. Even poor sides in League 2 would bring a couple of hundred fans to Aggborough, of which one or two might politely be described as head cases. Poor sides in the Conference might bring a couple of fans full stop. I remember a forgettable home game against Welling United when the away team took a shock lead and their travelling support stood in front of us (three tasty forty somethings with shares in Brylcreem, fake leather and Elizabeth Duke) started laughing. Expectation levels clearly aren't high in the DA16 part of London.

Truro had come into the game on a mixed run of form. After winning five of their first six games they had only managed one victory in the next five. When Halesowen's Aaron Griffiths was brought down by Arran Pugh in the 7th minute, and ex-Aston Villa starlet Stefan Moore stepped up to score his 19th of the season, you sensed this patchy run was about to continue. Although Andy Taylor did his level best to address the balance by testing Yeltz 'keeper Nick Buseey on more than one occasion, Truro's task was made even harder in the 39th minute when on loan Steve Adams was dismissed with a straight red card for a late challenge on Halesowen's Jamie Hood. The fans behind the goal shuffled feet and sunk hands into coat pockets. "Diving bastard" came the inevitable response, although it wasn't said with much conviction. The cries that went up when stud clattered into bone cleared the nearby trees of nesting ravens.

At half time, with the wind chill rising and rain starting to spit, we sought shelter and refreshment in one of the portakabins which doubled as a food kiosk. It would be almost rude for a Cornish pasty not to be on sale here, as the food is very much entwined in the local heritage. Historians claim the pasty was originally made as a lunch for the area's Tin Miners, with the thick crust allowing them to hold the food without getting dirt on it. In 2002, the Cornish Pasty Association submitted an application to obtain Protected Geographical Indication (PGI) status for the Cornish pasty, which gives the same protection to other regional items such as Stilton Cheese and Arbroath Smokies. In short, if it isn't made in the area, you can't label it so. My local kebab house in London N5 sells the "Arsenal Burger" although it is debatable whether such protection status is being sought.

Given the unimaginative fare usually on sale at football grounds (are we really that gastronomically undemanding as a nation?) the pasty selection offered a welcome and tasty alternative but the kiosk was an unqualified success not for the locally baked produce *per se* but the tuck shop at the end of the counter which sold a wide variety of confectionary products. Now don't get me wrong, there is nothing particularly innovative about selling chocolate bars at a football match. Nearly every club I have ever visited has sold king size Mars Bars or Snickers (a euphemistic and interesting deployment of the word 'King' if ever there was one - 'greedy bastard' size would be seemingly more appropriate). The difference here was that rather than stuffed in a box next to the hot pie rack, the sweets were laid out in a tuck shop style for handling and review, which instantly transported me back to school and those sneaky moments spent frittering dinner money on Wham Bars and Fizzy Laces. I half expected to hand over my money to the lady behind the till and find a few conkers and a marble collection mixed amongst the change.

City's manager Sean McCarthy made a double substitution after the break as a depleted Truro side looked to test the visitors with increased firepower. The tactic looked to be working as Truro's midfield completely overran their opponents, resulting in a series of corners, near misses, and small overexcited children behind the goal jumping around like they'd been drip-fed Tartrazine. Despite the continued pressure, the breakthrough didn't come. This was partly down to the heroics of Halesowen's enormous centre back Henry Eze, whose muscular legs made an otherwise baggy pair of shorts seem skin tight. In fact, so distracted was I by Henry's physique that I was tempted to ask for a photo of it afterwards as proof, like a man stumbling upon the Bodmin Beast and needing documented evidence. Needless to say I didn't. Aside from the disquieting homoeroticism of walking into a male changing room and asking to take "one for the collection", I didn't fancy leaving Cornwall bereft of teeth.

Truro's gallant push for an equaliser eventually paid dividends - for Halesowen. Caught badly exposed, an interception deep in their own half allowed Simon Johnson to take advantage of Jake Ash's clearance, cut inside a flat footed defender and drive past Truro's oncoming 'keeper. It was harsh on City who had dominated the half but the danger of pressing forward with ten men was there for all to see, especially given the pace of the Halesowen frontline. Truro striker Les Afful, who rarely survives a match report without the use of the word 'diminutive' in close proximity, pulled one back on 70 minutes, by sliding a pull back into an empty net, much to the chagrin of the Halesowen 'keeper. "That's an action replay of what happened last week" he complained to the gleeful Truro fans near the touchline. It was ambitious to expect any sympathy. Maybe if he told us his girlfriend had bought him the box set of Nick Berry's *Harbour Lights* for an anniversary present he might have found some sympathisers.

The game finished 2-1 to Halesowen. Yeltz manager Matt Clarke declared it a "massive win", showing the regard others have for this small Cornish side in their debut Southern League season. For whatever reason the local fans seemed a little more reserved in their recognition; only 429 turned out, which was well down on the season average. It was cold and the Pirates Rugby team were playing down the road but Truro need to be consistently hitting the 700 or 800 mark to sustain their upward progress. Ultimately the local people will decide whether a strong semi-professional team is wanted in Cornwall, not a rich benefactor. The ashes of too many ambitious non league teams have been scattered over the steps of Her Majesty's Revenue and Customs to really think anything else.

London APSA v Stansted

Essex Senior League – Step 5
Thursday 10th December 2009

Final Score: 1-3
Attendance: 25

FIFA, football's governing body, has 208 associations affiliated to it, representing almost every country and nation state on earth. The 2010 World Cup, which featured all but a handful of these associations, has now been whittled down to 32 teams for the show piece event in South Africa. Conservative estimates predict viewing figures for the tournament to be around 3-400 million; FIFA's generous speculation might put the total at three times that. Either way, there can be no denying the game's incredible social, cultural and economic relevance throughout the globe. As Lawrence Kitchin once noted "football is the only global idiom apart from science".

England enter the tournament under a fanfare of expectation. Their conspicuous absence from Euro 2008 fuelled national debate on failing standards, lack of grassroots investments, and mildly xenophobic concerns about a domestic saturation of foreign players. The latter argument rather ignores that fact that, 1966 aside, England have constantly failed to deliver in major tournaments, even when overseas players in England were rarer than a Julie Andrews fart. The 1970s, an era of apparent maverick genius, was a particular nadir; it exposes a nationalistic wound when you play second fiddle to Scotland for an entire decade. The recent transition of the England team in a few short months from national embarrassment to imperious Anglo-Romanic warriors also puts to bed many of the shibboleths engulfing the national game. The Three Lions are touted as one of the favourites to lift the World Cup, yet there has been no paradigm shift, no major policy change and no kneejerk jingoism, simply the appointment of a proven world class coach. Unfortunately for the hand wringing traditionalists he happens to be Italian but irony shouldn't get in the way of such trifling matters.

The debate about foreign players in this country - that the national game prevails in spite of not because of it - is partly a microcosm of wider societal opinions on immigration and the changing demographics of our nation. Immigration is not new to this country but the post 9/11 *realpolitik* of right wing ideology has amplified the issue to distorted levels. When England last won the World Cup there were around 100,000 people of Indian subcontinent descent living in the UK and 75,000 from Black African and Black Caribbean populations. The 2001 census suggests these figures have grown to 1.8 million and 1 million respectively. The growth of these migrant communities has had an inevitable effect on the game in this country. A cursory glance at 'the Boys of '66' will show a roll call of white faces. It is quite feasible that England's starting line-up against the USA in South Africa will have at least five players of black ethnicity.

The prominence of black players in today's game is quite staggering given the indifferent and at times outright racist attitudes towards their participation in the national sport, even though the roots of migrant players in this country are deeply planted. Arthur Wharton, generally recognised as the first black professional footballer in England (indeed, the world), played for Darlington as early as 1885 and there have been countless other examples of 'coloured' players gracing English clubs both pre and post war, but it wasn't until the second generation children of 1950 and 1960s West Indian and African migrant workers started playing the game that black participation in English football became an outwardly social problem. What was perhaps a sporadic, even novelty, issue became a major racial discourse which manifested itself in discrimination and violent personal attack.

Paul Canoville's award winning autobiography *Black and Blue* provides a stark reminder of just how appalling this abuse was at times. As the first black player to play for Chelsea in the early 1980s, at a time when the club had a hardcore neo-Nazi following, his experiences are nothing short of disgraceful. Racially targeted by fans to the point of feeling physically sick, his career at Chelsea ended unceremoniously after punching a 'famous' teammate who called him a "black cunt." So engrained was racism on English terraces at the time that far right groups produced their own league tables, discounting goals black players had scored. Unsurprisingly, Canoville's experiences were not merely an isolated example in a racist pocket of south west London. Every black player of the era recounts similar tales. Dave Hill's studious account of John Barnes' move to Liverpool FC[1], a club with a historically 'white' veneer in a city divided along racial lines, exposes a community with similar racist views. Only this time it wasn't the

---

[1] *Out Of His Skin: The John Barnes Phenomenon*

vitriol of a vocal minority but an entire stadium, throwing bananas, making monkey noises and chanting 'niggerpool'.

That black players now account for one in five of all professional footballers in this country and are seen as role models across the land is testament to myriad community and social agencies aiming to improve race relations in the UK. It would take a book of some length and analysis to truly answer how the sociology of the crowd and the player experience has changed in such a relatively short space of time, but part of the issue seems to be less tolerance by the authorities toward racially aggravated behaviour inside grounds. The same analogy can be drawn with football hooliganism. It is highly unlikely people are simply less violent nowadays, it's just authorities will no longer accept feral gangs running riot on match days; a slap on the wrist is a lot easier to deal with than a lifetime ground ban and a £2,000 fine. At a personal level, I remember first-hand the monkey chants aimed towards a young Walsall player at Hereford's Edgar Street some twenty years ago, which was retrospectively frightening owing to the apparent normality of it all. The only emotion I was left with from that game was one of frightened pity as the fledgling defender left the field in tears. It was testament to progression that less than ten years later, at the same ground, someone in the crowd called one of the visiting Fulham players "a fucking black bastard" and was greeted with little more than sharp inhalations of breath and shakes of the head. "I'm sorry" followed shortly afterwards.

The successful emergence of indigenous minority players is not unique to England. A similar pattern has emerged across Europe with Turkish players in the German Bundersliga and (north) African players in the French Ligue One. This isn't to say racism has been eradicated from our terraces or those abroad, because it hasn't. Spain, Italy and the Balkan states have an appalling recent record of racist chanting and, domestically, Tottenham, Millwall, Blackpool and Preston supporters have been indicted with similar charges over the last 24 months. Whether racism will ever be expunged is a debatable point. Of more interest is how people work through this prejudice and, crucially, if it still acts as a barrier to participation in our national sport. The success of black players in this country suggests that great strides have been made. If we accept this and cast the net wider, the question is not so much how black players have made such an impact on the game but why Asian players, specifically Indian, Bangladeshi and Pakistani, haven't.

The question is a complex, conspicuous and ongoing issue. The racial and cultural transformation of the professional game - the opening Premiership season featured just 22 players from outside the UK and Ireland, now there are some 300 or so - has meant arguments along purely racial or skin colour lines have become diluted. Moreover, these arriving foreign players are split along cultural and religious backgrounds too. A new signing paraded to the Stretford or Kop End nowadays is as likely to be a teetotal practising Muslim as a grizzled product of Glasgow's East End. If football, albeit reluctantly, has accepted these individuals into its fold, demonstrably signalling the end of a white British cultural cartel, why does the Asian community still appear so terribly underrepresented at every level of the national game?

The issue was first significantly reviewed in the ironically titled *Asian's Can't Play football* by Jas Bains and Jav Singh in 1996. Their findings, based on interviews with youth team coaches at professional clubs, revealed that just over half of them thought Asian footballers were "physically inferior" to players from other groups. Their follow up report ten years later, the more optimistically titled, yet equally pessimistic *Asian's can play football – another wasted decade* sees little change in attitudes and urges the FA to act soon or lose a large percentage of our national youth for good.

The findings are supported by anti-racist organisation 'Kick it out'. Leon Mann, speaking in 2007 to www.sportingo.com, on behalf of the organisation, talked of the barriers he saw in place:
"Racism, either explicit or implicit, still prevails in football today. We still get reports of racist incidents. Asians are being discriminated against through the lack of understanding by clubs, coaches and players. There is enough evidence that Asians are interested in football, but the reason why you don't find more Asian players is that they fear verbal and physical harassment. Coaches need to be aware of this. You also have a lot of stereotyping, such as Asians are not tall enough, they're not strong enough, and they've got different dietary habits. Black players used to face the same problems, but they persisted and now they've broken through. Asians can do likewise."

These views appear consistent with the experiences of the few Asian players who have broken through into the professional ranks. Zesh Rehman, the Bradford City defender, seems to agree. Speaking to grassroots website www.clubwebsite.co.uk he argued Asian players face a lot of stereotypes, such as "being scared of the weather or having the wrong diet." Other Asian players, such as Walsall's Netan Sansara, who has played for England at U18 and U19 levels, point to less subtly racist issues. Talking to *The Times* in 2008 he spoke frankly of his football experiences.

"At first I didn't enjoy it because there was a lot of racism. I used to go home and tell my mum, 'I don't want to go back.' It was horrible. I used to get called 'Paki' - even from my own team. A lot of people don't realise that it goes on. Even now, I don't think people at Walsall know what I went through. If you get called 'Paki' every day, of course it's going to get to you. I just used to smile and say 'I'm not Pakistani, I'm an Indian' but it was hard to laugh it off. They said it was just banter and eventually I tried to accept that, because if you complain too much people can say, 'He's using it as an excuse.' But 'Paki?' Banter? No chance."

Racial stereotyping and discrimination alone are without doubt preventative barriers to participating in team sports, especially team sports with an alleged institutionalised racist undercurrent. However, it would be overly simplistic to view the problem solely in these terms. The emergence of black and overseas players in the national game suggests that other agencies may be at play, not least from within the Asian community itself.

Perhaps the biggest difference between black and Asian cultural values is those placed on academia and sport. A 1990s Manchester University study on ethnic minorities and sport headed by Professor Gajendra Verma reported that Afro-Caribbean children were often channelled into sport at the expense of their school education, whilst Asian communities tended not to value physical education and sport as much as other ethnic groups.[1] There appears to be overwhelming family pressure on young Asians to concentrate on studies or help out in often gruelling family businesses coupled with the reluctance from parents to fully assimilate into the host culture. Keith Vaz, the Labour politician, supports such claims, arguing that the Asian community has never regarded sport as being a career on a par with other professions in public life. Netan Sansara supports this view to an extent, arguing family on his mother's side never really understood how a person could become a sportsman for a living; playing football was just something one did at weekends.

---

[1] G. Verma and D. Darby, *Winners and Losers: Ethnic Minorities in Sport and Recreation.* London: The Falmer Press, 1994

No doubt part of the reason for this apparent apathy is the lack of football role models for the Asian community. There are notable examples other than Sansara and Rehman - Michael Chopra, Anwar Uddin, Adnan Ahmed, Harpal Singh - but these are exceptions to a very rigid rule, often playing in insular environments with little recognition beyond their immediate club. What may also be lacking is basic guidance on a route into the game. Abdul Basit, an award-winning coach and community cohesion officer for Bolton Wanderers, believes that more education within the Asian community would make a big difference. Speaking to *The Times* in 2008, he argued "The Asian interest in football is absolutely huge but it's about showing young players a pathway into the professional game," he said. "There's a lack of knowledge about how you become a footballer. Some kids think they might get scouted playing in the street, but if you're not playing for a team in an organised league you won't get spotted, end of. We need to get Asian kids of seven or eight into the academies and to create more Asian coaches to put into the communities, because it can be difficult for outsiders."

If there was one person who might have a clear and valuable insight on a "pathway into the professional game" it might be Zulfi Ali, founder of London All People's Sports Association (APSA), one of the National League System's leading Asian clubs. Ali's philosophy, according to their website, is simple; to bring about the birth of an Asian team which will compete in the mainstream and be the standard bearer for the Asian Football Community.[1]

The club was formed in 1993, around the same time as the inception of the first Asian Football League (AFL). The club's roots can be traced to a group of friends from Newham's East Ham College, who merged with a local youth team, Young Muslims, who, like many boys in the area, were no longer eligible to play under 16's football. The club, under Ali's guidance, were crowned inaugural Asian League champions, under the name Ahle Sunnah. For a number of years the team continued to participate in various Asian run competitions though it was not until April 1999 that the club looked at moving into the non league structure, triggered by a trip to Pakistan via a Manchester based group called APSA. The trip brought together Zulfi Ali and, current Vice-Chairman, Anjum Khan who both shared the same vision; to create an Asian team which would be able to compete in the football

---

[1] www.londonapsa.co.uk/page.php?iid=3

pyramid and provide an inspiration and motivation for the Asian football community. Following the Pakistan trip, Ahle Sunnah continued their dominance of various domestic tournaments, including wins in the Umbro International Tournament Manchester, Business Houses League and Cup Premier Division, the Asian Football League and the UK Asian Championships.

The success of the club brought with it national exposure. The BBC and Channel 4 filmed a number of documentaries on APSA (originally referred to as London Anglo-Pakistani Sports Association); including a feature on the game against the Pakistan national team in Oxford. Despite this progression, by 2002 the dream of playing senior non league football had not been realised. Their fledgling efforts were not helped when plans to use the Newham Terence McMillan Stadium fell through owing to the ground not being up to Essex Senior League (ESL) standards. Help was soon on hand though. With the help of Aveley FC and the financial assistance of Asian franchise business Kebabish the hard work finally paid dividends as the team entered the ESL in August 2003.

The first season at Step 5 proved a steep learning curve. Although eventually safe from relegation, there were obvious squad deficiencies, which saw major personnel changes for the following campaign. Sporadic moments of glory, such as a 2-2 draw against league champions Enfield Town, showed potential but a lack of depth once again proved crucial in curtailing any realistic ambition of either challenging for the title or promotion. The season still proved a partial success, as APSA won the UK Asian Championship at Stamford Bridge.

Progressive years have provided significant milestones for the club. In 2006 APSA became the first Asian team to play in the FA Cup and in 2007 progressed to the next round by winning a local derby against Sporting Bengal United in a seven goal tie. This progress has been coupled with a successful youth development programme. The club have brought the under 14s through to under 16s in the most senior youth leagues in London and then on into under 18 level. A recent return to the Terence McMillan Stadium has also bought the club back to the heart of the community where it feels it belongs.

I arranged to meet Zulfi on a particularly cold Thursday night in Newham, before their Essex Senior League match with Stansted. The ground is a brisk twenty minute walk from Plaistow tube station and the still echoes of the winter night gave the low rise council blocks a distinctly haunted quality. There were no lights to be seen, just lifeless blocks of prefabricated concrete; an unkempt graveyard of social housing policy. After passing a string of 24 hour shops, takeaways and all night laundrettes - a Hanna Barbera style repeat backdrop for inner city London - I finally reached the ground.

The Terrence McMillan Stadium is primarily used for athletics. The Newham and Essex Beagles club are based there, as well as a host of other sports organisations. The main stand offers a variety of facilities such as indoor football and basketball, as well as conference rooms and business suites. There are also a few hundred covered seats built into the complex, providing the only really vantage point for spectators, unless you fancy standing and leaning on the rails at the front, exposed to the elements and their mercurial charms. The other three sides of the pitch are simply roped off, save a couple of dugouts on the opposite side of the stand. Hospitality facilities are modest; a small portakabin operates as reception, refreshment kiosk, toilets and buffer from the elements. This was much needed before the game, with the large windswept area being more exposed than a Northern hen party in Benidorm.

Owing to local traffic problems, the game kicked off late, much to the annoyance of the groundhoppers gathering like moths by the brightly lit tea counter. Groundhoppers occupy an incongruous part of football fandom, like a jigsaw piece blatantly placed back in the wrong box. They are, for the most part, trainspotters with a football fixation. Whilst something of a huge generalisation - some are admittedly just blokes who love watching football - the groundhopper can be mapped by a few notable observations. It isn't so much physical appearance (although some do conform to stereotype of excess gravy stains and World of Beige storecards) but more the predilection with finite detail: goal scorers, attendances, shots on goals, kick of times, programme quality, player stats, ground observations, which may seem part of any football fans insatiable arsenal until you realise the sheer veracity with which this information is collated. I spoke to one of the guys huddled next to me to get a fan's perspective on the evening.

"I come here because it's local, a decent game of football, and easy to get to in the week. I travel all over the country watching Premiership games right down to park league and reserve matches. Sometimes I'll go to two or three in a day. This is my 186th of the season this evening."

186? I don't think I've been to that many matches in my life. I love football - I couldn't imagine my life without it - but this went rocketing beyond anything I could subscribe into a whole new stratosphere of obsession. It is almost a hypnotic state of mind. The presence of groundhoppers at matches throughout the country proves how universal the appeal of the game is though. To imagine the men stood behind me had such an important common denominator with me was almost unfathomable. At the same time it made me philosophical. It is too easy to mock someone for their chosen lifestyle, to pour scorn on a harmless pastime. For all I knew, this chance meeting was a porthole into the future, a pre-emptive note, that unless I start taking the idea of relationships and domesticity a bit more seriously I will be sat out in the rain as an ageing obsessive, carrier bag wedged between feet, notebook in hand, cast away in the depths of a long forgotten county league one fine frosty February morning surrounded by the only family I have. Let's face it, I was already halfway there.

Stocked up with enough coffee to make an elephant twitch, Zulfi lead us to one of the quiet offices in the grandstand for a chat. The room also afforded an excellent view of the game which had just kicked off. More importantly, it was warm.

"My interest in football, like most lads, started at school but it wasn't until college that the passion really came through, which resulted in me starting a team up. One thing I noticed straight away was the fear factor among some Asian lads when playing in or against certain teams at a certain level. My experience was slightly different from my peers in that I started working for a bank and was one of the few Asian footballers there. This meant people knew me and, more importantly, knew that I played football - I was one of the lads, so to speak."

I have always been a big believer in sport, particularly football, being a great social leveller. You can take any person from any class, race or background and, as long as they had football to talk about, would get on famously. It is probably one of the reasons I studied Recreation Management at university. I had a Gordon Brittas style view of the world that people would be unified under the roof of a sports centre in the shared euphoria of sporting experience, at least until someone loses their change in the vending machine trying to buy a Mars bar and all hell breaks loose.

"At this time I was still heavily involved in local Asian leagues though, which were very informal and very basic. Often we played on free pitches with no nets with friends or friends of friends. The problem I found is that, whilst playing in an Asian league is nice, you need to get out there and compete in senior leagues if you want to make a proper name for yourself. The obvious problem with these ambitions is that they come at a price; anyone wanting to enter the non league pyramid at a decent level needs cash and, most importantly, a suitable ground."

As we talked, Stansted went 1-0 up. The APSA team, despite its underlying principles, only had a handful of Asian players on display. I asked why this was. Zulfi was realistic about APSA's current status and their chances of progression.

"The team used to be predominantly Asian and Afro-Caribbean and whilst the aim of the club was, and indeed is, to develop young Asian players, we need to be realistic and select the best players available at Essex Senior level, not those that fit a certain racial background. We can only bring the best players through from youth and Sunday leagues, so it is important to maintain a focus on developing young players, particularly those who are too scared to step up a level for fear of not being the main man. Being top player in the Asian leagues and then becoming an also ran in the semi-professional system can be a problem for some lads. It's an ego thing and needs to be addressed. London APSA is currently a shop window. Players come here and then move on. The top sides in this league pay money - APSA don't - so realistically it will be hard for us to get in the top six, never mind win it. At the same time we won't just take on a benefactor and hope for the best. There is little point in spending or borrowing money to go up, just to get relegated again the next season. APSA is a big family club which will grow slowly by spreading the word, but you need to have a good team backed up by a good advertising campaign. This will take time to develop. There are a lot of wealthy people in Newham who share the same passion who want to get involved and hopefully, over the years, all this will come together and we can have a team that the Asian community can be truly proud of. The first and hardest steps have already been taken."

As halftime approached, the conversation inevitably led to the issue of Asian players, or rather the lack of, in the modern game. Reading other people's theories was one thing but Zulfi was about as qualified as anyone to give an honest insight to the matter

"I can only speak from personal observation, but 15 to 20 years ago Asian players weren't interested in the game for a variety of reasons: racism was rife, hooliganism was everywhere, and being Asian was not something that mixed well with this. It is also a generational thing. The first wave of Asian settlers in this country weren't into football. In fact it wasn't until their children, or even their children's children, were born did this interest pick up. The current young adult generation of Asian players in this country has a passion for the game. They take their kids to matches or to the park to play football. I also believe racial attitudes have improved considerably on the pitch. Apart from the odd comment, particularly after 9/11, I have never really heard any serious racial abuse going on in this league or otherwise. This is not to say it doesn't go on, but at this level I really haven't seen a problem. Going forward - and where APSA comes in - kids need to get involved at a young age. We would like to see more and more Asian players, right down to under seven level, feel comfortable about playing the game in a mixed environment. It's not about 'Asian teams' at that age, but about getting Asian players to play with other lads from all backgrounds. Many young Asians are not used to mixing with white kids and lack a lot of confidence when they are faced with doing so. Hopefully we can encourage people that this is normal, through coaching schools or tournaments at established Premiership grounds, that it is important to integrate, as it makes people accept you. I know from personal experience that football is good at making people see you in a positive light, as one of the crowd, not an outsider."

The whistle went for halftime. This signalled my time to let Zulfi go and to reacquaint myself with the cold. As tempting as it was, no self-respecting football fan should watch a match from a portakabin or sat on a desk in a conference room, so I shuffled down to pitch side, ending up near a couple in their 40s. I didn't ask why they were there. I thought at first they might be on their way to a dinner date - the woman looked slightly too well dressed to have just popped down to keep her husband company - but given he was resplendent in tracksuit and trainers, this somewhat dampened the theory. The romantic in me wanted to assume they simply popped down to watch a local match. The reality is they were probably there watching their son. Although most crowds tend to follow a fairly sturdy demographic, diversity at games never fails to amaze me. I remember standing in a perfect storm watching an imperfect match at Woking, chatting to a rain soaked couple in their 50s so middle class they could have been extras from *The Good Life*. Clearly the Bridge Club's loss was Woking's gain.

I watched the second half of the match from the main stand. The official attendance was announced as 25. Not over a loudspeaker I might add but by a lad smoking a fag near the clubhouse who I happened to enquire of. APSA equalised with an outrageous lob from the half way line, but you had an impending sense that Stansted, riding high in the league, would still pull the game around, which they duly did with two quick-fire goals. The away team were stronger, better organised and one step ahead of their opponents in most departments. It was as simple as that. I spent the last 15 minutes of the match talking to two elderly gents who had just taken podium places at the 'London's most Cockney pensioner' awards. It transpired they were part of the management team of Takeley FC and were sussing out their future ESL opponents. Like APSA, Takeley were not applying for promotion at the moment partly due to ongoing ground developments and, partly, due to a lack of funds that promotion to Step 4 would necessitate. "One day - but not at the moment. We don't want to go up without being fully prepared." I sensed an Arkela in a previous life.

I left the ground in a sanguine mood. If the England 2018 World Cup bid and its multicultural message is to take on any real meaning it could do a lot worse than to draw on the experiences and virtues of teams like London APSA as pioneers of racial integration, particularly in areas that have previously been overlooked or marginalised. Zulfi was, if nothing else, a realist and his pragmatic approach based on the founding principles of the club were to be admired. Given the complex, and at times diametric, values of football culture and Asian culture, there is no doubt that progression will be slow, particularly when faced with an institutionalised football mind-set that at best is naïve and at worst plain prejudiced. Efforts to recruit Asian youngsters, indeed all youngsters into the game, need to be made by empowering and educating those on both sides of the debate. Tournaments to recruit local Asian talent, such as Chelsea's Asian Soccer star, are no doubt well-meaning but don't really address the more salient issues, such as why so many Asian players are overlooked in the first place and what responsibility clubs have in nurturing children at a young age irrespective of their early background and skill level. A constant theme I touched on with Zulfi is that sporting equality needs to work on encouraging integrated not separatist ideas of participation. With APSA there may be the necessary conduit to mobilise such a philosophy; although unashamedly promoting football to the Asian community it is doing so in the context of a national mainstream league and a multicultural environment, which was previously unchartered territory for many Asian players.

My one hope were I to return to APSA in twenty years' time is not necessarily that they are playing League football or passing opposition teams off the park, but that the fan base reflects both the efforts and the demographics of the management team. It is the least this type of social innovation deserves, especially when done for a love of the game and the people you represent.

New season - new optimism at Ebbsfleet United

Get your pies here - the refreshment kiosk at Enfield Town

Llanelian Road - the breathtaking home of
Colwyn Bay FC

FA Cup fever comes to Wealdstone

RIGHT The players walk out for Wealdstone's big day against Rotherham United

BELOW Standing room only at Truro City

Main Stand - Chelmsford City FC

FC United fans at Stocksbridge

An expectant crowd looks on at Needham Market FC

A chilly day at Biggleswade Town FC

The main stand at Needham Market

Rainworth Miners' Welfare FC

Rainworth Miners' Welfare FC

LEFT A unique vantage point at Dudley Town FC

Dudley's main stand in disrepair - the site is now an entertainment complex

Dudley's main stand during better days

DUDLEY TOWN 1, BRIDGNORTH TOWN 0.
SATURDAY 24th SEPT. 1983

Dudley's heroic 76-77 FA Cup team

Stansfeld celebrate their title win

The main stand at Coney Hall FC

Bath City fans celebrate play-off final victory

Packed house - Bath City entertain Woking

Poole Town v Newport IOW

Wessex League Premier Division – Step 5
Saturday 9th January 2010

Final Score: P-P
Attendance: N/A

As the train glided silently through the Christmas card Hampshire landscape, I had one of those rare moments of absolute contentment. Slumped in my seat, head resting on the window, my mind racing faster than the carriage carrying me, I gazed upon the icing sugared fields and towns drifting past my gaze. The snow, a visual morphine, had given everything a magic dusting, turning the prosaic, even the ugly, into something ethereal, stirring memories of childlike awe when the world seemed magical. Thoughts and images scrolled on parallax like an 8mm film through my head: who lived in those houses, who drank in those pubs, who ploughed those fields, where did those roads lead to? I flashed past houses homes to a thousand people I would never meet in my short lifetime, yet felt the warm affinity of human kinship flood my body like heroin injected into the soul. It was a perfect moment. Then we arrived in Basingstoke.

Snow can do funny things to the mind. It can also do funny things to football. As I write this, we are enduring the coldest winter in 30 years - parts of Oxfordshire registered minus 17 last night - which has had a decimating effect on the nation's fixtures over the last few weeks. Of today's matches only three games survived in the Premiership and seven in the entire Football League. Non league fixture sheets had more casualties than The Somme; the pools panel have probably never felt more useful. This does of course raise practical questions about scheduling games in such unforgiving conditions. Unfortunately, pragmatism and traditionalism have never been good bedfellows. Mere mention of a winter break brings certain sections of the football community out in a rose tinted rash; "winter football is part of our sport's heritage, you can't mess with tradition", they cry, even though many contemporary football practises have about as much heritage and tradition as the MK Dons.

The problem with burying your head in the sand - or the snow in this case - is ignoring the problems this presents with fixture congestion. Games will either be cancelled due to frozen pitches or dangerous access routes. Bigger clubs can cheat the weather with under soil heating, pitch protection or armies of volunteer fans tooled up with shovels. Many non league clubs simply don't have the luxury of these options and are at the mercy of the elements offering clemency. Given the rigid timeframes football operates to postponed matches always need to be slotted in before the deadline end of the season. Since mid-December, a cursory glance at the various national fixture lists shows some teams, particularly those at Steps 5-7, have barely kicked a ball. This can result in the farcical situation of teams playing three, or even four, times in a week to make up lost ground. It would be bad enough for full time professionals (and, I should point out for parity's sake that Rotherham in League 2 have now gone nearly a month without playing) but for part-time players it becomes a mission bordering on insanity. As a result, the respective leagues start to lose their integrity. A snowbound team challenging for honours is going to be compromised by the jading effects of rearranged fixtures piling up, particularly if they are participating in any cups. It is not unusual to look at some of the regionalised leagues and see a huge disparity in games played once winter subsides which in turn makes fans question just how serious any campaign can be with such a backlog of matches. Additionally, revenue will be affected as fans face the financial and logistical reality of attending a month's worth of fixtures in a week.

The obvious solutions appear to be extending the season by a month and taking January off, perhaps coupled with a slight reduction in the amount of games played in a season.[1] It's not as if non league players will be summoned to international summer tournaments and the concept of a season finishing in early May is a fairly recent phenomenon anyway. I can't bring myself to propose a December free of football, or more accurately a Christmas free of football, as frankly it's the only thing that keeps me, and no doubt thousands of others, sane from the consumerist banality of it all. Besides, the real inclement weather doesn't seem to kick in until the new year, so I stand by my convictions, if only to convince myself.

Unsurprisingly, the weather was beginning to play havoc with the scheduling of this book. I already had to cancel a visit to MK Wanderers due to a frozen

---

[1] I actually observed this on a non league forum and, with the sheer vastness of clubs, there was no one solution that would benefit every team, partly owing to ground share logistics and partly owing to the differing number of games respective sides are obliged to play in a season.

pitch and when the Wessex League suspended all games indefinitely, my rearranged trip to Poole Town only added to my own personal fixture pile up. With only a finite number of Saturdays available, cancellation after cancellation was leaving me running out of free weekends to meet the teams I felt would add credence to my travels. Given I had no leverage over the weather I took the decision to plough ahead with my appointments irrespective of the games going ahead or not. I figured it was the people and the places that really made the stories behind the teams, so I set off from London in the knowledge I would not be seeing Poole Town play today but talking instead to the people at the very heart of the club.

I had arranged to meet Mark Bumford, Poole Town's Commercial Director, on arrival. I had been in correspondence with Mark for some months beforehand and he was extremely keen to talk about his role in the club and their ambitious plans for the future. I was met instead by club owner Chris Reeves, who looked like he could be Jeremy Clarkson's older brother. He certainly had the wheels to grace the Clarkson bloodline - a two seat sports model which the players jocularly referred to as a 'hairdresser's car'. Chris explained that Mark was at the ground and offered to take me on a quick tour of Poole Town history, starting with the Poole Speedway Stadium. Poole lies on the south coast of Dorset and with a population of around 140,000 is one of the largest settlements in Britain not to have a professional football team. The area is particularly noted for its stunning coastal scenery, bustling tourism trade and recreational marine activities. The town's marinas are littered with yachts, speedboats and jet skis, giving the impression of a Simon Le Bon garage clearance. Poole is also home to a peninsular called Sandbanks which, according to recent reports, has the fourth highest land value in the world. Harry Redknapp has a house there. Dubbed "Britain's Palm Beach" it is an area of outstanding natural beauty. These aesthetic qualities stretch to the residents as well; two of the last five British Miss Worlds hailed from this tranquil coastal town.

Our first pit stop was Poole Stadium, current home to the Poole Pirates speedway team and the local greyhound meet. Poole Town (or Poole FC as they were known until 1934) moved to the stadium in 1933, though the club can trace its roots back to 1890 from the merger of two local sides, Poole Rovers and Poole Hornets. The club turned professional in 1926, joining the Southern League Eastern Division, and despite only finishing 14th were distinguished by a 3rd round FA Cup tie at Everton, where they lost 3-1 in front of a 65,000 crowd, courtesy of a Dixie Dean hat trick.

Fortunes were soon to change though. During the depression of 1929-30, Poole found it impossible to fulfil the last four games of the season, at which point their records were expunged. Out of 33 Southern League sides, only twenty one formed the following season. As a consequence, Poole dropped into the Western League where they were to stay until 1957, coming runners up in 1946-47, 1949-50, 1953-54 and 1955-56, before eventually winning the title in 1956-57 and promotion back to the Southern League. In 1962-63 the club reached the FA Cup first round proper, holding Watford to a draw at Vicarage Road and then losing the replay at Poole Stadium in front of 11,155 fans. After two decades of consolidation and relative obscurity, the club resurfaced in the cup - this time the 1981 Anglo Italian cup for semi-professional clubs, reaching the Final before losing to Modena, until recently in Serie A, 4-1 in Italy. Further FA Cup glory was experienced in 1983-84 when Poole reached the FA Cup 1st round proper, drawing 0-0 at home to Newport County in front of 5,000 fans, before losing the replay 3-1 with a couple of goals coming from a certain John Aldridge.

By the early 1990s the club were an established Southern League outfit - one level below the Conference National. In 1994 a major turning point occurred in the clubs affairs when they were effectively forced to leave Poole Stadium and ground share with local side Hamworthy United. Chris recalled the moment vividly:

"For reasons beyond my comprehension, the forefathers of Poole Town failed to take up the offer of a lease on the stadium from the local council some years prior. When the speedway company who owned the lease on the stadium went into liquidation, the club effectively had no right to be there. Around this time, I was introduced to Derek Block who wanted to put money up for the stadium, allow Poole Town to play there, and push the club forward. This was music to my ears - until it transpired we had very different views on how the club should be run. It got to the point where we realised the business relationship would never work, so much so that Block called an AGM to remove me from the board. Freddie Rowe, a long term fan and investor in the side, got in touch with me on hearing the news and offered his shares in the club, which would allow me to turn the tables and remove Block from the board. Unfortunately, this just wasn't feasible. By doing this, the club would have nowhere to play and would almost certainly fold - it would be cutting my nose off to spite my face. I wasn't going to stand by and watch the club die just to service a sense of retribution, so I stood down. This gave me time to re-evaluate the situation and, with the assistance of Clive and Arthur Robbins, I formed a consortium which purchased the club back off Block. It was in everyone's best interests - Derek realised fairly early on he had underestimated the size of the project - but meant that Poole Town were now homeless."

Chris represents the lifeblood of the club and has seen it all during a lifetime of support. As a teenager, in the days before digital TV or internet streaming facilitated the ability to watch live games from the comfort of your bed, he would get his football fix from radio commentary of the big Division 1 games, but soon realised that that his passions were greater served by going to watch his local team play. From his first live introduction at Poole Stadium he was hooked; by the time Chris was in his late 20s he had become a regular contributor to the club programme. "I remember when our then manager was sacked and I wrote a scathing article in the club programme attacking the board. Rather than take umbrage, the majority shareholder agreed with what I was saying and asked me to join. He seemed to like the fact I wasn't afraid to pull any punches. I wasn't exactly your archetypal football executive; I had just got married, owned a house with no furniture and drove a second hand car. The other directors were horrified."

The club's eviction from Poole Stadium clearly had a marked effect on the team. In the 1995-96 season they adopted the kind of affinity usually reserved for the likes of East Stirling or schoolboy teams who appear nervously on local news for showing "courage in the face of adversity" (i.e. they're terrible and have never won a single game, but get a roll call opportunity with a bloated local ex-pro for showing that it's the taking part that counts). Going into their game against Bashley, the Dolphins had managed to lose every one of the 39 previous matches and were in danger of becoming 'the worst side in history" based on seasonal performance alone. The national press, with one eye on the macabre, came down in droves to see if the club could pull off the unthinkable and go through a whole campaign without gaining a single point. Unfortunately, a 0-0 draw punctured any hope of some scurrilous headline making. Not that an eventual 41 defeats out of 42 wasn't bad but the notoriety of the team had dropped markedly, going from record breakingly bad to just plain rubbish, a bit like Eddie the Eagle Edwards when his crapness was usurped and he became the second worst long jump skier on earth. Better to be a spectacular loser than a nondescript also-ran. The Poole Town fanzine 'Tatnam Talk', which at nearly one hundred fact filled pages is thicker than a footballer's tie knot, recalls the moment with a series of press cuttings, including one surreal picture of the team celebrating in the dressing room afterwards as if they had won promotion to the Football League.

To compound what was now an *annus horribilis*, the club dropped out of the Southern League and were made to leave their Hamworthy home. Salvation came in the form of Holt United, with the club kicking off the 1996-97 season as ground sharers and members of the Hampshire League Division 1. Despite finishing runners up in the 1998-99 campaign, the Hampshire League was restructured into a Premier and Division 1 split. As Holt's ground was not up to Premier League standards, Poole were effectively relegated, an irony given it was the club's most successful season in years. Unabashed, the team gained promotion to the Hampshire Premier the following season and with attendances of over 200 provided a general consensus the club were too big - from a fan base and infrastructure perspective at least - to be playing county level football. Chris acknowledges these years were some of the toughest the club has endured but, like all optimists, realised what a galvanising effect it had, not least in demonstrating how much the team meant to the local community. Many supporters gave up their own time to mobilise the club and ensure it carried on despite operating in adverse conditions with little prospect of immediate salvation.

"Even when Poole were at their lowest in the county leagues, we still ensured there was a playing budget to give the team and the supporters the best football they could watch. It was also important that we kept the profile of the team as high as we could, as it would be all too easy to have slipped off the radar like so many others before us. This way, if and when an opportunity for progression came along, we were in a position to take it, not polarised financially or in terms of personnel."

Such an opportunity presented itself in 2005. After a series of strong campaigns in the Hampshire Premier, the leagues were realigned for the 2004-05 season which placed The Dolphins in the Wessex League Division 2, from which they were subsequently promoted. A search for a new ground had been ongoing for some time and the club's continued rise up the pyramid crystallised the need for Poole to have a home of their own. Despite reaching out to the local council, finding new premises - either in the town or on the outskirts - was proving extremely difficult. Then, out of leftfield, a chance conversation with the club's physio led Chris to a derelict weed strewn site owned by Oakdale Middle School. Chris recalls the moment fondly:

"To be honest it was just a slum, a jungle. There was a changing room - or at least a semblance of a changing room - and an area of unused overgrown wasteland. I thought at first it might be someone's idea of a joke but subsequent conversations convinced me that with hard work and endeavour we could create something here and finally give the club a home back in the centre of Poole."

Chris drove us to the ground where Poole still play today, Tatnam Farm, so called because they're used to be, well, a farm there. There are permanent safety barriers around the pitch with a small stand to the opposite side behind the dugouts which houses just over 150 seats. In addition to this are floodlights, a small club shop, tea hut, licensed bar and refurbished toilets, the latter built by ex-player Tony France.

Chris looked around wistfully, "I wish we had some before and after pictures to show you because words can't do justices to what this place used to be like." I walked on to the pitch to grab a few photos of my own. The snow crunched under foot on what was becoming a bitterly cold day. Away from the dozing comfort of a train carriage my senses were a lot more visceral. I was reminded of the last time I felt such frozen isolation on a football pitch. It was winter 1989 and the South Shropshire League was playing the Newtown League in an annual mismatch tournament. The Newtown League contained three Welsh U14 players. Our backbone was drawn from the Young Farmers Club. It was a fiercely cold evening even with two coats on. The prospect of playing in what was tantamount to underwear made my mouth dry. On the coach over to Wales I had an ominous feeling I would be coming home in a body bag, especially when one of the head coaches announced that "gloves are for poofs". I would have been happy to come out right there and then.

The whole thing was a farce from start to finish. I don't recall the losing score line - my brain suffered mild frostbite - but it was in double figures. To compound matters, the game was played on old generation Astroturf which tended to leave anyone wearing those 1980s satin hot pants masquerading as football shorts with indescribable friction burns. For some inexplicable reason, I was playing at centre back despite being a proven goal scorer in my formative years. I suspect my sudden positional switch was drawn from the old school manual of English schoolboy coaching; anyone classified as "big and quick" can play in defence. It was to prove a foolish tactic not least because I gave up after ten minutes and prayed for salvation. After the tenth goal went in, and the temperature fell to minus look-no-sensation-in-my-hands, I am fairly sure I started to cry. I have never been so glad to hear a final whistle. I have also questioned the existence of a higher deity ever since.

We met Mark at the ground modelling the latest line in Poole Town merchandise. As Commercial Director, his job is to promote the club throughout the area. "It's a particularly important role, given some people in Poole still think we play at the old stadium, some think we play outside of the borough and some, incredibly, think we went out of business years ago. My role is to convey to the 140,000 or so people in the town that we are very much alive and kicking, playing good football in a good league."
Mark's route into the club was slightly unorthodox. Many fans remark they have sought solace in their local side when disillusioned with their long standing allegiances, but often these remarks are aimed at top flight teams. Mark's frustrations were aimed at another non league club.

"I've been following football for 30 years, during which time I supported Oxford United. About a season and a half ago, I questioned why I was driving my family up the motorway from Poole spending large amounts of time and money to watch them play, particularly when I left feeling short changed. By chance, I went to see Poole Town play in the FA Cup against Merthyr who were two leagues above. Poole won 3-0 and I realised there was something special about this team. Moreover, I realised I could save a lot of time and money supporting my local side who seemed to be so in touch with the local community. Part of watching football is feeling you really belong to the club and I wasn't getting that at Oxford. At Poole there was scope to make a difference so I offered my services and was invited to join the board of directors. It's a voluntary role, but the place is so friendly and the rapport with the fans so good that I can honestly say Poole Town has become my first love. It's a pleasure to be here. To me, it's what football should be about."

Like many non league clubs, the first obstacle in getting people through the door is convincing them a viable alternative exists to their usual Saturday routine. Poole is the best supported team in the Wessex Premier with an average home attendance of 300 fans, up 17% on last season. This still represents a modest turnout for an area with such a large population and - with all due respect to Bournemouth - no obvious big side nearby.

"I think there are several issues here," said Chris. "Firstly, we lost fans and coverage when we dropped down the leagues, but - and I think this is true of football as a whole - crowds also suffer because there are so many other things for people to do nowadays. In the 1950s it was very different. Stadiums up and down the country would be sold out. I recall a note in the 1957 supporters' club handbook which bemoans the fact that our reserve team games had dropped below a thousand. It was a different era. It's also probably fair to say that Poole is not really a hotbed of football. It has quite an ageing population and has never had a League side for generations to pass support down to. That said, there are a clutch of fans in the borough and a lot of local derbies in the Wessex League. Our crowds also need to be put into context. Only two clubs in the Southern League South and West have better gates than us and probably only a handful better us in the Southern Premier. The fans are certainly out there. They may be walking round town wearing Premiership shirts but I don't necessarily believe that these people go and watch these teams play, either because they have been priced out, watch from home, or maybe have just lost interest. These are the people we need to engage. We used to get crowds over a thousand in the '80s, there's no reason why we can't again."

I was shown round the main building complex; if indeed complex were too lavish a word. Inside the archaic structure, which looked more like a Cub Scout hut, were the changing rooms, bar and boardroom offices. It was about as far from the famed marble halls of Highbury as one could possibly imagine - indeed, the only thing marbled here were the tea stains on the worktops. After being walked round the changing rooms in the guise of a coroner showing a detective the murder scene, we went into the main club office. It was a slice of football heaven. Spread over the four walls in genealogical freeze frame stood the proud history of the club, from its two-tone brylcreamed beginnings to present day high definition first team. Along the way there were cameos from football's glitterati; match reports from the Anglo-Italian cup: Ron Atkinson's Man United team of the mid-1980s who played Poole in a pre-season friendly; Brian Clough's Nottingham Forest, mud splattered and steaming on an early summer's quagmire. The tapestry is complete with pendants from non league clubs around the country, some no longer with us; their fading badges an obituary forever remembered alongside their illustrious counterparts.

One photo particularly caught my eye. It was the 2008-09 league winning team which featured a man who looked like a gangland enforcer. Chris laughed. "That's Steve Richardson. He's 44 now and still incredibly fit. I like to think one of the reasons he stays with us is because all the players are very well looked after here. They are paid a decent fee (around £50-£80 a week) as well as expenses. We also stick by our promises and ensure there are good training sessions, good physios, good food and that the kit is washed and laid out on pegs for them the night before. It makes them feel special, makes them feel wanted and, I hope, part of a family unit."

The group consensus at this point was to step out of the cold and get some lunch, where we could talk about the future of the club. As we trudged back to the cars, I was shown one last memento of the stadium. On the wall at the back of the man stand was a plaque dedicated to all the supporters who had helped build it. If it had the air of a pantheon it was with good reason; some of those etched in gold on the wood had now passed away. Clubs live on after their fans die but in some cases are remembered forever, their memories a testament to the human endeavour behind our game and the place it has in our hearts.

Although there was clearly a lot of pride in the collective effort that transformed an overgrown allotment into an award nominated Step 5 ground, Tatnam Farm is not suitable for the club's long term vision. Last season, despite running away with the league, they were denied promotion to the Southern League as the ground did not meet Step 4 requirements, and owing to developmental restrictions, is never likely to. In keeping with Poole Town's somewhat chaotic recent history, plans to move to a new stadium have been both protracted and frustrating. In 2008 the club submitted proposals for the creation of a new £1m stadium at Branksome Park which would satisfy Step 4 criteria and beyond. The local borough council were prepared to subsidise the project to the tune of £250K, understanding the importance of retaining and developing a local football club with ambitious plans. Although no official line came out, the plan seemed destined to be rubber stamped until, to everyone's shock, the council's planning office rejected the proposal, claiming the land site would represent a loss of open space. It was a controversial judgement, not least because of the arbitrary nature of the objection and its contradictory foundations; Poole Borough Council advertise the virtues of engaging the community via recreational projects and this would have provided a very real template to showpiece.

The stadium plan has now moved to plan B, or more specifically, Canford Arena to the north of the town. Plans are not yet finalised, not least because there are question marks over whether the somewhat remote location fits in with the ambitions of the club. Logistically, it ticks all the boxes, with the underlying infrastructure - access, space and additional leisure facilities - already in place, but there are green belt issues to address. Talks with planners and landowners have seemed promising and, crucially, the move has the backing of the FA and Dorset County FC (DCFA).

On paper, this has all the hallmarks of another provincial red tape saga, nestling innocuously in the local free press between stories of petty crime and farmers markets, but to view these issues as local - or at least irrelevant beyond the immediate borough - would be myopic. Teams like Poole Town are not always there just to make up the numbers and their success, or conversely their demise, can cause ripples that affect the national game. On paper there may be little to associate the behemoths of the game with their park football counterparts but their fortunes are often inextricably entwined, crossing paths like orbiting planets in a parallel universe. Although money is increasingly negating the need for youth development, many larger clubs still rely on bargain buys to balance their books and often look to the semi-professional game for the next Jermaine Beckford or Kevin Phillips. As part of the pyramid system, non league clubs have consistently nurtured young talent and provided a catchall for players who drop out of the professional game. Some disappear without trace; others, such as Charlie Austin, Poole Town's recently unearthed prodigy, re-emerge better, wiser and with renewed conviction. Chris took up his story.

"We picked Charlie up from Hungerford, another Step 5 team, after his parents moved to Poole and were looking for a similar level club for him. He was originally on the books at Reading but didn't make the grade so dropped into non league football. His father had been to watch us play and Charlie came down for a trial. He was a largely unknown quantity but from the minute I saw him take a sublime first touch I thought to myself 'this lad can play'. My instincts were proved right. In his first full season with us he scored 46 goals. We put him on a one year contract after that, gave him a £1,000 signing on fee, and upped his wage to £80 a week and £10 a goal. In the pre-season he went to train with Bournemouth and came back even better, scoring 18 goals in 11 games. By this point he had emerged on Danny Wilson's radar at Swindon, owing to him being known in the area and part of the Swindon youth setup as a kid. We obviously couldn't stand in Charlie's way as he was desperate to go, but negotiations were difficult. Andrew Fitton, the Swindon Chairman, seemed aghast at the prospect of paying a Step 5 club a fee for a player's service but I took the attitude that if they don't pay we won't sell him. I gave Andrew time to think about it and he eventually offered a modest transfer fee which we accepted. We also included add ons and caveats should he be sold on or become an international; Charlie is being talked about as a future England U21 striker and with 8 goals in 8 starts for Swindon Town it's not hard to see why (Charlie would finish the season with 19 goals from 33 games and was the source of a dedicated interview before Swindon's play off final on SKY Sports) We are also blessed with two potential replacements for Charlie in Carl Preston and Russell Cooke, so hopefully his loss won't affect our ambitions too much."

Ambition is becoming an increasingly dirty word in football, particularly when it is backed by unchecked sources of money. Poole's ambitions seem slightly more grounded. Chris admits he has personal reasons for wanting promotion, which stem from a desire to succeed at whatever he does, but the club is also realistic about where they can go. Mark was quick to point out that given how far the club had fallen survival had been based on good business sense and creativity. The club has been consolidated by credibility and would aim to be as successful as it could by applying a sensible proportion of funds to playing staff, rather than risk throwing money at a situation that could backfire. "We are, in many respects, a self-made club," said Mark, "and with the move to Cranford Arena, there is no reason why we couldn't reach the Conference South. We don't need or even want to operate on the single benefactor model as the game is littered with examples of clubs going bust when the benefactor pulls out. Our infrastructure is solid here - we have been in the black year after year and we work on the principle that the club belongs to a group of people with shared responsibility, not a single person. Also, and I think this is crucial; the idea of someone coming in and pumping millions into the club removes the fun. Where's the satisfaction in buying your way through the league?

Our satisfaction comes from being self-reliant and, contrary to popular belief, we are not the Chelsea of Step 5. Our facilities are basic but functional and our wage structure has integrity. Where we are lucky is with the fans and their unswerving loyalty and support. We appreciate how blessed we are to have such dedicated people around us and we would like to maintain this degree of intimacy if and when we get promoted. It is important that you make yourself as transparent as possible, to allow fans the opportunity to talk to you and, at times, let off steam at you. All of us are members of the fan's forum, as are some of the players and nobody hides behind a pseudonym" (which is true - I read one of the players personally and objectively responding to criticism after a recent defeat to Wimbourne Town).

"Of course," added Chris, "the bigger we get the harder it will be to take on the views of every single fan, but Mark and I always attend the supporters' meetings and always give feedback on commercial activities. This close relationship isn't without its pitfalls though. Recently there was uproar on the forum after we sacked some members of staff." This sounded serious. Who was it? Director on the fiddle? Player found drunk at training?

"No, it was the tea ladies". Marvellous.

As a model of 'the football business' Poole Town are exemplary and, in Chris and Mark, they have two of the most endearing people you could wish to have behind the scenes. This may sound like sycophantic praise, and quite possibly it is, but from the first day I contacted the club to request an interview they were falling over themselves to help me. The cynical side of me might say that, as Commercial Director, it is in Mark's interest to facilitate anyone giving them free publicity but I would like to think his assistance was out of a genuine love for the club. If all this hard work *is* a façade, if Poole Town do eventually get their promotion but sell out to a wealthy backer looking to cash in on healthy demographics, it would be a tragedy not just for the people of Poole but for English football in general. As I caught the train back to London and chugged back through the Dorset countryside I allowed myself time to daydream again; in this dream such a thing would never happen.

Stocksbridge Park Steels v FC United of Manchester

Northern Premier League – Step 3
Saturday 23rd January 2010

Final Score: 1-1
Attendance: 761

When I first suggested the idea of a group day out to a non league game I expected to be met with howls of derision. I had been regaling my friends with details of provincial match visits for the last five months and having experienced the delights of *al fresco* drinking on the terraces or watching SKY Sports with club directors in the bar afterwards, I felt it could be a cathartic process for those who found themselves talking increasingly about the negative aspects of the game rather than the positives.

In reality these observations were a little *faux naïf*. The principle talk over email leading up to the game was of a big boozy day out with the lads, though for some this represented a first ever fore into the non league scene and, for my friend Darcy - whose wildly untamed facial hair and manic eyes hinted at a glittering career as an ID parade suspect - a first visit to a football match in nearly thirty years. Either way I was pleasantly surprised at how this seemingly low key event had attracted nearly fifteen people to head to the Castle Inn at Bolsterstone through some of the most stunning scenery South Yorkshire has to offer.

The choice of match was of course heavily engineered. My oldest and closest friends still reside in Sheffield, a legacy of twelve years spent living in the Steel City, so the match was always going to be based in the locality. I ran a few options past my friends: Sheffield FC, Hallam FC, Worksop Town, but the fixture that raised most interest was the clash between "South Yorkshire's premier non league club" Stocksbridge Park Steels and the enigma that is FC United of Manchester (or FCUM as they are acronymically known, which has strong underlying sentiments if pronounced in a certain way).

If there are many indictments of modern football the creation of FC United of Manchester is surely the most damning; not least because of the two fingers it has given to the self-professed "biggest club in the world", Manchester United. Premiership supporters have long been the plaything of the financial gods, at the mercy of omnipotent forces like the crew of the Argo in their quest for the Golden Fleece. Only this time their fate is sealed not by a bored looking Zeus but a leviathan of far greater power: the sports speculator.

What makes FC United rather unique in an ever increasing world of supporters' owned clubs is the evolution of a team driven by moral indignation rather than harsh practicalities. Unlike AFC Wimbledon and Enfield Town, who saw their clubs moved out of their immediate boroughs, or AFC Telford who saw their club liquidated, FC United have formed out of pure objection. That the club they object to is possibly the most decorated in recent football history makes the move even more significant. FC United first and foremost are a shot in the arm, a barometer of the football climate, a timely reminder to the authorities that silverware alone is not enough, certainly not when the principles of a club are being compromised for the sake of generating money for a privileged few.

Of course, this rebellion was never simply about the Glazier takeover, or at least was never meant to be. Former Secretary Luc Zentar went on record at the time of the clubs creation to say he was sick of football and what it had become, specifically the way supporters were treated. "It's a Gestapo-like environment," he told the ESPN website, "I can't stand the fact that it costs £36 to get in to a ground with no atmosphere, where you can't stand, can't shout, can't fart, can't even sit with your friends."[1] Clearly he was not alone in his analysis and retrospection suggests the Glazier takeover compounded rather than caused the formation of the club in June 2005. What is clear is the fractious relationship Manchester United continues to have with their fans. As of January 2010 concern around the club's perilous financing had crystallised over a £500m bond issue, designed to refinance a debt of £716m costing £42m a year in interest payments alone. Like TV violence which desensitises through its ubiquitous nature, football finances are simply abstract figures to the vast majority of normal fans, a fiscal sedative which barely raises an eyebrow. And who can blame them? Football parlance is so strewn with vulgar examples of opulence it is difficult to feel anything damning anymore; when something becomes *de rigeur* it loses

---

[1] www.soccernet.espn.go.com/feature?id=33663&cc=5739

any shock value: £80m players, £20m wages, billionaire owners, even Monopoly didn't stretch its credibility so far. To cite a point, it has been suggested that the professional fees involved in refinancing Manchester United's debt cost in excess of £50m.[1] Fifty million. Fifty million pounds. You can't say it without sounding like Danny DeVito in *Twins*. At best this might have the more morally outraged guardian do a double take but in the context of modern football practises this is just over half a Ronaldo or the openly operational debt of many Premiership clubs. Fans take it on board, utter the odd platitude about football finances, and then go back to watching televised football in their replica shirt. It is not until these figures are put into the context of the wider game that the sheer obscenity of it all hits home; £10K for new changing rooms so amateur players don't have to shower in the cold; £15K to stave off a winding up order that would bury 100 years of local history when a club folds; £20-50K to keep a modest Step 5 side in business for a year. £2M to build a new community stadium with leisure and educational facilities for local people. £80K to buy endless rounds of cocktails in a west end bar full of voluptuous young women…

On the surface, it is hard to see why this debt is such a problem. The Glaziers have effectively taken out a huge mortgage on Manchester United, plunging them into the red, but in reality this isn't a problem as long as they keep on winning trophies and carry on managing the interest payments. Furthermore, given the power of the Manchester United brand even if the Glazier's do go down with a bad fall an investor will invariably step in with a wet sponge and a can of freeze spray. Analysed in terms of on field success, the takeover appears to be working. Since the Glazier's hotfooted into Salford, United have retained the Premiership and won the Champions League whilst dazzling sell-out crowds around the world. This is merely a superficial level though. Behind the glory grabbing headlines, the main source of supporters' ire is channelled into long term concerns. Firstly, how these ambitious financing plans affect the price of following the club and, secondly, how Manchester United - debts and all - will compete in a market that is so cash rich.

It would be easy to place FC United into this troublesome equation as a panacea for the disgruntled fan but the *raison d'être* for this newly formed faction goes beyond concerns of profiteering, and potentially beyond the

---

[1] www.fourfourtwo.com/news/england/46825/default.aspx

concerns of fans who would be appeased by Middle Eastern backers jetting into town and 'doing a Man City', as if parity at the hand of the petro dollar were order of the day. When we arrived at the Castle Inn a few FC fans were already sampling the local ale, and spotting a badge quicker than a pisshead spots a kebab shop, I introduced myself for a quick chat. There are several rules of etiquette on introducing yourself to rival fans, not least that you don't wear a Stone Island hat coupled with an Armani three quarters length whilst acting as if you are sussing them out. Otherwise it could leave you lying on the floor spitting innocent protestations through a blooded mouth. Thankfully I am charmingly naïve at times and once I mentioned I had been speaking with Supporters Direct and had Chairman Andy Walsh's number, any concerns of going home in an ambulance were allayed.

I sat opposite the oldest chap in the group, a grey haired don with an accent richer than a chocolate soufflé. "I'd been a season ticket at Old Trafford most of my life, but I started following this lot when I couldn't afford to go any more. What's more I don't like the idea of being forced to buy tickets for cup matches just to ensure you can watch league games. It's a complete rip off. In fact, I don't like being told how to support my club which is exactly what Man United were making us do. The 'regime' in place is exactly the right phrase."

"It's not just about the money though you understand," added another. "Most of us were pissed off with the way the club was selling itself out, the way it treated its fans. Quite a few people I know stopped going when they dropped the words "Football Club" from the badge and others have drifted away over time after a series of nonsense rules were bought in coupled with a complete lack of understanding regarding what the club was supposed to be about. Old Trafford still sells out but the real fans, the working class fans from Salford and surrounding areas, are being replaced by day-trippers or those simply who can afford it. FC United is all about remembering, celebrating and endorsing what Manchester United is supposed to be about; a community club run for the everyday fan. We don't hate Manchester United. In fact we are all still passionate about what the club was and still look out for their results. We are just annoyed at what it has become and can't be a part of it anymore."

For many neutrals, herein lies the contradiction. It is easy to see FC United as a conduit for channelling emotion, a notion of idealism for what football - or a specific club - should be about. Where critics have been very vocal is in the selective and somewhat hypocritical manner in which FC base their grievance. Manchester United dominated the 1990s under the stewardship of Alex Ferguson and a golden generation of youth team players but they were also ably assisted by the financial returns associated with being a PLC. As a PLC their club were always susceptible to a buyout, which finally materialised in 2005, irrespective of how financially reckless it may have seemed. The moral, it would seem, is that you can't have your cake and eat it. The counter to this argument is that the ownership is a contributory factor and nothing more. For the guys sat round my table, it was a about a malaise, a disenfranchise from a club they loved, a slow and steady sell-out to satisfy corporate interests. Yet despite all this they still openly supported Manchester United. So were FC United just a parallel fantasy, a plaything to exorcise the evil spirits of consumerism? A chance to stand and swear and be joyously vociferous whilst cheering on a team that you believe embodied the real spirit of Manchester United?

"Even if it all changed, if the Glaziers left and ticket prices went down and all the other bullshit was wiped out, I couldn't go back now. FC United has become a club in its own right not just a protest movement. I know a lot of people tell us that if we are so pissed off with Old Trafford we should support a local non league side but this is missing the point. They wouldn't be our team. We might have a soft spot for them but it isn't the same thing. FC United was designed by accident, for fans who wanted to be part of a club that not only supported the spirit of Manchester United but made every member and fan feel like they were part of a club, not a business enterprise. It's a very unique feeling. Plus the football is so much better than any of us ever envisaged. If you had told me ten years ago I would enjoy coming to places like Stocksbridge instead of Highbury I would have said you were mad, but I have never enjoyed my football so much. You still get to have a drink with your mates and enjoy the game but you aren't being ripped off. You also get the chance to stand where you want with who you want and say what you want. It's how football used to be."[1]

[1] On Saturday 27th February, before the home game against North Ferriby United, FC United hosted a supporters' rally aimed at putting supporter ownership at the very centre of the debate on the future of the game. The rally was called "Beyond the debt." As well as representatives from the club, guest speakers included Guardian journalist David Conn, in addition to representatives from Schalke FC, Supporters Direct and IMUSA. The principle aim was to evaluate and review an alternative model of how the game is structured and the role of supporter owned clubs within this framework.

By a stroke of luck, another member of the gathered away contingent was Club Official Vinny Thompson. Rather than extend the already well-trodden rhetoric, Vinny was keen to focus on the other good works the club were embarking on, particularly the anti-racism campaigns and the community days.

"A lot of people won't know what goes on behind the scenes at FC United but we do a lot work with marginalised communities and young kids. If you are going to be a real community club the community need to recognise you mean it. We are having a Youth United Day later in the year. If you want to have a balanced look at our club, I recommend you come along."[1]

As 3pm approached and the pub was a considerable walk from the ground, we decided to head out before the beer caused an onset of mild ambivalence. The landlady of The Castle had shown us a shortcut to the Bracken Mood Stadium through a field and as we trekked across the narrow dog shit strewn pathway looking like a hooligan firm on a three peak challenge it occurred to me just how unorthodox and rural some non league clubs actually were. There were no sign posts, no street lights and no indication at all that a football club laid just round the corner. The Pennines dominated the horizon, speckled with soft fuzzy lighting and fleeting shadows, the single file silhouettes ahead made us look like characters in a *Band of Brothers* montage. Ironically, when the footpath gave way to a housing estate like a river running to the mouth of the sea we felt even more lost.

"Are you taking the piss?"

"No."

"We're definitely going the wrong way."

"It's this way."

"Bollocks."

And so on.

Eventually we saw a trickle of people in front of us and latched on to them. When the Miners Arms hovered into view - as menacing and beat up as the name suggested - we knew we had arrived at our destination.

The first thing that struck me on entering the ground was the sheer volume of FCUM fans - conservative estimates would put the figure at 500 - but it

---

[1] www.askbury.co.uk/news-feature/63/sport-news/39428/youth-united-day

was the complete visible lack of Stocksbridge supporters that made the occasion slightly disquieting. For all intents and purposes this felt like a FC home fixture. NPL attendance stats suggest this is not a rarity. Most clubs that FC visit break all gate records and away crowds of over 1,000 have been reported on rare occasions. It all felt rather surreal.

Most of the FCUM contingent were sheltered behind the goal in the covered terracing and looked an impressive site with their fanfare of noise and flags. We took our place on the side of the ground next to the main stand on what was possibly the deepest terracing on the face of the planet. You almost had to throw your legs over to climb up; giving the feeling you were on the set of *The Borrowers*. Woe betide anyone falling forward celebrating a goal; the drop to the next step would be like falling off the side of a cliff.

I had only been to Stocksbridge once before, to meet a girl for a date. Lust, like football support, takes you places you would seldom otherwise travel and my overriding memory of the day was being acutely aware of my southernness, so much so I felt like a land baron during feudal times, up from London to sodomise the farmhand's daughter. Formed in 1986 with the merger of Stocksbridge Works FC and Oxley Park Sports FC, Park Steels had channelled their resources into the Bracken Moor Stadium in order to meet ground grading criteria for any subsequent rise through the non league pyramid system. Work included the opening of a social club, refurbishment to the dressing rooms, erection of floodlights, the building of a new stand and extension to the social club new canteen area, making the ground one of the best junior stadiums in South Yorkshire.

The appointment of management team Mick Horne and Trevor Gough in 1991 signalled the start of the club's rise through the non league ranks. In the 1993-94 season they won the Northern Counties East League (NCEL) Premier Division but were denied promotion to the Unibond League on ground technicalities. Promotion eventually came two seasons later, with the club entering the Unibond First Division, achieving consistently high finishes for what was still a fledgling outfit.

In the 2002-03 season Paul Jackson equalled an FA Cup record of ten goals in one game, during the Steels 17-1 thrashing of Oldham Town. Steels had their best FA Cup run the following season reaching the third qualifying round before eventually losing away at Shildon. Having consolidated in the Unibond League, the club then embarked on a period of successful but ultimately fruitless campaigns; in 2005-06 they missed out on promotion after losing to Kendal in the play offs; in 2006-07 they missed out on a play off position after being in the top three for almost all of the season; in 2007-08 season Steels finished in 5th place losing to local rivals Sheffield FC in the Play Off Semi-final. In 2008-09 the football gods finally smiled (or took pity on) Stocksbridge and, following a 3rd place finish in Unibond Division 1 South, Park Steels won the Play Off Final against Belper Town, meaning promotion was ensured to Step 3 for the first time in their history.

The 2009-10 season started well, with the team occupying a play off place for the first few months of the campaign, albeit having played significantly more games than the clubs around them. Going in to the game, the Steels' form had slumped with only a handful of wins since the start of October, which made predicting the outcome against an indifferent FC United side very difficult. FC themselves missed out on the Unibond play offs last season by virtue of Kendal Town scoring an 88th minute goal in a game elsewhere which, like its infamous mint cake, no doubt left a foul taste in the mouth.

The game started at a frantic pace, which met with nods of approval from my mate Steve, a man who refuses to accept the 1980s finished two decades ago, both from a football and sartorial perspective. "The standard of tackling is brilliant - proper old school," he enthused, conjuring up blissful images of a hungover Bryan Robson clattering into a central midfield tackle before relaxing in the players' bar afterwards with a pint in one hand and a SKY Sports reporter in the other.

The FC United contingent sang loudly and proudly throughout the first half, with a repertoire of old Stretford End anthems and a few new numbers, mostly about how much they despised the Glaziers and the whole supporter sell-out. To the innocent observer - and there were plenty of them stood next to me - it would seem that FC United's support was based as much on their dislike of recent history than their aspirations for their future. Also, a few of the neutral crowd shivering in the shadows of the ageing main stand were simply not convinced.

"It all seems a bit false," my friend Lee commented, a dyed in the wool Evertonian, "they're just Man United fans with a chip on their shoulder. As soon as the Glaziers go they'll all come crawling back." Whether this claim has any substance is a moot point. Whether an Evertonian can be objective on such matters is another. FCUM fans I have spoken to admit that every person that turns out to watch them has their own reasons. Some openly admit that it is purely a Glazier protest, some still go to Old Trafford, and some will never set foot there again.

Despite bucket loads of endeavour, the game didn't really spring into life until the half hour mark when Joe Yoffe latched on to a hopeful punt upfield (I wonder how many times that stock phrase has been used in local match reports over the years) and was taken out by Steels 'keeper Ben Scott on the edge of the area. The referee gave a yellow card and a free kick and, judging by the abuse being hurled at him from the away end, his number to a local garage specialising in slashed car tyres. The incident injected a bit of needle into proceedings, which clearly carried on after the half time whistle as the referee did his best to appease a few heated exchanges with mortarboard style efficiency. My friends were clearly enjoying the live theatre given we were yards from the players' tunnel.

"That big fucker just called the referee a cunt," said one gleefully, like a child hearing his grandparents swear for the first time in public.

When the tunnel gates reopened, I wandered down to the clubhouse to see if they were letting anyone in, as the sheer number of away supporters had forced the bar to temporarily close on safety advice. A queue was forming near the front door and the atmosphere was becoming tense. Hovering near the stewards to assess the situation inside an older FC fan, who had been giving the stewards grief for the last few minutes, decide to vex his frustrations on me.

"Don't think you're getting in this fucking bar ahead of me, pal," he said without any note of humour. I chose the most neutral response I could and smiled at him.

"Yeah, you can fucking smile." I melted into the melee out of eye contact. He looked hard and I once got threatened by Quakers. The doors remained locked. The eloquent protagonist, who was now picking a fight with anyone who would listen, decided his best route of entry was to abuse the door staff even more, which garnered disapproving responses from his fellow supporters. Eventually (and somewhat incredibly) everyone was allowed in, sending a tidal wave of Stone Island crashing through the doors and up the stairs. The queue was already ten deep at the bar so I took an opportunity to stand in the warm for a while and eat a Kit Kat, which by any stretch of the imagination is a truly emasculating statement. As more and more fans spilled in, tensions grew. The same guy who had been causing a scene downstairs was now squaring up to a fellow FC supporter who had accused him of being an embarrassment. It didn't go down at all well. I have been attending football matches all over the country for over twenty years and it was the first time I had ever seen a fan strike someone following the same team. The inevitable surge ensued, followed by a lot of accusations and threats. Interestingly, at least more than one caught up in the pointless shoving match tried to bring a sense of occasion to proceedings.

"This is FC United - we don't want any of that bullshit here," came the rallying cry. Unfortunately the bullshit had already been dumped on the clubhouse floor and was stinking the place out. I felt genuinely uncomfortable, which for a non league match was a first and, I would hope, a last. There wasn't a home fan anywhere in site so I headed back out to the terraces to regale my friends with recent goings on. As much as I disapproved of proceedings, I am a sucker for tittle tattle.

It was starting to get distinctly colder by the time the second half kicked off but this didn't stop a few hardened souls seeking out two entrepreneurial urchins who were leaning over the wall behind the terraces and offering them money to pick up some cans of beer. From at least two levels this was a blatantly illegal act but it seemed to add to the general *bon homie* of the sparsely populated home end, if indeed any definitive segregation could be identified. The arrival of the beer bought back memories of scheming efforts to smuggle 20/20 into school discos, usually consumed swig by swig in a circle of friends behind industrial waste bins. Naturally these covert operations were all rather pointless. A teacher can invariably spot a dribbling 15 year old quicker than an Arsenal talent scout and such events usually peaked with a crescendo of blue vomit and suspension notes.

FCUM started the second half strongly and nearly broke the deadlock through Jake Cottrell, after good right wing play by Phil Marsh, but the midfielder took a touch too many and blazed the shot over the bar. The impressive Carlos Roca, a Mancunian born Spaniard with slightly feral features, began to control the midfield and on 61 minutes scored a well taken goal, dummying his marker, cutting inside another, and firing under the Steels 'keeper. The 500 or so away fans went ballistic, although not as ballistic as my friend Darcy when we told him we weren't leaving early to go the pub.

At this point Stocksbridge looked a defeated team. Their cause was hardly helped when Brett Lovell, the gargantuan Steels centre back who was clearly out of the country when Arsene Wenger introduced dietary discipline into the game, was sent off for a series of clumsy rather than malicious challenges. This (large) gap at the back allowed FC to expose increasing weaknesses and Marsh again came close after being put through by Jake Cottrell. With some of the home fans sensing defeat, and the bitter weather making the prospect of a warm pub increasingly inviting, a few of our group decided enough was enough.

"Well I'm staying to the end," said one lone voice intent on getting his money's worth. Obviously the *Stand By Me* mentality wasn't unanimous, as half of the freezing group trudged out under a fog of breath. Those that did stay were no doubt glad of their convictions. With two minutes left, substitute Mark Ward played a free kick into the box and following a scramble (obscured for large parts by the main stand) Andy Ring bundled himself and the ball over the line despite the goalkeeper's claims it was kicked from his grasp. I would write "cue wild celebrations" but this would be a downright lie. At best there was a short burst of cheer somewhere to our right. The final whistle bought with it applause from both sets of fans. To FCUM's credit, their fans gave everything for 90 minutes and as a spectacle for those attending their first non league matches their presence no doubt gave a cutting edge to the occasion. As we filed out a few of my friends started checking for the latest scores on their phones.
"Anyone know how United got on?" said a broad Mancunian voice.
"Yeah it was 1-1 mate, weren't you watching?" came the sarcastic response from a rapidly retreating home fan.

Despite my penis having shrivelled to the size of an acorn in the freezing South Yorkshire midwinter, I decided to chance a quick toilet break before heading back over the fields to the pub (I was also harbouring irrational thoughts about getting the old fella out on the walk home with a potential Bodmin Beast type predator waiting in the wings). Inside the tiny cloakroom, there were stickers plastered all over the walls saying "Hate the Glaziers - love United" although it wasn't particularly explicit which United it was referring to, perhaps for good reason. Although it was a seemingly innocent act, it crystallised the biggest problem I have with today's game.

FC United may be a non league club but their fans are predominantly drawn from the professional ranks and are used to travelling in large numbers around well marshalled and segregated grounds. At risk of generalising, I suspect many have little prior experience of regular non league attendance or etiquette, which means there is a diametric clash of football terrace culture. As a consequence, we get a spectacle like this where the sheer volume of numbers and associated demeanour is vastly different from the usual trickle of away fans that would usually turn up. I have to go on record as saying it was only a tiny minority of those away fans who seemed intent on throwing their weight around and it is quite feasible that any club bringing large numbers - perhaps for an end of season play off or Championship decider - could be peppered with the odd unsavoury character. But these actions, combined with the blanket posting of anti-Glazier graffiti all over Stockbridge's ground, suggests that FCUM need to learn a degree of courteous restraint. In truth, a lot of neutral fans couldn't care less about the Glazier saga at Old Trafford. In fact, many who have an open dislike for all things Man United probably find the whole episode highly amusing. As my mate Danny pointed out, "they probably don't give a toss what anyone else thinks of them", but I would argue this is the whole crux of the issue. If FCUM are to be embraced by the non league community and welcomed with open arms at away grounds they need to start acting like a non league club rather than be seen as a collection of embittered Man United fans stampeding round the semi-professional provinces ramming an agenda down everyone's throats. This may seem a draconian summary, and for the vast majority of fans who embrace FCUM as a new dawn of supporters' empowerment it will seem a little unfair, but the actions of a misguided few can leave an overriding impression, as any football fan who has been labelled a hooligan by simply mentioning their love for the sport will no doubt testify. Personally, I applaud what FC United are trying to do. Their underlying principles - to give football back to the people - is a benevolent and worthy one and one hopes that those who sign up to this embryonic club do so out of love for the game rather than hate for its failings; for the immediate future, and with a true and separate identity still needing to be forged, FC United will remain, to the casual observer at least, a distinctly esoteric outfit, clouded with suspicion.

The next day at work, I emailed everyone who went to the match and asked them what they thought. There was the usual banter and persiflage but one response stood out as summarising what the layman - or layfan - thought of the day.

"I'd like to go to Stocksbridge again sometime," came the reply, "but this time to a real non league game."

Chelmsford City v Oxford United

FA Trophy 3rd Round
Saturday 30th January 2010

Final Score: 1-3
Attendance: 1,347

One of the more complicated debates doing the rounds in pyramid football concerns the status of the Conference National as a 'non league' division. At the time of writing, one of the popular threads on the effervescent www.nonleaguematters.co.uk forum asks "at what point does the Conference officially leave non league?" Prior to automatic Football League promotion in 1987, the Conference was almost exclusively semi-professional with a clear dividing line drawn between the teams in this division and their professional counterparts in the four levels above. As promotion and relegation ensued, previously full time clubs found themselves competing with part time outfits and by the time the two up two down system was introduced in 2002-03 the Conference was awash with ex-League sides who had maintained their professional status.

The start of the 2009-10 Blue Square Premier (the sponsored moniker of the Conference National) was possibly the most high profile ever, with three of its member clubs (Luton Town, Oxford United, AFC Wimbledon) having played in the top flight of English football in the last 25 years. Additionally, five clubs were Football League members when promotion and relegation began in 1987 (Cambridge United, Chester City, Mansfield Town, Wrexham, York City), two had been promoted and came back down (Kidderminster, Rushden & Diamonds) and one was voted out in 1972 (Barrow). In all, if we are to effectively include Gateshead as an incarnation of an ex-Football League side, 12 out of the 24 teams that make up the current division are ex-League sides, with a similar or even higher percentage operating on a full time basis. A consequence of this transitional phase has been the increase in average attendance throughout the league. The 1986-87 season saw an average attendance of 919 in the GM Vauxhall Conference, compared to a respective figure of 1,992 for the same league in January 2010, an increase of over 100% but still well below the average of 3,843 for the Football League in the same period. What these figures don't show is the huge disparity between the best and worst supported sides in the Blue Square; Oxford's crowd against Luton Town on 8th September 2009 drew in an astonishing 10,613 spectators, whilst Hayes & Yeading recorded only 291 for their January 2010 clash with Forest Green Rovers. Notwithstanding, seven Blue Square teams have better average attendances than their League 2 counterparts this season and, unsurprisingly, all seven are ex-Football League sides. Conversely, five of the bottom six supported sides in League 2 have all been promoted from the Conference over the last twenty years or so. Old habits it seems, die hard.

For non league purists, this statistical composite has raised questions over the Conference continuing to masquerade as a non league competition. Technically it remains non league but this is mere semantics. Many non league fans are drawn to the semi-professional game precisely because it isn't subject to the same bureaucracy and commercialism as the full time game, but increasingly Step 1 football is adopting more and more of these attributes, not least with regards segregation, match day costs, and online censorship; it may be coincidence but several larger non league clubs have removed links to fans' forums for reasons that may be speculative but nonetheless cause intrigue. Then again, what are the alternatives? The current structure of the league is a direct result of automatic promotion and - to a lesser extent - feckless management at boardroom level. It is quite conceivable as I write this page that Darlington and their 25,000 seat stadium could be plying their trade in the Conference next year. On paper it's a farcical state of affairs. Yet, as the cliché goes, the table doesn't lie and is as much reflective of modern football's financial belligerence as it is a marker of a club's true standing in life. As long as clubs continue to operate beyond their means or, even worse, can be exploited and left for dead by half arsed legislation, then the Conference will continue to accept the poor and needy of the professional game like some kind of incumbent workhouse, regardless of a member's glittering past. If the authorities were to rename the Blue Square "League 3" few would be genuinely surprised, although it probably would mask the polarisation between the biggest and smallest clubs in the division where, much like the Premiership, you begin to have leagues within a league. Even with the necessary infrastructure, one would be hard pushed to see teams currently averaging 5-600 spectators ever progressing beyond their current status.

When Chelmsford v Oxford United was drawn out of the hat for the third round of the FA Trophy, it may have been the glamour tie of the round but possibly not the most interesting for this book. Given the wide spectrum of media starved clubs at my disposal it might seem odd to profile a match featuring Oxford United, but any attempt to look at the non league scene as a whole needs to recognise the changes that have occurred over the last twenty years, specifically the presence of teams that wouldn't look out of place in the Championship. On a tactical note, I also needed to cover an FA Trophy match, preferably one featuring a potential giant killing, so it ticked several boxes.

The last (indeed only) time Chelmsford City had appeared on my radar was back in the late '90s when they were sponsored by Red Card energy drink. The sponsorship campaign was huge. Nearly every bus shelter in the land during the 1997-98 season had a series of stern faced City players standing underneath a variety of non nonsense quotes. My favourite (and by favourite I mean the only one I recollect) read "If Man United were playing down the bottom of my garden I'd draw the curtains" though to this day I am not sure what this message was trying to convey; drink Red Card and develop an indifference to top flight football? If you look hard enough on YouTube there is a clip of Red Card's marketing manager, David Atter, extolling the virtues of the sponsorship deal on the now defunct *Under the Moon* show.[1] It looks like a bad acid trip at first, as David stands there in a Chelmsford shirt drawing graphs while a bald man plays keepy-uppy in the background. Danny Kelly, chief adjudicator for proceedings asks the question most viewers would be curious to know: why choose Chelmsford City? The romantic in me wanted an answer rooted in grassroots passion, but the inevitable matter of fact response - they are the nearest club to the factory that makes the drink - took the gloss off it somewhat.

Ironically, despite being thrust into the national psyche, it was a time that represented a low point for a club that had gained a nearly man tag in non league football. The original amateur Chelmsford club formed in 1878[2] moving to their famous New Writtle Street ground in 1925 (although the website does reference this as 1922), before folding and reforming as a professional outfit in 1938. During the post-war boom years, City were overlooked for election to the Football League despite having an enviable team, stadium and supporters base (crowds of 15,000 plus were not

---

[1] www.youtube.com/watch?v=7GcH917pHhs

[2] According to official club historian David Selby, Chelmsford Football Club and Chelmsford City Football Club were separate entities and therefore had different dates of formation. He does concede, however, that it remains the subject of much debate and argument amongst fellow Chelmsford City historians.

uncommon) and were often usurped by clubs who were better contacted or caught the national imagination with dazzling cup runs. By the start of the 1960s the club were under the stewardship of ambitious chairman John Coward, who had a simple goal: to gain promotion to the Football League. Quite how this was to be achieved within the framework of an arbitrary voting system is unclear and the project never really got off the ground despite efforts to improve the Writtle Street Stadium. The start of the 1970s promised renewed optimism. The Southern League title was won again in 1972, with a glamorous cup tie against Ipswich Town the following season drawing 15,557 spectators to City's ground. Around this time, the club employed the services of a local PR company to boost their reputation and chances of election to the Football League. It was to prove a fruitless task and the clubs spiraling finances drastically affected performances on the field, despite two famous faces gracing the Chelmsford line up in Nigel Spink and a maturing Jimmy Greaves.

Despite a series of strong Southern League campaigns throughout the '80s, the club never reached the heights of the top non league division, the newly formed Alliance League (now the Blue Square Premier), partly owing to the tough one up one down system that was employed from the respective regional feeder leagues. Like many teams beset by off field problems, Chelmsford nearly folded in the early '90s, only to be saved at the last minute by a supporters group led by Trevor Wright. This was only a temporary reprieve though. Relegation followed shortly after the buyout and the club saw their Writtle Street ground sold off by the official receiver in 1997, meaning eviction and a subsequent ground share at Maldon Town. In an eventful season, City then moved to Billericay's New Lodge after a falling out with their new landlords. Despite finishing runners up in the 1997-98 Southern League Southern Division they were denied promotion by a technicality as New Lodge was not deemed sufficient for Southern Premier football. Controversially, their landlords gained promotion to the similarly placed Ryman League Premier Division which, aside from causing a degree of resentment, was a possible catalyst for the FA to review the uniformity of ground grading across the leagues.

During this period a number of ground proposals were submitted but none got past the drawing board. By a quirk of fate, the New Lodge was eventually given an A grade listing, meaning the club's second place finish in 2000-01 allowed them entry back to the Premier Division. A switch to Ryman League football in 2004-05 bought with it more local derbies and the news all fans had wanted to hear - an opportunity to move home. Chelmsford Borough Council had agreed, independent funding pending, that the club could return to the city and play their football at the Melbourne Park athletics stadium. This was joyous vindication for the army of volunteers who had kept the side running through its darkest days and on January 2006 the club returned to the borough after an absence of eight years in front of a crowd of 2,998.

The prospects for Chelmsford are bright. As the county town of Essex with a population of 120,000 it clearly has potential to accommodate League football. The team currently play in the Conference South, having missed out in the play offs last season to Hampton and Richmond Borough. Were promotion achieved this season it would mark a progressive period in the club's history, following their winning Isthmian League campaign in 2008. No doubt a large chunk of the club's recent fortunes are down to Jeff King, the man responsible for taking Canvey Island from the Essex Senior League to the Conference National during his long and successful tenure. King left Canvey Island under a cloud in 2006, claiming that the sub 500 crowds they were getting was affecting his ability to invest in the club. "If people choose not to go, we can choose not to waste our time and money," King told BBC Sport. "It looks like people in Canvey Island don't want to support a team in this league."

In retrospect, Canvey Island may have seemed a slightly strange choice to start a football 'project'. With a sub 40,000 population and a mere hop skip and two footed challenge from Southend and its own relatively successful side, it was always up against established opposition. Perhaps more significantly, a lot of south Essex has the claret and blue of West Ham running through its estuaries, partly a result of post-war migration and the displacement of bombed out East End communities into the neighbouring border counties. In Chelmsford, there is no doubt far more potential and the appointment appears to be reaping the rewards of King's contacts and investment already.

Despite this, Chelmsford are not a club rolling in money, or at least don't project the image of being so. When doing some background research for the match, I navigated to the official club website[1] whose banner page was

---

[1] www.chelmsfordcityfootballclub.co.uk

an open plea to help raise funds for ground improvements, specifically a roll on roll off roof for the terracing behind the goal. On the subject of the website, it is undoubtedly one of the best I have seen at either League or non league level. A particularly nice touch is the extended match highlights you can watch via the web portal, providing you can forgive the slightly amateur commentating, which sounds like a teenager reluctantly reading out his English essay to a full classroom.

In an attempt to safeguard their future, plans are in place to protect City's future by becoming a Community Interest Club. This move would ensure that all money from the club goes into the community rather than open to the vagaries of ambitious takeover plans or asset stripping. Chairman Marshall Wallace appears to embrace and nature the concept of a mutuality organisation at the heart of the community. Speaking to www.totalessex.co.uk in March 2009 he advised;
"We want to protect the club for future generations to come. We want to be able to achieve League status and we need to protect the assets of the club to reach that. It matches the club's ambitions on the pitch at the moment and we need to protect the assets now rather than later. Like any other company it will be run by a board of directors and there will probably be some supporters' representatives on the board. It's encouraging people to put money into the club."

Clearly Wallace isn't just paying lip service to these claims. Later this year there will be a specially arranged fans' forum where he and Head Coach Glenn Pennyfather will respond to any queries from supporters, as well as outline the latest of City's ongoing community work.

Getting to Chelmsford's ground from the railway station is something of a mission. You could get a bus, but then you could eat a kebab when you were sober. What we can do and what we should do are often wildly different scenarios. All things considered - the freezing weather being one - a taxi was the safest option. After fifteen minutes winding through housing estates and roundabout systems we arrived at Melbourne Park. I have to confess I am not a fan of football stadiums that double as athletics grounds. This is an invariable disservice to the time, effort and emotion that has gone into relocating the club back to the heart of Chelmsford but it still feels like a team just lodging there, like a mate kipping on your sofa after his bird has chucked him out. At a practical level, the natural gap caused by the running

CHANGING ENDS Mike Bayly

track means the stands are too far back from the pitch, which is an intimacy I have been spoiled with over the years. After all, a game isn't a game if you can't engage in witty banter with the away goalkeeper (i.e. keep telling him he's fat and shit or, as I saw at one ground, that you know where he lives, which has distinctly sinister *Here's Johnny* overtones). It's not that the ground isn't nice - it is: it just all seems a little staged. The club have certainly made the ground their own by virtue of a new clubhouse, changing rooms and social facilities, but it is still essentially an athletics stadium. The now departed and demolished New Writtle Street was generally considered one of the best amateur grounds of its day, as lovingly documented by Mike Floate is his book *New Writtle Street – the Final Season*. I suspect many fans still wistfully compare their old home to the current incarnation.

We took our place (I say "we" - a female friend with a season ticket at Arsenal had accompanied me for the day out of unquenchable curiosity) in the main stand. By the main entrance, a very draconian sign advised anyone caught swearing would be thrown out. I have never understood this hard line approach; football is supposed to be cathartic and vociferous, not a George Bernard Shaw play observed in quiet introspection. Evidently the message had got through to the fans around us; I didn't hear a single profanity the whole time I was there.

The players entered the pitch behind a large parrot to the sound of *Waltzing Bugle Boy*, which gave the aura of being sedated by a powerful hallucinogenic; it was more like an LSD-tinged Ealing Comedy than a high profile cup match. The game itself kicked off at a fast pace, with City's Ricky Holmes nearly getting the home team off to a flying start inside the first five minutes after missing a one on one when clean through on goal. Holmes was heavily involved again as the half wore on, setting up a couple of decent half chances which, in fairness, took some sterling work from United's Ryan Clarke to keep the scores level. Oxford eventually took the lead in the 37th minute when Kevin Sandwith's excellent chipped cross allowed Francis Green to spectacularly beat the City goalkeeper.

Half time soon came. As the players marched off past the shot put nets it gave me time to reconcile what was turning out to be a very strange afternoon. Firstly, there just didn't seem to be any atmosphere. There had been sporadic singing behind the goal to our left but from a crowd of 1,300 plus you would expect something more. The fans sitting around me seemed decidedly stoical and there was an air of indifference hanging over the match. Oxford United were League Cup winners less than 25 years ago, playing in front of more than 90,000 people at the old Wembley, so you could possibly forgive them for not being overawed by the occasion today. Furthermore, Oxford's aim this season by any realistic marker is to gain promotion back to the Football League. Chelmsford, likewise, have promotion ambitions of their own and as two fans sat behind me were quick to comment when their team went one down "I'm not too bothered about this to be honest - it's the league that really matters." From a match perspective, I was also disappointed at the standard of football on show. It's hard to directly compare but it seemed very hit and hope at times and certainly not the level you would expect of the supposed best side in non league football. Certainly it was nowhere near as enjoyable or as fluid as other matches attended this season of a much lower grading.

The turning point of the match came halfway into the second period when Jack Midson scored two quick-fire goals, tapping into an empty net after good approach play for the first and two minutes later killing the game as a spectacle by lobbing Harrison in the City goal to make it 3-0. It was a score line that flattered the visitors and it signalled the end of my afternoon's viewing on what was becoming an increasingly cold and protracted day. As we left the ground to catch a taxi back to the station, a distant roar indicated Chelmsford had pulled one back. It actually transpired we had missed two penalties in our haste to leave, the first converted by Chelmsford's Dave Rainford and the second, in injury time, missed by the same player. Penance I guess for committing the cardinal sin of leaving a ground early but the train was warm and the journey home through the Essex countryside only mildly more monotonous than some of the football on display.

In retrospect it was hard to know what to make of the match I had just witnessed. My overriding instinct was that neither team were overly concerned about the game in hand and this was reflected in the response of some of the supporters, some of whom didn't even bother coming out of the bar to watch the second half. Like the FA Cup, there is a strong possibility that the FA Trophy is becoming a devalued competition, certainly if you are anything but a mid-table side with little else to play for. I could be wrong but I am partly convinced that as the mobility between all leagues has increased over time, particularly with the introduction of play offs which gives so many more teams a fighting chance of going up (and down), so the emphasis has shifted away from these knockout competitions, irrespective of the prize on offer at the end. It might also be a change of mindset amongst supporters that as the non league game continues to grow in terms of coverage, so the small time mentality is slowly eradicating and with it a realisation that a trip to Wembley is no longer the prestige day out it used to be. Granted, commentators on FA Trophy Final day will ruminate on how much it means to the fans that have turned up and for many sides, especially those further down the pyramid, it would be hard to dispute this. A more relevant observation, however, is that most fans sat there would probably trade their seat for a promotion to the league above and I am fairly sure the same couldn't be said ten or twenty years ago. I was at Wembley in 2007 when Kidderminster lost to Stevenage and there were similar musings then.

If I were a betting man, I would place money on Chelmsford being in the Football League in the next five to ten years. The infrastructure and support is there to host League football, the question is whether they do it in a way that engages the fans in a long term vision rather than a speculative injection of cash for short term success. The one truly commendable aspect of their operations is their efforts to engage the community in everything they do. The club run youth teams from under 7 through to under 16 and have a variety of community led programmes which aim to reach out to "potential Chelmsford supporters" both young and old. No doubt this attitude is a legacy of their nomadic existence prior to their return home and an attempt to engage a local public who may have drifted away when the Writtle Street ground was sold off. At a slightly more clinical level, it makes good business sense. Theirs is a story I will continue to watch with interest.

The following week, Chelmsford manager Glenn Pennyfather spoke to the club website and accepted his troops were beaten by the better team. In a crash course on prophecy he added "Full credit to Oxford, they're a super side and it's going to take one hell of a team to stop them doing the double of the league and the FA Trophy."

Oxford drew Kidderminster Harriers at home in the next round and lost 2-1.

Biggleswade Town v Hitchin Town

Southern League Midland Division – Step 4
Saturday 13th February 2010

Final Score: 0-3
Attendance: 315

One of the great things about writing a book of this nature is visiting towns and villages that ordinarily one would have no godly inclination of venturing to. Biggleswade, nestling on the River Ivel in Bedfordshire, is such a town. The name Biggleswade - a glorious name at that - is thought to be derived from the Anglo-Saxon name 'Biceil' and 'Waed', the Saxon word for ford. In modern day terms it sounds suspiciously like a character from the fantastical world of Harry Potter, perhaps a friend of Albus Dumbledore, long term terrace stalwarts of AFC Hogwarts, the wholly Wizards' owned supporters team. My previous experience of Biggleswade was distinctly lacking in magic, having spent the night sleeping at the train station after drunkenly missing my stop at nearby Hitchin (by quirk of coincidence, today's opponents). Unlike most vagrants staked out under the stars, I had been shopping at the Paul Smith store in Covent Garden before embarking on light refreshment in the nearby pub, so my prostrate demeanour on the station bench - designer bag pillow and v-neck jumper duvet - must have given the impression of a distinctly incongruous and eccentric drifter.

With a population of just over 15,000 and flanked by numerous other professional and semi-professional sides, it is surprising that Biggleswade boasts not one but two established non league teams. Biggleswade United re-formed in 1959 and are the generally acknowledged reincarnation of the original 1929 club who play in the Spartan South Midlands League at Step 5, one below their rivals Biggleswade Town, who were promoted from this division last season. On paper, Town are the bigger side. During the 2008-09 campaign they averaged 118 spectators compared to United's 50, but matches between the two attracted some impressive gates, with 365 and 123 turning out respectively. According to local supporters, there is no love lost between the two sides, though any claims to local bragging rights may well be based on a recent change in fortunes; as recently as 2007 Biggleswade Town were playing in front of sub 20 crowds, with an average well below their local rivals. So what brought about such a change in fortune?

Formed in 1874 as Biggleswade FC, the club became one of the founder members of the Biggleswade and District League in 1902-03. The 'Waders', as the club are known, first entered the FA Cup in 1904 and were comprehensively beaten 7-1 by a strong Watford side, then members of the Southern League. Biggleswade FC remained in the Biggleswade and District League until 1914-15, joining the Northants League after the war in 1920-21, which is now known as the United Counties League (UCL). The highest position the club attained was third place in 1935, although in 1929 they finished top of the Northants Alliance, which was a subsidiary competition of the League.

After the Second World War the Waders spent five seasons in the Spartan League, before re-joining the UCL in 1951. In 1955 they joined the Eastern Counties League before it reverted to the UCL in 1964, where they remained until 1980, joining the South Midlands League. After a few seasons in Division 1, promotion to the Premier Division was finally achieved in 1986-87. The club struggled during the first seasons back in the top flight but things began to look brighter - literally - when floodlights were installed at the Old Fairfields ground in 1989. Unfortunately, the 1990s continued in the same vein. During the 1996-97 campaign the club finished bottom of the South Midlands Premier Division and only the lack of clubs around them with adequate facilities to fill the division prevented relegation. The following season saw the merger of the South Midland and Spartan Leagues, with the club suffering relegation and then promotion in what was becoming a turbulent end to the century. Plans were progressing for the long intended move to a ground of their own and, although a site had been identified, the club were to remain at Fairfields for another five years.

The 2008-09 season proved one of the most memorable for the club in their long yet relatively undistinguished history. For the first time in 134 years the Waders had a home of their own and, after a breathtaking climax to the season, the Spartan South Midlands League title was claimed by a single goal on goal difference. The club were now playing at the highest level in their history, in a new stadium and with a new verve.

Getting to Biggleswade's new Carlsberg Stadium from the station is like travelling through various stages of geographical and architectural evolution. The station bridge leads into the exotically named Saffron Road, a pleasant Victorian suburb with a joke shop called "Let's Party" nestled in the middle. It looked more like an organic supermarket from the outside and its location hinted towards a target market of commuters or day-trippers looking for their next tickle of amusement. Either that or it catered for a slim demographic of revellers about to board the Kings Cross train in urgent need for a gorilla costume. From Saffron Road, I turned into Hitchin Street and through a modern well maintained upper working class housing estate (Man United stickers in the downstairs bathroom window and a visible lack of Laura Ashley furnishings in the window leads me to draw such sweeping conclusions) which then gave way to a slightly tired looking trading estate. Opposite the entrance to said estate, and sat affront a MOT shop, sat a beautiful Victorian house, poised like a Faberge Egg next to a dog turd. Quite how (or why) this sublime piece of brick built heritage remained was a mystery but it offered a stunning dichotomy from the prefabricated contraption behind it. After leaving the trading estate, I headed under the A1 bridge and away from civilization. The main road headed towards a vanishing point in the distance, with acres of fields either side of me. At this point I began to feel like Forrest Gump, heading off on a pointless trek across the country, mildly concerned that I would be found two days later confused and incoherent on the outskirts of Welwyn Garden City like some kind of non league Piano Man. After another hundred yards of walking, a building homed into view which bore a passing resemblance to the sugar refinery in the laughably bad 1970s horror movie *Empire of the Ants*, which I only sat through on the off chance I might get to see one of Joan Collins' breasts.

The building in question was the newly erected Carlsberg Stadium, Biggleswade Town's new urban fringe ground. The club play in green and white, so it was rather fortuitous that the Carlsberg logo blended in so seamlessly with its lager can coloured surroundings. Next to the main sign signalling the entrance to the complex was another advertising free entry for kids under thirteen accompanied by an adult, which is always a sensible policy for a club looking to turn heads away from the lure of the SKY Sports digibox under the TV. The ground itself is reached by traversing a long muddy track, affecting the look of a construction site and the prospect of a fat bloke with an arse crack and a hard hat seeking the foreman's position to enter the premises. From an aesthetic perspective, one would politely describe the outside of the stadium as 'functional'. For those seeking a non league ground of character and charm it might prove a disappointing journey.

Of course, it's easy to scoff. And many do. Biggleswade's ground, much like the proposed Runcorn Linnets' development, has been derided in certain quarters for its bland soulless architecture, out of town location and 'sports complex' business concept (The Carlsberg Stadium has all weather pitches for hire and other corporate facilities) but with limited budgets and faced with overwhelming pragmatic concerns, there can often be little room for sentimentality. No doubt every fan and club official would like a stadium in the heart of the town with consideration given to architectural tradition but the cost and availability of prime real estate, coupled with the cost of designing and building anything other than an out of the box blueprint, means these choices rarely present themselves. It is also a sign of the times that more and more clubs are moving to purpose built stadiums out of town to either cash in on land value or address local environmental problems; one of the biggest losses to our national game occurred when Shrewsbury Town left their beautiful Gay Meadow Stadium and moved to a prototype of modern football architecture in the Meole Brace district of town, partly to address the continual flooding of their ground on the banks of the River Severn.[1]

Thankfully, there are shining examples of where new stadium development can be functional, innovative and environmental. Dartford's Prince's Park, for example, is a stunning showcase of how a (non league) ground can break the design mould. As well as looking fairly spectacular (it reminds me of a scaled down version of Monaco's Stade Louis II) it has a grassed roof, solar panels for hot water, a sunken pitch to reduce noise and light pollution, and a small lake to collect rainwater for recycling purposes. The main building also has timber cladding for insulation and has been described by the local council as one of the most ecologically sound stadia ever built. Admittedly the ground is funded and owned by the local council, increasing the scope of the project, so direct comparisons with those on a limited private budget are a little unfair.

I met Club Secretary Andy McDonnell in the club official's bar inside the impressive new clubhouse structure. Andy was one of the first people I contacted back in August after I read details of the new ground on one of the many non league blogging websites. It was the first club I had been to

[1] For years, stray balls from misplaced cross field passes were retrieved from the River Severn by Fred Davies in his coracle. Legend had it he charged 50p a time. If this is even vaguely accurate, Fred would have retired a very rich man.

where I got a true 'access all areas' tour of the stadium and pre-match day experience. The Hitchin Town Secretary Roy Izzard was standing at the bar with a coffee and I was keen to point out that the game had sentimental reasons for me, as I spent the first two years of my life living in the town (not that I can remember anything of it. The only photographic documentation I can find of this era, aside from being sat on a hideous wicker chair dribbling, shows me standing next to a kid with an Afro haircut playing catch). Roy was an extremely pleasant chap, with a demeanour that spoke of a wardrobe home to more than one Barbour wax jacket.

Hitchin Town are a relatively big side to be playing at Step 4, at least in terms of history and fan base, a fact acknowledged by Roy. Despite being relegated from the Southern Premier least season their average crowd of 338 was the 7th best in the division. I have never believed a club has a divine right to be in a particular league and that a team's standing generally reflects their management, youth development or wider financial issues. There are times of course when clubs are relegated for reasons beyond their control, such as league restructuring or revised ground grading but, as a rule, the pyramid doesn't lie. Those who flirt with higher or lower leagues for a brief period of time usually do so for good reason, namely because they are working under an unsustainable short term model or are now suffering the fallout from one; Canvey Island are a good case in point here. Hitchin's current form suggests an immediate return to Step 3 next season but ambitions are clearly higher. Whilst never a non league giant, the club came runner up in the old Isthmian League in 1968-69 in what was then one level below the Football League and regularly made the latter stages of the old FA Amateur Cup. Their splendid website[1] also carries a 'Did you know?' section (to which the answer is almost always 'certainly not') which points to a distinguished history, particularly their appearance in the first ever round on the first ever day of the FA Cup in November 1871, drawing 0-0 with Crystal Palace.

After I had met the match officials, looked at the trophy cabinet and reviewed some of the historical press cuttings on the wall, Andy took me on a tour of the complex. It was certainly well appointed and light years ahead of other Step 4 sides I had visited. In fact if you took the building in isolation, it wouldn't look out of place in League 2. As well as the main clubhouse with bar, flat screen TV, and function room, there was a gym,

---

[1] www.hitchintownfc.co.uk

laundry room, VIP area, and two state of the art changing rooms. "It's certainly over specified," Andy observed, "but we wanted to plan ahead. Plus the function room is an added form of revenue on non match days." I stopped short of actually engaging any of the players in conversation in the changing rooms, firstly because I am not gifted in the art of casual manly chit chat and secondly because I feel uncomfortable exchanging pleasantries with anyone just wearing pants.

The tour then took us out into the new ground, which looked so fresh you could almost smell the paint on the metalwork. The main stand does have a flat pack air to it but the seats give an extraordinary amount of leg room and there are also good disabled facilities which are lacking at many non league grounds (although quite how you would get a wheelchair down the main entrance to the stadium in the first place is another matter altogether). There are fenced off areas behind both goals and a small covered terrace near the dugouts on the opposite side of the ground. Adjacent to the ground are two artificial 5-a-side pitches and a further expanse of land will be used to build full size pitches for training and hiring purposes. Compared to their old beat up Fairfield ground, which could best be described as 'characterful', it was palatial.[1] We sat in the main stand and Andy took a few minutes out to test the PA system (is there a covenant at football grounds that Kylie's *The Locomotion* must be played at least once a season?) before we chatted about the teams recent change in fortunes.

"We played at Fairfield since 1874. The Cricket and Football Clubs shared the same ground, but the fixtures and commitments started to overlap. We found that certain games couldn't be played on certain dates; in short our season had to end on the 1st May and start on the 1st September. Aside from the ground looking tired, it was obvious the club couldn't progress in its current state, so plans were submitted to the council for the new stadium. We ground shared at Bedford for a couple of years and then moved in here." I asked if the council had been willing to assist with the relocation. "The ground, which probably cost around £2m to build, has been financed almost entirely by the Chairman. There was no original subsidy from the council or the Football Foundation. The council saw no benefit in funding the project and the Football Foundation tend to work in mysterious and

---

[1] Details and pictures of the old Fairfields ground can be found at www.pyramidpassion.co.uk/html/biggleswade_town.html

drawn out ways. If they had helped us out, there were certain tie-ins and caveats which probably wouldn't have helped us become independent in the long term. That said, we are in line to receive some funding from Central Bedfordshire Council which will amount to around £15,000 or 0.83% of the total cost of the ground. Although it is a very small part of the total spend it does technically mean there will be some assistance, so it's only fair to put that on record."

"So the club is really propped up by the chairman's money?" Andy paused. "Well, yes we are. But then just about every club I know operates in the same way, or at least those with any ambitions of progressing. It can be a dangerous model but it's no different to any other business. When we played at Fairfield the crowds were very low and the gate receipts barely covered the cost of the officials. In fact it was only the raffle money that kept us going at times. It wasn't very sustainable. Now we get crowds of 100 plus and the community seems to have rediscovered its interest in the club. The new raffle system and the bar bring in much needed revenue and we are in a position to take advantage of other business opportunities like 5-a-side hire and so on."

As we were talking, Andy walked me round the rest of the ground. Of particular interest were the turnstiles, which were apparently donated from Sheffield United's Bramall Lane, offering a true slice of football history juxtaposed against the modern face of football progress.

"The ground is a grade D at present, which is good enough for this level and Step 3, providing we get the ground up to grade C by March the following season. This would involve adding another turnstile and improving crowd segregation. Whether we do this, or when we do this, is another matter. We are surviving at present in this league but we need bigger gates to really push on. One of our major incentives is to get children in at a young age, by providing free admission with an adult. But this is only the tip of the iceberg, so to speak. I think in truth the whole club needs to start thinking more commercially."

The social club was now bustling with fans from both teams. Looking around there were also quite a few random affiliations on display; Luton Town, Stevenage, MK Dons, as well as the more predictable allegiances to Chelsea and Tottenham. I made short work of a Cornish pasty, had my fourth cup of coffee, and then wandered outside mildly lightheaded to the club shop. The club shop was like an Aladdin's cave - assuming of course your idea of a treasure trove is old match day programmes and second hand footballs. I thumbed through the collection of journals with clammy handed anticipation, marvelling over the obscurity of some of the team names. Godmanchester Rovers stood out, not least because it shows Alex Ferguson isn't the only deity where a Manchester is concerned, but my favourite team name from this, or indeed any sweep of English football, is undoubtedly Romulus, the Greek God of hopeful punts. As a role model for a club, Romulus is an interesting choice. One the one hand, a fierce warrior and founder of the Roman empire, on the other, a man raised by a wolf and a woodpecker who killed his own brother for jumping over a wall. Amongst other notions, it suggests an organisation that has draconian ideas about pitch transgression. Romulus FC, so legend has it, were formed in 1979 by a small group of parents in Sutton Coldfield looking to form a football club for their children and have progressed in a relatively short space of time to the same league that Biggleswade now find themselves in. Interestingly Romulus ground share with Sutton Coldfield Town, who are also in the Zamaretto Midland League. Rumour has it Sutton fans dress as Spartans when the two clash (actually I made this bit up).

I took my place by the side of the main stand for the start of the match, near to the 180 or so Hitchin fans who had made the short journey up the A1. It was a deceptively cold day and after five minutes I retreated to the main stand in the optimistic belief that sitting down might actually warm me up. I make no bones about it; I am pathetic once the sun goes in, like a kind of reverse Dracula. From the onset, Hitchin looked like the stronger side and underlined their championship credentials with a masterful display of pass and movement. Aesthetically, it would have been nice if this play had resulted in a masterful and well taken goal, employing all the principles of total football, but the first goal was a complete farce. Richard Howell found Harry Hunt, whose speculative shot was parried by the Waders' goalkeeper and then allowed to be fumbled over the line. It was clearly an omen of things to come. Hitchin were now dominating, with their central midfielders winning a lot of the ball and their wide men causing havoc with their ability to move into and create space. A few minutes later it was 2-0, with Biggleswade's 'keeper Ashley Timms going a long way to padding out next Christmas' *Goalkeeping Gaffs* DVD. Playing a free kick across the area, Hitchin's Jamie Arlick intercepted and simply prodded the ball home with the 'keeper completely stranded. Not that the score line flattered the visitors. They were better in all areas of the pitch.

At half time I sought thermal solace in the clubhouse and a chance to thaw my frozen feet with a cup of tea and a custard cream. A lot of fans were hovering around the TV checking out how the other local sides (namely Luton, Stevenage and Watford) were getting on, although it was hard to gauge if they were fans or rivals. That was until one rustic tinged voice piped up "I hope those buggers don't get promoted to the Football League" when Stevenage's halftime score line scrolled through, which clarified at least one standpoint on the matter.

Biggleswade started the second half with a lot more conviction and played some neat football on the floor but Hitchin still looked the superior outfit once they had possession. A few minutes into the restart, the halftime raffle results were announced, with prizes including a four pack of Carlsberg, a bag of Toffees and a box of Jelly babies. The same competition at Arsenal had a car as first prize. Mind you I don't drive, so on the announcement that mine was a winning number, I felt like Charlie discovering the golden ticket and received my Jelly Babies with barely concealed delight. The game played out at a leisurely pace and was broken up by a series of substitutions which did little to alter the overall flow of the game. Biggleswade did come close when Brett Donnelly hit a post but it was only ever going to be a consolation. Just to prove the cock-ups in the first half weren't a fluke, Hitchin added a ridiculous third on 75 minutes when Leaun Lewis' shot deflected up and looped over a stranded Timms, a bit like West Germany's horror goal against England in the 1990 World Cup Semi-final. Only this time the only tears were coming from a small child next to me who had clearly grown weary of the cold and the inevitable home defeat.

Andy came and sat with me for the last few minutes of the game, his hat and long coat giving him a striking resemblance to Sylvester McCoy's Doctor Who. At the final whistle the general consensus was that the better team had won, and won well. Biggleswade Town have clearly come a long way from playing in front of a handful of spectators on a shared pitch but if there is one concern it is where the team goes from here. Like all clubs, a rise through the leagues will inevitably attract new support but with so many other sides in the area there is a constant battle for a share of the supporter pound. In order to sustain a title push and make the operation more self-sufficient you suspect the average attendance will need to rise considerably, though now the team have a sparkling new home with excellent facilities this increase may come, especially if they maintain a policy of encouraging children to come along for free.

Walking back along the deserted main road through the cold dusky evening, the half-light gave the distant housing estate a soft spectre like aura. I hurried on to catch the train back to north London, avoiding a childish pedantry to pop into the joke shop and engage in some physical humour. When you spend your weekends travelling round the country in the freezing cold, at the mercy of delayed trains, non-existent bus services and last minute match cancellations, only to spend 90 minutes stood on open ended terracing being buffeted by monsoons and arctic winds, your life is full of enough tragic comedy to last a lifetime.

Needham Market v Wroxham

FA Vase Quarter Final
Saturday 27th February 2010

Final Score: 1-2
Attendance: 601

Any psychologist reading this book may note a degree of catharsis in my writing, as if I were reliving old memories or exorcising old ghosts. In truth, they would probably be right. As a certified egoist, I am no doubt exercising a certain degree of indulgence in matters of a personal nature. But then all writing - good or bad - is inevitably shaped by personal experience, just as it is with all forms of expressive art. The skill, of course, is finding a fine line between subplot integration and self-obsessed rambling. Whether I can achieve this feat is a debatable point: you're looking at a man who still subscribed to *Whizzer and Chips* aged fifteen years old.

My next game of choice - a FA Vase Quarter Final clash between Needham Market from Suffolk and Wroxham from Norfolk - offered a chance to revisit a county where I spent many a happy seaside break at my grandparents' home in Felixstowe. Felixstowe is about as far flung from your traditional British seaside town as one can imagine. It has the obligatory arcade and sinister oxymoronic fun pub on the sea front but the beach is largely shingle and anyone heading there for a traditional kiss-me-quick weekend jaunt is liable to be gravely disappointed. What made Felixstowe so appealing to my youthful eyes were the less obvious attractions: the huge industrial port which invigorated memories of *Stanlow* and *Sealand* by OMD; the ferry, a veritable bohemian shanty town, heavy with saline camaraderie and a graveyard to skeletal oil splattered rowing boats and moored fishing leviathans. My granddad often took me there, a man of considerable local repute with his own fishing charter and holder of an MBE for services to Customs and Excise (or Revenue and Customs in its current incarnation). Ostensibly, the area was an ugly collection of rotting wood and unkempt sea vessels; to me it was a childhood utopia, a snapshot of a world that one only read about in escapist juvenile literature. I have always been drawn to the seemingly moribund, the weeping beauty in a fractured landscape or the visceral emotion of industrial monochrome. And for me, Felixstowe ferry represented an esotericism I have never found elsewhere. My only regret is I have not been back in so long.

The FA Vase is the showpiece event for clubs playing at Steps 5-7 in the National League System. The tournament developed out of the FA's abolition of the old Amateur Cup in 1974, when it was deemed the distinction between 'amateur' and 'professional' no longer held any specific relevance. Over 200 clubs entered in the first season, with Hoddesdon Town beating Epsom & Ewell 2-1 at Wembley in front of 9,000 spectators. The major draw of the competition is that a small town or village side can quite feasibly reach Wembley, providing a tangible opportunity for immortality every season. Although a cursory glance at previous winners shows some familiar names on the non league circuit (Halesowen Town, Forest Green Rovers, Tamworth) there are also those hallowed occasions when teams that have lived in obscurity their entire existence suddenly penetrate the national psyche, like Rainworth Miners' Welfare in 1982, Wimborne Town in 1992 or Diss Town in 1994. Needham themselves have experienced a lot of FA Vase success - or heartache depending on your perspective - in recent years and reached the semi-finals in the 2007-08 season before losing to eventual winners Kirkham & Wesham (now known as AFC Fylde).

Needham Market lies about ten miles from Ipswich and a pleasant 90 minute journey through the Suffolk countryside from London's Liverpool St. The main station is a beautiful piece of Victorian architectural heritage, opened in 1846, closed down in 1967, and then reopened in 1971. The main Grade 2 listed building, which is no longer in commercial railway use, was described by Gordon Biddle, the famous railway historian, as "one of the best in East Anglia".[1] The whole station forecourt looked extremely idyllic, like you had stepped on to the set of *Oh Doctor Beeching*. A few Ipswich fans passed the other way to make the short journey to Portman Road for their home match against Bristol City. Other than that, the place was deserted. I am a hopeless football romantic at the best of times so I am not sure entirely what I was expecting on arriving at this tiny provincial backwater. Needham Market barely has 4,500 residents but for some reason I had images of bunting and brass bands, streets lined with garrulous ruddy-cheeked supporters and face painted children running amok in a celebration of unrestrained communal excitement.

The only people I found were standing under a bus shelter on an otherwise deserted road. Nailed to the side of the shelter was a community notice

---

[1] *Britain's Historic Railway Buildings*

board advertising a few local plays and a Metallica tribute act, 'Mentallica'. At the very bottom an A4 poster flapped in the wind giving details of today's game. "Support the boys by making some noise" it enthused. The Neighbourhood Watch flyer next to it tempered the furore with its stern committee glances.

I took a shortcut up a lane by the side of The Swan public house and after five minutes' brisk walk found myself at Bloomfields, the home ground of Needham Market FC. The site is named after club stalwart Derrick Bloomfield who has given more than 60 years' service to the club, culminating in a testimonial match against Ipswich Town in 2004 and a long service award from the FA for his unswerving commitments. NMFC originally played at Young's Meadow but moved to Bloomfields in 1996 after former player Arthur Rodwell made the club a beneficiary of his will. The move also brought with it acceptance into the Jewson (now Ridgeons) League Division One and kick started the club's plans to grow. With the combination of a successful lottery grant bid and a dedicated volunteer work force, the club have built up a stadium that is now fully owned and a centre point for the community.

The match had only passed a pitch inspection at 9am and with the rain still coming down the stewards hovering around outside expressed concern that the game would still go ahead. I prayed it would. Aside from the lengthy journey and moral sapping prospect of a cancellation, I really couldn't afford the time or the money to come back again so soon. I tried to put on my most earnest face as I passed through the turnstile, as if to subliminally tell the referee and anyone with a degree of officialdom to make the game go ahead. The other option was to stand there like a cross between Brian Blessed and a town crier and let it be known I had travelled all the way from the city of London for this game and come hell or high-water it would be played today, lest blood be spilt.

I took advantage of arriving early to take a wander round the ground. The new clubhouse was a grand modern structure which housed a large bar and function room, as well as upstairs boardroom and disabled facilities. The rest of the ground was a little more down to earth. The main stand which straddled the halfway line housed around 200 seats and a small covered area - the Fred Nunn Memorial stand - stood opposite. The area behind the far goal was just fenced off grass but the section behind the clubhouse end of the pitch was a wonder to behold. Technically it was a 'covered standing area' insofar as it had a roof and you could stand under it but more noteworthy was the ladder, two tables, and a patio chair which were stored underneath it. It may seem an insignificant observation but it perfectly summarised the peculiarities that go to make up the fabric of the non league game.

Before the game kicked off I grabbed a few minutes with Needham Market's Club Secretary Mark Easlea in the upstairs of the new clubhouse. Mark used to play for the club but had to retire from the game at an early age following a bad injury. In an effort to maintain his association with the game and the club, he offered his services to them in an official capacity. "Needham is largely run by a volunteer workforce and for me this is what football is all about; a club at the heart of the community, for the community, run by people for the love of the game. We are lucky that we have so many fans that are prepared to give up their time and lucky that we have financial backers who are prepared to invest in the club without being unrealistic. We are only a small side. We lose a lot of fans to Ipswich Town but it's important to offer an alternative to those fans when Ipswich are playing away or, in their worst case scenario, if Ipswich become too expensive to watch. We won't and can't compete with a side that big but we do have our place, which is reflected by in the way we are run. As a Step 5 side we have applied for promotion and should have the necessary facilities to get the grading (which is capricious by nature and constantly under review) for Step 4 football. Beyond that only time will tell if the fan base is enough to sustain anything higher. We certainly aren't going to overspend if the interest just isn't there. Needham is a small town. We have to be realistic."

Although such realistic talk is assuring in these boom or bust times, Needham Market need only look a few miles up the road for one of the most astonishing non league ascendancies in recent years. In 1995 Histon were playing in the Eastern Counties League Division 1, a level below where the Marketers are now. By 2007 they had reached the Conference National and had knocked Leeds out of the FA Cup. Although much of the responsibility for this rise was down to club Chairman Gareth Baldwin, Histon were always keen to point out that they were not simply a one man band. The experience of managerial team Steve Fallon and John Beck - the same John Beck who took local rivals Cambridge United from the 4th division of the Football League to the 2th division play offs in the early 1990s - has undoubtedly played a big part, as has staying part time; even with their acceleration through the pyramid, Histon have a budget that represents a fraction of their peers at Conference level. There are of course sceptics who refuse to believe that no club could do what Histon did without a serious cash injection. There is an acceptable compromise of romance and reality that points to a sustainable business model, the much touted but invariably abused phrase that seems to underpin the ideals of all football clubs. In this case, it actually seems to be working. However, this paradigm will soon be put to the test. Baldwin has now left Histon and consensus seems to be that the Stutes (a name which harks back to their original Histon Institute name) will freefall through the league unless his replacement is prepared to take on a benevolent position in proceedings. Only time will tell if Histon really are the prototype model for hard work and ambition or just another single benefactor story glossed over by hard sell.

Back in the clubhouse - where I was surreptitiously helping myself to fistfuls of homemade food - I asked Mark about the game today and what the Vase meant to his club.

"Obviously it would be incredible to reach Wembley, both for the occasion and the financial injection and of course to promote the name of the club but, in truth, and I can only speak for myself, I would prefer that we got promotion to Step 4. That is our long term goal."

It probably wasn't the answer I was expecting to hear. I had assumed that for Step 5 sides the FA Vase would be their showpiece event but Needham Market represent a small cross-section of teams actively seeking promotion to the next level and, like their larger counterparts who need to prioritise their season, cup competitions appear to play second fiddle. No doubt for those not seeking promotion the Vase may take on more precedence, but this is a speculative guess. The truth is every team is different and every team has its own views on what does and does not constitute a successful season.

Going into today's game, Needham Market lay second in the league behind Cambridge Regional College (CRC). There has been a degree of controversy over CRC's application for Step 4 promotion, not least because they are viewed as a Cambridge United 'reserve team' even though in reality they are the youth team arm of the club. CUFC's argument is that boys aged 16 to 18 will gain far better experience of senior football by playing in the non league setup, though whether this should extend to allowing promotion for such a youth outfit through the leagues is a moot point. Mark, as well as other fans I canvassed opinion of, argued that such a notion is rather unfair, given the pulling power and finances a team such as Cambridge have. Personally, I tend to agree with them, although do sympathise with the wider standpoint.[1]

The ground was filling up now. I left the warmth of the clubhouse and headed out into the bright but chilly winter afternoon, which was occasionally drenched in warmth when the sun found a gap between the clouds, like a fleet footed striker finding space in the box. I stood to the left of the main stand, just in front of two men holding Anglia's loudest fan competition. The whole stand had a very geriatric feel. Wroxham fans bedecked in blue were speckled amongst the Needham faithful. Old men coughed and pointed. Old women sat with blankets over laps and thermos flasks full of soup. It looked like a studio audience from *Bullseye*. When the teams ran on to the pitch, two pensioners on the back row hammered on the corrugated wall of the stand with their gloved fists and walking sticks. There was a very British MovieTone quality about the moment; I almost expected Tom Webster to materialise with a hapless but well-meaning quip. Wroxham, lying well behind Needham in the Ridgeons Premier League, had the better of the opening ten minutes, but it was the home side's Damian Hilton who had the first real chance of the game, placing his shot wide after good build up play. Wroxham maintained their superiority throughout and belied their mid-table position with some slick passing play, with wide man Steve Spriggs looking particularly dangerous. Their superiority finally paid off when Paul Cook turned his marker in the box and stumbled over a Pip Boyland challenge to win a penalty. The decision went down badly with the home faithful, though as an objective neutral free from partisan feeling, it looked a fairly reasonable shout. But then I'm no referee. Mind you nor where the 200 people sat behind me and they all seemed to get a perfect view, which given the average age of the crowd was no mean feat.

Shaun Howes duly dispatched the spot kick to deservedly put Wroxham 1-0 up. The fifty or so Wroxham fans went wild. Observing the hugs and fist

---

[1] There is a very eloquent piece about CRC's ambitions at the following URL
www.cambridge-united.co.uk/page/NewsDetail/0,,10423~1894709.html

pumping juxtaposed to the looks of despair on the home fans sat next to them, it occurred to me just how rare a scene like this must be to the lay football fan. Local derby quarter final cup games usually smack of segregation, policing, and pre-empted talks of violent clashes, so this was a snapshot of a more tranquil side to our national game.

Needham rallied after the goal and the veteran Scott Howie (he of Norwich City and Coventry City fame) pulled off a fine save from Danny Phillips' long range effort. According to various internet sources, Howie is now a running his own tax consultancy for footballers and was a former Economics student, words that don't always sit comfortably in the monosyllabic world of the professional footballer. Mind you, as Brian Glanville's famous book advised, *Goalkeepers are different*. England stopper David James loves art and writes for *The Observer,* for example.

The halftime whistle signalled a rush for the refreshment kiosk which had formed two queues: one for drinks, one for food. Despite being clearly labelled, I remained blissfully unaware until getting to the front and finding I couldn't be served a coffee. Part of the reason for my *faux pas* was down to the large number of visiting neutrals who had made the trip down to Suffolk. Once I see an unusual football shirt I am transfixed, like a form of human trainspotting. There were Kings Lynn fans, a Norwich shirt and other tops whose badges I was unable to make out. I have always found non league attire, particularly scarves, akin to some kind of magic amulet. On my return from Colwyn Bay, a group of lads approached me on the tube in less than friendly overtones and asked if I was a West Ham fan. It was a reasonable assumption, giving the claret and blue scarf wrapped round my neck. When I showed them it was actually a team from the Unibond League their demeanour changed. One even shook my hand and said well done, as if I were in some way living with a critical affliction. Given its pacifying qualities, perhaps the police should consider such clothing the next time an inner city riot takes place. It's a lot harder to throw a Molotov cocktail at a copper if he's wearing a Fisher Athletic bobble hat.

For the second half I took up a position behind the goal Needham were attacking, in the hope of getting some goal mouth action. Wroxham probably felt they should have had a second penalty only five minutes into the second half when Rhys Barber looked to have caught Spriggs in the box, but the referee atoned himself with the home crowd by waving play on.

Spriggs, who was looking the best player on the park, was now causing Needham some serious problems, with a series of quick, skilful and penetrative runs. Needham thought they had levelled midway through the half when Danny Philips put the ball in the net but was ruled offside. The breakthrough finally came on 67 minutes when Wroxham's Gareth Simpson tripped Damien Hilton and the striker put away the resulting penalty. For the home fans one sensed this was more relief than elation. Indeed one might even say that expectations were such that the equaliser was almost expected. Needham Market's home record this season had been almost unrivalled and, with no home defeats, the concept of losing today, especially to rivals from Norfolk, was not so much unpalatable but incomprehensible. The goal clearly spurred the home side who kept the pressure on the away goal in what was turning into a proper pulsating blood and guts encounter. I stop short of writing "high octane" as it only seems to be deployed by tabloid papers describing any Hollywood film with lots of explosions. At this point, it seemed for all the world Needham would get a result but Wroxham went back in front five minutes later when Paul Cook broke away and played it square for danger man Spriggs to side foot home into an empty net. "Come on Yachtsmen!" went up an elated cry from the main stand. Given Wroxham is fifteen miles from the Norfolk coast, I was a little puzzled at first where the relevance of this nickname came from until I read up on the Wroxham Broads, which forms part of the wider Norfolk Broads networks. Unfortunately, I couldn't disassociate this from "Watership Alan", possibly my favourite Alan Partridge episode in which he does a promotional barge holiday video for Hamilton's Water Breaks. My apologies if this reference means absolutely nothing to you. That's what I get for wasting three years of university watching videos instead of going to lectures.

After Wroxham went ahead they seemed content to soak up the pressure and the final ten minutes was a tale of Needham pressure punctuated by a series of unnecessary free kicks. In the subsequent website match report on the Needham Market website[1] (which is an excellent standard for Step 5 football) there were subtle suggestions of gamesmanship and dubious injuries but, speaking as someone who saw one of the Wroxham backline have his head split open by a stray elbow, I am not sure if this was wholly justified. The truth is Wroxham were the better team on the day and Needham, by their own admissions, were well below par. At full time, the

---

[1] www.needhammarketfc.co.uk

majority of the 601 crowd no doubt went home unhappy but, unlike Wroxham, they still have a promotion push to play for, which may have meant both sides approached the game with a different mentality. I wish both sides all the best in their respective campaigns and hope Needham Market can finally achieve their Step 4 dream. They are a well-run, likeable club with a fantastic volunteer support group and a professional outlook that is clearly geared to a higher level of football. As for Wroxham, they will do well to beat Whitley Bay, who are the undoubted favourites for this season's competition.

The trains back to Ipswich only ran every hour, which meant a considerable wait in the inviting looking Swan pub opposite the station. It was a clear sign of how cold it was outside as I chose to stay in the warm and watch the Six Nations rugby match between England and Ireland. I still don't understand the sport. I don't see any skill or fluidity. I just see thirty massive skinheads in tight clothing rolling around on the floor kicking each other, like a homoerotic Sex Pistols gig. Of course, one can't apply such literal observations to football. Oh no. As J.B Priestley notes in his book *The Good Companions*, to talk of football in such a meaningless way "is merely to say that a violin is wood and catgut, that Hamlet is so much ink and paper."

The train back from Ipswich to London was freezing. A group of drunken Bristol City fans sat in our carriage and were talking excitedly about an Ipswich supporter who had just been bottled. They looked hard. I felt like Richard returning to the mainland after a spell in utopia, in Alex Garland's The Beach.

I pulled my cap down and feigned sleep.

Rainworth Miners' Welfare v Arnold Town

Northern Counties East League Premier Division – Step 5
Saturday 13th March 2010

Final Score: 1-1
Attendance: 102

Football and social history are inextricably linked. Our football stadiums past and present provide a reminder of an architectural *zeitgeist*, generations of dedicated support show the importance of a club's place in the community, and programme notes and memorabilia document a game that influenced, and was influenced by, changing socio-economic variables. Amongst the wide variety of football institutions still running in this country few are imbued with the same historical legacy as the Miners' Welfare Club, which serves to remind of a past that is all but eroded away.

Miners' Welfare schemes had their origins in the 1920s and 1930s and were funded by weekly contributions, deducted from the miners' wages. The initial monies were used to build and run the schemes of which some ran as 'institutes', implying they also had an educational and recreational purpose. But essentially they all had one thing in common; to represent and look after the wellbeing of the miners and their families. Almost inevitably, various sporting clubs - football, cricket, and bowls - grew out of these organisations and began to flourish.

Whilst researching the history of the Miners' Welfare organisations, I stumbled across an article on the BBC Website about the demise of Denaby & Cadeby Miners' Welfare near Conisbrough, in South Yorkshire.[1] The piece focused on the 'Pin the Pits' campaign, started by local artist Rachel Horne, who was born in Conisbrough during the Miners' Strike of 1984. The campaign aims to get Ordnance Survey to mark regenerated pit sites with a half pit wheel symbol on their reference maps, thus giving recognition to former coal mining sites and their historical interest and importance. Further down the article was a note about Denaby United FC, who folded in 2002 following eviction from their ground by the Denaby & Cadeby Miners'

---

[1]

www.bbc.co.uk/southyorkshire/content/articles/2009/07/08/rachel_horne_miners_welfare
_feature.shtml

Welfare. It seemed like an interesting story so I contacted Rachel and arranged to meet her for a coffee one evening on one of her trips back to London. As we talked over herbal tea and cappuccino with more froth than a *Daily Mail* reader, it became clear she was a passionate and skilled orator. "The miners and mining communities always had a great sense of camaraderie and knew how to create a voice for themselves. An expression of this was through the sports teams and every pit village or town would have its own sports clubs and teams. Of course, not everyone who played for the clubs had to be a miner, but they invariably were, and these organisations were a central part of the working community. I remember going to see Denaby United when I was about ten years old. There must have been 1,500 people there, even though the ground was run down and dilapidated. In its heyday, people would travel from longer distances to watch them play as they were a good side. Now the team, and almost all trace of it, has gone. The welfare club made a big mistake evicting them from the ground and I, along with many others, still don't know fully why they did it. There is a movement to get the club reformed and hopefully it can be woven into a wider campaign to raise awareness and money for the Miners' Welfare movement and the preservation of our heritage. The social club is still going but it's increasingly on its last legs; it is important all aspects of village life are preserved as there is a culture here we need to embrace and remember."

I asked just how important the Miners' Welfare movement was to the area, given the pits had now closed.
"They are still tremendously important but the problem now is also one of image. I can't help thinking that in the eighties it was cool to be working class but in the nineties and noughties it was almost looked down upon to be from this social group. Denaby is a poor area blighted by high unemployment, drugs and all the other social problems that go with the loss of so many jobs. It is almost laughable to be from Denaby, as everyone sees you as rough and part of a benefit culture. The problem is people rarely look beyond this. Recently the village held a football match to raise money for a local lad who lost his life and it really galvanised the community. It also showed what a powerful cohesive tool sport can be if handled in the right way."

For an outsider such as myself, armed only with social theory and a few radical journals, it is impossible to imagine what this kind of lifestyle must be like and how deeply the closures must have affected everyone there. By Rachel's own admission, it took her over five years of study to fully appreciate it and that's from someone who was born and raised in the area. "There is a big call for people in the community to move away or work elsewhere, but generations of people have been born in the area so the preference is to stay close to their roots and look out for one another. I think this notion of togetherness is completely undervalued. Part of the problem is giving people an identity back and giving them something to focus on, such as the upcoming annual Gala with brass band, which was always a very traditional part of mining life. This, along with perhaps a sports or football team that keeps the area on the national or global map, is hugely important. We want to celebrate our past but also look to the future and that's a lot easier if people are proud of their community and outsiders know we are still here and still going strong."

Quite how important Denaby United were or are to this small community in South Yorkshire is still undecided. On the last ever game played at their Tickhill Square ground, there were reports of just as many people in the social club watching a match on SKY as there were in the ground, which would have been no mean feat given the 300 plus attendance at the match. One thing does appear to be certain though. There are those who believe teams of this nature still play a pivotal role in providing a foci for the community, as well as elevating otherwise obsolete or forgotten areas into the national consciousness. If ever proof were needed of that, we can look no further than Rainworth Miners' Welfare FC, in nearby Nottinghamshire. Rainworth (pronounced Ren-nuth in the local phonetic and giving the club it's 'Wrens' nickname) is a village of around 8,000 people, lying four miles south east of Mansfield. The area grew when the Rufford Colliery was sunk, although, like many others in the area, it closed in 1993. Rainworth is famous for two reasons. Firstly, notorious murderer 'The Black Panther' was captured and arrested there in 1975 and, secondly, their football team reached the FA Vase Final at Wembley in 1982.

On arriving in Rainworth it makes the first story plausible and the second completely incredulous; the ground is a three hour journey from London but a million metaphorical miles away in every other respect. After chugging into Mansfield on a regional train which was one day away from a firm handshake and a gold carriage clock, I decided to catch a taxi from The Swan, one of those chain pubs synonymous with cheap food, cheap beer and middle aged grandmothers wearing white Hi-Tec trainers. I had arranged to meet my mate Danny there but he had inexplicably missed his stop at Worksop and ended up in Lincoln, much to the merriment of the train crew, who were no doubt starved of entertainment on what is surely the dullest passenger route in the UK.

The taxi dropped me at the ground at around 1.30pm. First impressions were of how smart and well maintained it was, in fact it almost had the air of a Crown Green Bowls club. The clubhouse looked new and fresh and the main stand pristine and proud like shining brass on a regimental blazer. The ground has come a long way in a short time, even though the club were first formed in 1922, underlying intentions to progress beyond a long history of country level football. Floodlights were not put in until 1991, though Rainworth were still the first club in the Notts Alliance, of which they were then members, to boast this facility. To comply with stricter FA Vase requirements covered accommodation was erected on the allotment side of the ground, with seating added later. By the early years of the new millennium many Notts Alliance clubs - including several Miners' Welfare clubs - had seen greener grass in the Central Midlands League, which formed the base of the non league pyramid locally. Rainworth, though, did not follow suit until 2003 and soon had their eyes on a place in the Northern Counties East League (NCEL). To reflect the ambition of the club, and comply with NCEL requirements, new dressing rooms, clubhouse and an all seater stand were installed shortly after, giving the site a very professional feel and a 2,000 capacity of which 221 is seated.

My tour guide for the day was Media Manager Gordon Foster who is very hands on with the club, writing the award winning programme, handling the team sheets and operating the PA system. Not much goes on at Rainworth that Gordon doesn't know about. His association with the Wrens was born from his previous job as church organist across the road.

"Historically I supported Mansfield but, of course, being a church organist sometimes meant Saturday afternoon weddings - the then vicar used to joke that if there was a 2pm wedding and Mansfield were at home the wedding march at the end was played at double speed. But a lot of our Saturday services didn't finish until just before kick-off so it was always chance whether I could attend or not. One day, I think it was around 1981 or so, I decided there was no way I would get into town before 3pm, so I came over to watch Rainworth play. They were playing Frecheville in round four of the FA Vase, during what became our well documented run to the Wembley Final. I liked what I saw, jumped on the bandwagon I suppose, and Rainworth has been 'my' club ever since, although subsequently I landed a job on the sports desk of the local paper which meant that, while I was still involved behind the scenes, on match days I was covering higher grade clubs like Sutton Town and Alfreton Town. Now that I have retired I'm back with my own village club full time. I've been coming ever since."

As we walked round the ground, which is being groomed for Step 4 football, Gordon pointed to a grass bank behind the small stand on the far side of the pitch.

"During the Vase semi-final that whole bank was full of people. In those days there were also huge open grass banked areas behind the Kirklington Road goal where the pavilion now stands. I sometimes wonder how we fitted that many people in here, but we did. They were really wonderful times. It so happened that Mansfield were having a bad time, so a lot of their supporters borrowed Rainworth's colours to share in the Vase glory."

Ask most people in the area about the club and they will invariably mention that FA Vase run of 1981-82 to the Final, where sadly they lost 3-0 to a strong Forest Green Rovers side. The crowd of 12,500 is believed to be woefully underestimated, with Rainworth bringing 10,000 fans of their own. Irrespective of the score line, the game marked many milestones; they were only the second true amateur side and the only Miners' Welfare team to ever make it to the Final.

The semi-final home leg, a 2-1 win against Barton Rovers, was played in front of a crowd of 5,071 - a record to this day for a match outside of the Final itself. At the time, there was no covered accommodation and the main pitch was simply roped off. The ground was three sided, with a cricket square and second pitch opposite. What makes the feat even more remarkable was the lowly level that Rainworth were playing at the time (namely the old Notts Alliance League) and the fact many of the players were either miners or worked in the mining industry. Although the traditional pyramid system was in its infancy back then and bore no resemblance to the feeder structure in place today, this would have been the equivalent of a Step 7 side reaching this stage of the competition, a feat unlikely to be repeated again. The occasion is gloriously and euphorically captured in the newspapers of the day mounted in the clubhouse and on the official website. There is a tremendous sense of pride and occasion that such a small club could make such a mark on the national game.

It was certainly a stark contrast to today. Rainworth have been averaging around the 100 mark for crowds this season and lose a section of their support when Mansfield Town play at home. If there was any legacy of that magical cup run it was in print and pride rather than punters; a few of the locals in the social club over the road didn't know who today's opposition were. It's a safe bet some in the village didn't even know a game was on at all.

I asked how Rainworth survived on relatively modest resources, particularly given their recent upward momentum. "We do have a chairman who backs the club and has money to put in, although he would not like to be seen as a 'sugar daddy' and club officials work hard to raise money from a variety of sources including having every home match sponsored," advised Gordon. "But like many clubs at this level money is always an issue. Even things like the printer for the programmes were a major outlay and needed careful consideration."

I approached this chapter on Rainworth with a particular interest in the club's experiences during the miners' strike of 1984. One of the lingering controversies of this period was that Nottinghamshire miners continued to work while others around them downed tools, citing the fact they would not enter a strike without the approval of a national strike ballot. From that moment, the working miners of Notts were targeted, giving rise to the flying pickets - organised squads of strikers, mostly from Yorkshire, who converged on Notts and dared men to cross the picket line. Inevitably, scenes turned ugly, with verbal abuse turning to physical threats and even attempts on lives.

Those who supported the strike argued the Nottinghamshire workers enjoyed favourable mining conditions and better wages. However, the Nottinghamshire miners argued that they did not participate because the law required a ballot for a national strike and their area vote had seen around 75% vote against such a strike. The conflict led to Notts miners being called 'scabs', although locals would argue that a scab is someone who crosses a picket line and there was nothing official about the picket lines set up in Nottinghamshire.

The division still runs deep today, long after the strike finished and long after the last pits closed. Matches between Yorkshire and Nottinghamshire teams at every level can sometimes still incubate a deep seated vitriol, even though some of the modern protagonists participating in the name-calling were too young to truly understand the complexity of the situation.

"I recall one occasion when our neighbouring club Blidworth Welfare played away to Grimesthorpe FC a while back. The fans and the officials were calling the Blidworth folk scabs and it was a truly evil and hostile atmosphere. They vowed never to play in Yorkshire again. For some people it's just an excuse to cause trouble but others seem to have very long memories and will never change their stance. It's a real shame. It shouldn't affect the football, especially as most of our players at the time had nothing to do with the strike. They are victims of a legacy of hate."

The tour continued with a look at the changing rooms and their immaculately laid out kit before ending with a glimpse behind the scenes at the press office and officials lounge, which looked like the kind of static homes you get in windswept holiday parks on the Welsh coast. I half expected to see frilly curtains in the window and flying ducks on the wall. It was all very well drilled and homely.

At this point Danny and his Danish friend Eskil arrived with rucksacks, looking like extras from a rambler's edition of *Countryfile*. Danny, a mix of occasionally incomprehensible Mancunian and unchecked facial hair, started to regale us with stories of missed train connections, inefficient taxi services and the general perils of provincial travel. As a disclaimer, it does tend to help if you pay attention to where you are bloody going. Eskil was visiting for the weekend and had wanted to go to a "real" English non league match. His last football experience on these shores had been Old Trafford. I glanced at the admission hut where a man was stood rolling a fag. Next to it a sign read "Do not let your dogs foul the grass - canine faeces can cause blindness and death"; this was about as real as it got.

Shortly before kick-off, we were joined by our mutual friend Ben, who lived in the area. His demeanour indicated a man grappling with an equation more complex than anything John Nash ever tried to prove.
"When Danny said you and he were coming here to watch a match in Rainworth I thought he must have been joking," came the bemused announcement. "Even I don't come to Rainworth, and I live here."

The ground was sparsely populated but there was a good atmosphere for one of the more local derbies in the league. A handful of Arnold Town fans in their amber and gold were making themselves known away to our left and a rotund Rainworth fan to our right was rattling the windows of the director's portakabins with his vociferous shouts of encouragement. Eskil, no doubt hungry from his impromptu tour of Lincolnshire, emerged from the clubhouse with a plate of pie, peas and mint sauce, expressing surprise that it was vaguely palatable. I wasn't sure how to take this; Denmark is hardly the epicentre of world cuisine and its national dishes sound like types of IKEA wardrobe. Stood in the ground of an old mining village with a can of Mansfield Bitter and a 20p raffle ticket I suddenly felt very proud to be English.

Rainworth went in at half time 1-0 up, courtesy of an Ant Lynam penalty. Prior to today's game they had lost five matches in a row which had seriously dented their promotion chances to the Unibond League. That the club finds itself in a position to challenge for such honours is a truly remarkable story; fifteen years ago they were playing at level 13 of the English pyramid system (or Step 9, if indeed such a thing existed). Under the stewardship of the marvellously name Rudy Funk, the club have gained two promotions and now sit at their highest ever level of the national pyramid. Romanian Rudy and his assistant Billy Millar arrived at the club during the 2005 close season, with the promise of delivering Unibond football and, given the commercial enterprises in place, this target is looking increasingly likely. Their attendance statistics would blend in fairly innocuously if they were promoted, particularly with any rise in crowds that tends to accompany promoted teams. Whether the club has the necessary fan base, infrastructure and funding to push on from there is another matter; when you compare nearby Mansfield's excellent Field Mill Stadium which dominates the town's skyline and their regular 3,500 fan base in the Conference National, the two sides are worlds apart.

We crossed the road at half time to the Miners' Welfare social club, a place where my blonde highlights and laptop had never felt more conspicuous. Old men sat in fours playing cards, discussing the heads on their pints, while others watched the TV in motionless silence. The notice board advised people to get their meat orders in by the following Friday. Bobby George, looking like he had just done an armed raid on a Cash Converters jewellery department, was advertising a garish promotional evening. The light from the patio windows cut through an air thick with dust. I have a feeling if Marty McFly went forward 25 years from 1985 to where we were sat now he wouldn't see a huge amount of difference.

For the second half, I took my seat next to Robbie Blamford and Eileen Wright who was the wife of the late Alan Wright. Alan is considered a Rainworth legend, having served as goalkeeper, committee member, groundsman and secretary, as well as being chairman of the old Notts Alliance and the driving force behind its successor, the Notts Senior League, which Rainworth were destined never to join, until his death in 2002. His endeavours are forever remembered in the wrought iron gates at the ground entrance, where his name is proudly displayed.

Being sat between two Rainworth stalwarts certainly gave me a different perspective on proceedings and the main stand generated some superb passion and atmosphere, particularly after Arnold capitalised on some poor defensive play by slotting in the equaliser. Even after several games at a variety of non league venues this season, the small details still touch me. With the Rainworth players trudging back to the centre circle, Robbie shouted to one of the muddied players if he wanted a lift home after the match, to which he got a slightly weary thumbs up. Unfortunately I had spent too much time talking to various people around the ground to include any kind of detailed match report but the lad in front of me, who was covering his first ever match for Radio Mansfield, was doing a splendid job. The game ended with a flurry of tackles and a couple of cracked heads courtesy of wandering elbows, though the draw was met with a degree of disapproval in what must be demanding times for this small but upwardly mobile club.

So, as I headed back to London, what had I gleaned from my day out in Rainworth? Well, not a lot really, or at least not what I was hoping to. The problem with an issue as emotive as the mining industry is a danger to over romanticise and overplay the relevance of certain agencies. From a writer's perspective, I would love to say that the Miners' Welfare team was a central hub of the community but I really don't have a foundation on which to base this. Based on my observations they are a modestly supported club with big ambitions and a Cup Final past which has possibly cast a spectre of under-achievement over them ever since. Many of the local population invariably follow Mansfield or other larger sides and if the club were simply called 'Rainworth United' there would be little to distinguish them from any other satellite team in the perpetual shadow of a more established urban behemoth.

But perhaps in this minor detail lies the most crucial point of all. Lexically, the club's prominence as a Miners' Welfare team is critically important, even if its *de facto* role in the community is largely debatable. The headstocks and winding gear are gone from this area now and the only constant or tangible reminder to the outside world of this once proud and important heritage are the people themselves and their football team. If, as Rachel Horne has suggested, the legacy of our pit towns and villages should be celebrated and remembered then there are few better ways to keep these places in the public eye than through the median of sport. Granted, it would still take a fan with a particular devotion to non league football to be aware of Rainworth, or any other Miners' Welfare side, but we live in a day of unrivalled sports coverage where provincial sides can become national heroes, if only for a day. We live in disposable, ephemeral times but the impact of a Miners' Welfare team reaching Wembley or making a televised FA Cup appearance could do wonders for the public profile of so many areas where the vagaries of economic policy have caused so many problems. For this reason, and for the preservation of our socio-industrial past, I hope Rainworth continue to march forward.

AFC Liverpool v Eccleshall

North West Counties League Division 1 – Step 6
Saturday 27th March 2010

Final Score: 0-2
Attendance: 135

It is probably worth noting in these days of saturated TV coverage that televised football used to offer a magical insight into a world that was far more mysterious than the omnipresent beast we have now. Now, match coverage is instantly available through a variety of 24/7 media; then - and by 'then' I mean the mid-1980s - football coverage was limited to the odd game or regional highlights package on terrestrial TV. This made the prospect of live football all the more salivating and gave adults leverage over star struck children desperate for a piece of match action. Before my obsession with football developed, my parents used to employ the same tactic with *The Dukes of Hazard*, turning a boisterous rebellious five year old into a William Brown on lithium; rooms were tidied, greens eaten, commands obeyed in the hope of watching two rednecks with mullets drive irresponsibly around the Southern States. Such was life back 'then'. Of course, my parents - my mother in particular - knew full well the stranglehold football had over me and could use it to devastating effect. Table not laid for dinner? You're not watching *Central Sports Special* later. Garden not mown? That's the trip to Gay Meadow cancelled. And so it went on. The nefarious regimes of Dickens' times had nothing on the manipulative coercion of Stanton Road, Ludlow.

And so, televised matches took on an almost ethereal quality. This was a more innocent era of fan interaction, where Ceefax and Teletext were a (neigh, *the*) vogue form of keeping up to date with latest match developments. I 'watched' the legendary 4-4 FA Cup draw between Everton and Liverpool in 1991 via such technology, taking notes and focusing on the flicker of a screen like an idiot savant. In later life, I would spend many a happy Saturday afternoon in Dixons watching Ceefax Page 302 - a biblical number for football aficionados - in the hope of seeing the latest scores and scorers, whilst my then girlfriend would engage in her own passions across the road in Top Shop.

The standout televised game of this era, perhaps for anyone of my generation, was the Liverpool v Arsenal Division 1 game on Friday 26th May 1989. The match had originally been scheduled to take place some weeks earlier but after the Hillsborough Tragedy of 15th April, which claimed the lives of 96 Liverpool supporters, many matches were postponed as a mark of respect. The match was rescheduled for 26th May and would be the last game of the season. Going into the game Arsenal needed to win by at least two goals to take the title. It was an improbable task.

I had a vested interest in Arsenal winning; not because I was an Arsenal fan but because I didn't like Liverpool, or at least I didn't like the fact that all the Liverpool fans in my class - and there were plenty of them - saw fit to continually deride the fact I supported Kidderminster. To me this was about revenge, catharsis, and every fibre, every sinew, prayed for an Arsenal win. When Alan Smith controversially put the Gunners 1-0 up I thought years of attending church as a choirboy may finally be paying off. But the clock ticked. And ticked. And ticked. Ninety minutes passed. The scored stayed 1-0. I had used up all my divine intervention and, besides which, had misplaced faith after praying Kidderminster would beat Maidstone in an earlier FA Cup replay which never transpired. And then, Brian Moore uttered the most seminal, most beautiful piece of commentary that has even been committed to tape:
"Arsenal come streaming forward now in surely what will be their last attack. A good ball by Dixon, finding Smith, for Thomas, charging through the midfield. Thomas, it's up for grabs now!"

People say they remember where they were or what they were doing when JFK was shot or when they found out Princess Diana had died. Most football fans can tell you every nuance of emotion, every minutiae of action when Michael Thomas scored to make it 2-0 and hand Arsenal the title. I was sat there in disbelief, as if in some out of body experience, dragged from the maelstrom of football hell and gently bathed in the tingling warmth of karma, its fingers caressing my skin and whispering unfathomable sweetness in my ear.

Beyond my own egocentric pleasures, the game had a far greater and long lasting impact on the British game. Many consider the match a turning point for an ailing game. Writing at the time, Jason Cowley of *The Guardian* noted how the Liverpool fans stayed and applauded the Arsenal team, which lay in stark contrast to the violence and negativity that had enshrouded the game throughout a turbulent decade. He later described the match as "the night football was reborn" and, in a wider context, could be seen as the moment at which people started to see the commercial possibilities of televised football. A new era was about to unfold which could only be good for the national game...

Twenty one years later and I am standing outside Prescot Cables ground on a bright spring afternoon, nine miles to the east of Liverpool. Their Hope Street home is a fine old non league stadium, with a superb grandstand, but is starting to show signs of ageing. The wrought iron gates at the entrance hint at a proud industrial past that has long declined. It is a strange and innocuous area, an eclectic mix of period housing and Coca-Colarised shopping malls, its new designer flats standing like concrete shoots of regeneration next to windswept clearance sites.

Today I am here to see Prescot's tenants, AFC Liverpool, the supporters' owned club run by Liverpool fans, for Liverpool fans. Now, we seem to have been here before. This is just Liverpool's version of FC United right? A copycat *modus operandi* for yet more disgruntled fans? Well, yes and no. The primary difference between AFC Liverpool and FC United of Manchester are the rationales for their creation. Yes, they were started by supporters who saw problems with the current situation at their club but, unlike FC United, AFC Liverpool do not have a specific untenable grievance with the parent club or its owners. In their own words from the club website[1], "It is aimed especially at those Liverpool fans priced out of Premier League football. Same colours, same songs, same community of Reds. It draws its support base from Liverpool fans. AFC Liverpool fans still support Liverpool and those who can afford to will still go to Anfield to support the Reds. The club is meant as a grassroots addition to Liverpool FC, not to be a replacement for it. We see ourselves very much as part of the LFC family - LFC's little brother."

There is a rather subtle irony here. The commercial mechanisms that served to drag football away from an era associated with malaise is now the very thing causing people to turn to the same bygone age when football was accessible to all. It was something I wanted to explore further with my hosts

---

[1] www.afcliverpool.org.uk/go/

for the day, Chairman Chris Stirrup and Finance Officer Darren Pilling. The formation of the club, its rationale and objectives have already been well documented by the wider press but I was interested to know more about the personal stories and how the club was faring now the fanfare had died down. During the drive up from Lime St Station to Prescot's ground, Darren told me the background that led to his involvement with the club.

"I had been attending every home game at Anfield since the 1970s. By the mid '80s, the national game was really on its arse and had nowhere near the interest it does today. Often, certainly for mid-week games, you could buy tickets cheaply and on the day, which always guaranteed a good local support. As the game moved into the 1990s, and the popularity of the sport increased as a whole, ticket sales, or more importantly, season ticket sales, started to increase dramatically. Getting a ticket for non season ticket holders became a military operation. My brother and I had a system we used on the ticket line which pretty much guaranteed we always got one, but it still took a lot of patience. What was becoming increasingly obvious was that the number of tickets available for general purchase was becoming less and less. This seemed to coincide with a change in the supporters attending Anfield. As season tickets became more popular, so the price went up. Anfield was still selling out but it was selling out to those who could afford it most. For a lot of people, buying a season ticket isn't really an option, certainly not at the prices being advertised. The choice was becoming painfully obvious: buy a season ticket or stop watching the club play."

Speaking to *The Telegraph* in 2008, AFC Liverpool founder Alun Parry put these concerns into perspective:
"I've been going to Anfield since the late Seventies when I was six years old. A season ticket in the Kop cost £45 in 1985, today it's £650, which I know is a lot cheaper than some other Premier League clubs, but in inflation terms Eighties prices should equate to £98 today. We aren't blaming the club, we realise they have no choice, but the sad fact is that a whole community is being denied the opportunity to grow up in the 'match-going' culture."
Darren was quick to point out that his own experiences also carried other concerns about the changing football environment, notably the way in which the erosion of terrace culture was killing the match day atmosphere.

"I was at a game one day and decided to stand up and make up some noise, in an effort to get behind the team. It was no different to what we had been doing for generations. Suddenly this fella behind me tells me to sit down as he can't see. We got into a bit of a heated debate which resulted in me being asked to leave the ground. I can understand where he was coming from, but that isn't what football support is supposed to be about surely? Anyway, all things considered, I was getting rather tired of it all. Then the opportunity came to join AFC Liverpool and, to be honest, I have never looked back."

So maybe there was more to it than just cost and availability of tickets? Chris Stirrup, the AFC Liverpool Chairman, took me on a tour of the ground and as we walked along the terrace in the shadow of the main grandstand he gave a pragmatic take on affairs.

"I think if you ask every fan that comes to see us play, each will have their own reason for doing so. I know why we set the club up, and what the club is supposed to represent, but that doesn't mean everyone who comes here has to have exactly the same view, or even the same commitments. We set AFC Liverpool up in order to give the community a team they could share in, mutuality if you like. Fans vote at the AGM so any motions that are put forward they have the say. For example, last season there was a motion on ticket prices, it was put forward to increase them, and it was voted against. Members also voted on the club's crest design. The Ebbsfleet model of voting on players playing etc. proved unworkable and as we are all Liverpool supporters, we have all followed Bill Shankly's saying that 'Directors are only there to sign cheques' so as members, and as a board, we don't touch the footballing side of things, that is all left to the manager. However, at this year's AGM there is a motion to decide that if the manager offers their resignation to the members, should the members decide or their elected representatives. So we are always looking for workable ways in which to consult the one member one vote situation. The important thing to retain through all this is that the club belongs to the community and is an affordable option for all age groups. We need to make sure kids in the area have a chance to watch affordable local football whilst retaining their ties with Liverpool FC."

During our chat, it was possible Chris had one eye on a flag to the far side of the ground which read "Red and White, not Stars and Stripes", a direct protest to the American ownership of Liverpool FC. Although the website clearly states the club is not a protest movement against Hicks and Gillett, it was in keeping with many Liverpool fans' view on the current regime. "If fans wish to come here and use AFC Liverpool to express their dissatisfaction with Liverpool's owners that is their prerogative. I am sure many do at Anfield as well. We are not going to turn people away for having such values. As I say, everyone here has different reasons for following us but, I am sure, all have one thing in common; they want to see us do well and they want a team they can really feel part of."

Quite how well AFC Liverpool are doing is a moot point, especially given the fanfare of media and supporter interest surrounding the club when it first launched. By their own admission, the projected attendance figures from day one of around one thousand were significantly out, even though a 2008-09 average of 316, including a huge 723 away attendance at Bootle, were easily the best in the North West Counties Division 1. This season crowds seemed to have dropped markedly and, at the time of writing, the average home gate of 150 represents a disappointing second season, especially given FC United - a presumable comparable - were commanding average crowds of over 3,000 when they played in the same division.

"I'm not sure we can be compared to FC United because they were formed for very different reasons, on the back of a very specific protest, which automatically galvanised interest. It was a form of supporter defiance I guess. AFC Liverpool simply wish to offer an alternate for fans who, for whatever reason, are unable to watch Liverpool play at Anfield. The truth is many fans would still rather go to town on a Saturday and watch Liverpool in the pub and, to be honest, we can't blame them. We also have problems attracting fans because of our location. Many locals will tell you that Prescott isn't even in Liverpool, so it's a long way for some people to travel for what is and, let's be honest here, Step 6 football. It is possible that once that first season interest wore off, coupled with the fact we didn't get promotion, supporters felt it wasn't worth investing the effort. I think everyone thought things would progress a lot faster than they did. This season especially, we have been particularly poor at home and, no matter how cheap the entrance fee, people aren't going to pay to see a team that continually loses, especially if it means making a long trip from home."

Like FC United, one question aimed at these supporters' clubs is why not watch someone else in the locality play. Like FC United, the same answer can be given that you can't simply switch allegiance to a side that you have no previous history with. Liverpool is also an interesting case in that it doesn't exactly have a luxury of lower league sides at its disposal, despite being a veritable footballing hotbed. The only professional sides in the city are Liverpool and Everton and the only other recognisable non league team from the area has been South Liverpool, who were stalwarts of the Northern Premier League and now play in the Liverpool County Premier League. One could point to Bootle, Marine and indeed Prescott as examples of semi-professional football in the area, but really they fall under the wider metropolitan country of Merseyside. What this does ultimately point to is a lack of - rather than maybe a need of - alternate options for supporters in the city.

"The aim of the club," continued Chris "is to find a home in the city of Liverpool, as we believe this will encourage more fans to attend games and give us a place to truly call our own. Obviously we are indebted to Prescot for allowing us to play here, but it is still seen as a temporary home. There are areas we have identified in the city, particularly areas cited for regeneration, and anything we do will be done under the community banner, providing recreational and leisure services to local people, as well as a football team people can feel part of. I suppose you could say there is a 'niche' there for a club of our size, but that isn't what we are about. We didn't start the club to expose a gap in the market."

I took an opportunity before the game started to chat to some of the fans in the social club and, as Chris had rightly said, their reasons for being there were varied; cost, match day experience, LFC club politics, lack of standing, it was an effective amalgam of everything that appears to be blighting top flight football. There were also some fans from the Prescot area who simply fancied watching a game of local football. Perhaps the most encouraging aspect of the gathered support were the amount of youngsters in the bar, sat with their dads in AFC scarves and hats or with their friends reading team sheets, which reflected the club's mantra of getting a lost generation of young local fans back into grounds.

AFC Liverpool's opponent today were Staffordshire based Eccleshall, who sat a few places behind their hosts in mid-table. Although the sole preserve of football support is a healthy mix of blind faith and optimism, it would take a fan of unique sanguineness to see this as anything other than an end of season mid-table clash. This was the first Step 6 match I had encountered on my travels and it certainly imbued certain characteristics that marked it out as being a more leisurely level of football. For starters, the league table had some decidedly pub league sounding teams in it; Stone Dominoes,

Holker Old Boys, Daisy Hill and, judging by the shape of some of the physiques on the pitch, players who liked spending a lot of time in said pub. Clearly AFC Liverpool are pertinently aware of the level of football they are playing at. In the official club programme, under the code of conduct section, there is a reminder that "When travelling away remember that you are representing the club and also our city. Respect where you are and also don't pass judgement on clubs where facilities are far more basic than you have become accustomed to in the Premiership."

Certainly the football on display was far more basic than anything fans had become accustomed to in the Premiership. At times, it was more basic than games they had probably played in themselves. There were moments of comic genius from the Eccleshall wingers, such as back heels that skewed out for throw ins or, in one forgettable case, were missed completely. There were occasions watching the game when I thought "I could do better than this" but, of course, reality would bear this out to be a lie. I am old, I am slow and I wouldn't last five minutes in the physical battle that was ensuing. Chris had pointed out earlier that the pitch hadn't been conducive to AFC Liverpool's passing game, which is why they had been faring so poorly at home. In places, the pitch was patchy and certainly the expectations of the crowd were tempered as any move that combined more than three passes seemed to be greeted with shouts of approval and encouraging rounds of applause. In truth, it was a very poor first half, although the crowd - 135 in total - seemed to take in relatively good spirits. I had a good chance to wander round the ground at the break and take in some of the idiosyncrasies that tend to delight at this level of football. Two young mothers stood on the terraces with a pram talking about the relative merits of maternity. An old man stood behind the goal on his own, like a sheep who had wandered off from the herd, contently chewing the cud of the day. Children kicked a ball up against the side of the main stand in an impromptu game of 'Wembley'. People drank pints on the terraces. Everyone knew each other personally. Chris and Darren were Chris and Darren the supporters with pie and a cup of tea, not Chris and Darren members of the board. It suddenly occurred to me that I wasn't watching a football crowd as such but a community day out. It was really quite touching.

I spent much of the second half talking to journalist turned lecturer and writer Chris Shaw, who was writing a book on Liverpool FC fan culture. His journeys researching the book had taken him slightly further than me: China to be exact. The furthest east I had ventured was Suffolk. Certainly the match here today offered a microcosm of Liverpool FC fan culture. The main terrace behind the goal had a variety of LFC flags such as the 'Boys Pen', the legendary section of Kop terracing where young fans once gathered in what was a rite of passage initiation and central to what AFCL are trying to recreate. As one fan noted of his experiences in there

"The tradition in the Boys Pen was to get in early, try to get to the front and then, if you were hard enough, try to escape. All that effort to get in and all we wanted was to make an escape bid. The Kop was our freedom. The Boys Pen was a transit camp to heaven. It was a rite of passage for any Liverpool kid in the '60s."[1]

On a more sombre note hung the Justice 96 banners (which also appears on the AFC Liverpool kits) to mark the ongoing battle to bring those responsible for the Hillsborough tragedy to account. There were badges and scarves and memorabilia documenting all of Liverpool's glorious history. But this was a million miles from Anfield, where misplaced passes were being booted into the gardens of leaden grey council houses and entire sides of the ground lay empty of spectators, their cracked concrete steps watched over by the ghost, rather than the spirit, of Shankly.

The second half got off to a bad start for the home team. Liam Coyne earned himself a yellow card for a display of petulance and from the resulting free kick Eccleshall's Lascanna Sidibe found space at the far post to volley home Gavin Wood's cross. Minutes later the Reds were down to ten men when Coyne received his second yellow card for dissent. By now, the referee had ensured no one would be buying him a drink in the bar afterwards - though when he inexplicably gave a penalty to Eccleshall for a foul by Patrick O'Driscoll, the chances of him wearing one increased tenfold. Gavin Wood put away the resulting penalty to do his fantasy football stats no harm at all. Darren stood with a look of thin lipped bemusement. Chris shook his head as the word 'joke' became stuck in his throat. "There's two teams on the park ref," spoke a shrill voice, as a young lad with a football tucked under his arm gained a terrace scholarship for humour. It wasn't, by any stretch of the imagination, a good game. But it was a good day out. In the bar afterwards, Chris was visibly annoyed:

---

[1] www.thisisanfield.com/forums/archive/index.php/t-10352.html

"Of course you're disappointed after a defeat, and by midweek most of it's forgotten about but it just seems to hurt that little bit more because it's our club and we care so much. You also want the fans to get value for money in order for them to keep returning. I'm not sure they got that today."

Well, possibly not. But what they did get today was an alternative, about as far flung from the Premiership experience as one could endeavour to get and, by any definition, that is all AFC Liverpool can hope to offer. The question is where does the club go in the long term? The second season has been disappointing in terms of performance on the pitch and attendance off it. The management team openly admit they are very much learning on the job and have the finances to secure the running of the club. The second question is for whom? If there are disenfranchised masses in Liverpool they are either sat at home or in the pub watching SKY or simply not bothered about a live alternative, certainly not one as far down the pyramid as AFC Liverpool. An average gate of 150 tells its own story. Also, if ticket availability at Anfield is such a driver for the club you wonder what will happen when (or indeed if) Liverpool FC move to their new stadium at Stanley Park, as this will effectively address one of the issues for AFC Liverpool coming into existence. On the flip side, ticket prices are likely to increase if the new stadium comes along and for those already priced out AFC Liverpool may be an attractive alternative, especially if they can move into the city, at which point only a true marker of their popularity can really be gained. Or maybe, as I suspect is the case after spending an afternoon in the company of this volunteer workforce, none of these aspects really matter. What matters, if Chris and Darren's rhetoric is to be believed, is that they are running a club that they hope will become a standard bearer for community football and supporter mutuality in the Liverpool area. Whether this means two hundred supporters believe in what they are doing or two thousand the objective and the passion remain the same. Paradoxically, one could argue that the larger the club becomes the more it loses the personal touch that makes it such a special alternative in the first place, but Chris is convinced that with hard work and good management it is possible to maintain supporter intimacy and input right up to the professional ranks. After all, if it weren't possible, the project would have a shelf life already. If only for their belief in what they are doing, one can only wish them success. Quite when this comes and in what form is another matter, but with one cup under their belt already and a dedicated volunteer force, backed by luminaries from Liverpool FC themselves, it should only be a matter of time before promotion is achieved. From there, and with the prospect of a potential stadium in the heart of the city, who knows?

As I left to catch the train home Darren came out with a pin badge, a memento of today's game, and muttered sarcastically, "non league football – don't you just love it?"
In truth I think they all do. More than they probably ever realised.

Notes
There is a fantastic description of the Boys Pen in this poem found on one of the Liverpool FC fans' forums . The author is listed under the pseudonym of 'Braces and Boots.'

Its fifteen minutes to kick off time
I'm in my seat, Block 109
I look around, I hear the noise
see lots of fathers with their boys.
The kids look happy, a marvellous sight
McNasty's burgers they all bite
they're all excited that's for sure
and with their dads they feel secure.

Although the surroundings have now all changed
the children's feelings are just the same
the middle classes have now arrived
but things were different for a sixties child.

I then look out across the Kop
to the right hand corner at the top
where up until the age of ten
I served my time in the old 'boys pen'.

For those of you who do not know
it was a place for kids to go
metal bars like a kind of cage
where little kopites came of age.

I remember the first time I went inside
Liverpool v Chelsea '65

a star struck boy who stood amazed
football was all we had those days.

You'd always see some kids from school
they came from all over Liverpool
little scousers every week
from Kirkby town right up to Speke.

The Kop was packed out in those days
but at half time, dad found a way
to fight his way through all the crowd
and feed his boy, he did me proud.

An 'Eccles cake' a sausage roll
a drink of Coke, god bless his soul
between the bars he'd pass it through
like feeding monkeys at the zoo.

And through those bars we used to stare
at all the kopites standing there
oh how we'd long to stand with them
and make that step from boys to men.

Some kids escaped now and again
it was a pretty dangerous game
it filled the kopites full of laughter
to see kids dangling from the rafters.

It had its own 'soprano' choir
you couldn't sing 'walk on' much higher
inside those bars kids sang with pride
but it sounded so funny from the other side.

When the match was over at 4.45
your dad would pick you up outside
dozens of kids, some big some small
stood opposite the pen by the old brick wall.

But that was how it was those days
no greedy players, no corporate ways

they recognised us 'kopite cubs'
we were the future of the club.

Then at last it came my time
to leave this little world behind
I was at an age when every lad
didn't want to go the match with dad.

And so I passed out to the kop
that love affair has never stopped
I take my son to the occasional game
but this 'dad and lad' thing's not the same.

You never see young lads no more
who go the match in three's and fours
this city's children rue the day
when they took the old boys pen away.

The money men arrived in town
and in their wisdom pulled it down
they called it 'progress' but we read their thoughts
who needs children when adults pay more.

I now drift back to present day
I take my seat, watch the redmen play
a diehard red, I'm the real McCoy
because I was groomed from a little boy.

That golden era has now passed by
but we all have memories you cannot buy
from apprentice kopites, now middle aged men
who served their time in the old boys pen.

Dudley Town v Bloxwich United

West Midlands Regional League – Step 6
Saturday 10th April 2010

Final Score: 4-1
Attendance: 65

Hmm. What do we know about Dudley? Well, it's got a castle; a grand 11th century building standing atop a hill overlooking the town centre. There's a zoo as well, situated in the castle grounds. For those of a geological persuasion, there are huge limestone caverns which can be traversed by canal, and a splendid recreation of Victorian *fin de siècle* industrial life at the Black Country Living Museum. The brochure looks glossy and reads well - a veritable Garden of Eden dotted with Aran knit sweater wearing sightseers and groups of school children caught halfway between the ecstasy of a school trip and the agony of a history lesson.

Like so many places cobwebbed by a distinguished past, the present serves to remind of how much things have changed. 21st century Dudley is a nadir of the written word, a regular entrant in Crap Town anthologies or scurrilous websites decrying Burberry checked youth culture. It is, thankfully, also the subject of more considered observation. Anthony Cartwright's novel *Heartland*, an account of race, politics and football set in Dudley during the World Cup of 2002, sets out to explore the fractious post-industrial relationships between White and Asian communities in the area and the prominence of far right ideology which has - one can safely assume - gathered momentum amongst the urban degeneration. The issue, somewhat prophetically, was crystallised only a week prior to my visit when the English Defence League came to Dudley and engaged in violent protest against the building of an £18m super-mosque.

On my previous visits to this part of the West Midlands, on the well-trodden train route from Birmingham Moor Street to Kidderminster, it always struck me what a desolate part of the world it was, a hymn to crumbling brickwork, twisted barbed wire and vacant industrial units with weather worn To Let signs. Mile after mile this grim scenery went on, like a Bergman film set, without a single oasis of visual pleasure, a landscape plentiful of graffiti and bereft of hope. As my taxi weaved its way through roadworks and then on to the various dual carriageway systems that carve Dudley up, I could see the same bleak panorama, as if the soul of the town had been boarded up. Gone was the heavy industry skyline and in its place a miscellany of corrugated warehouses, business parks and retail units; the area has gone through a lot of changes in recent times.

It remains a big place though, if not a prosperous one. There is a general consensus, at least on the internet, that Dudley is the biggest town in England without a Football League side. If you Google "Dudley Population" it comes back with a figure from a variety of sources hovering around the 195,000 mark. However, there is considerable debate over where exactly this figure comes from. Local author and publisher Greg Stokes, who's raised the issue in a conversation on this very theme, argues that whilst Dudley may be the biggest administrative area without a Football League club, the Town that spawned the club only has a population of 65,000. Looked at in that context, the statistic is less remarkable. The waters are muddied further when you talk directly to Dudley Borough Council. According to the 2001 census, the population of the Dudley Metropolitan Borough stood at 304,615, although, as Greg is quick to point out, this incorporates a wider geographical area that many residents would never refer to as the Town of Dudley, or at least not the area that spawned Dudley Town FC. When I went direct to Donna Roberts at the Strategic Research and Development arm of Dudley Council, we started getting into ward boundaries and super output areas, but the upshot was that a commonly agreed figure of Dudley's population was almost impossible to obtain, not least because one would need to define the area itself. However one views it - quantitively or otherwise - there is no reason in theory why the area can't support a professional team. Although speckled with various amateur and park sides, the main clubs in Dudley are Dudley Town and Dudley Sports, both in the West Midlands Regional League (WMRL) Premier Division, and Dudley United who play in the division below. Given the size of the area, the relative lowly level of its teams (the WMRL is at Step 6) makes this anomaly even more surprising.

My destination today was the Dell Stadium, home of Dudley Town FC, the oldest of the town's major clubs. If football is considered art at times then art certainly imitates life. Like the town itself, the club has suffered a similar downward spiral in recent years, but not for the reasons that blight most sides. Some fans claim their club is held back because their ground is a hole.

Dudley Town have been held back because their ground almost fell into one. Like a child stood on the precipice of knowledge, Darth Vader lunchbox in one hand and Black Country tour guide jotter in the other, I feel a history lesson coming on...

Back in the 18th century, Dudley was a mining town. Only here they mined for limestone, which was carved out and used to remove impurities from iron ore. The mining effort produced a complex system of caves and by the mid-19th century over 40,000 boats would carry limestone through the caves along the tunnels, propelled along by miner's feet pushing against the tunnel ceiling. Today, a few remain as tourist attractions but most have been filled in. Now enter Dudley Town FC.

The club was formed in 1888 and played their games at the Shavers End ground in the Birmingham League. The club remained dormant after the Great War, but was reformed in 1928, entering the Cradley Heath and District League and then the Worcestershire Combination. In 1932 they moved into the Sports Ground, built as part of a project to provide work for the large unemployed population during the inter-war years. Over 16,000 people attended the opening match - a clear indication of the potential support available to a rising team.

In the early 1930s Dudley dominated the Worcestershire Combination, but the financial strain of a move to the Birmingham League saw the club fold shortly before the Second World War. After the war, the club was once again resurrected; re-joining the Birmingham League which was later renamed the West Midlands Regional League. The 1960s onwards marked a high point in the history of the club, both in terms of performances on the pitch and interest off it. 8,200 saw the Robins play Worcester City in 1964, over 7,000 turned up for a prestigious friendly against Wolves to celebrate the install of new floodlights in the ground and nearly five and a half thousand witnessed a hard fought FA Cup 1st round proper tie in 1976 against York City which earned a creditable replay. Perhaps of most significance during this halcyon period, was the match (or even 'matches' if apocryphal stories from an older generation are to be believed) Dudley Town played against Manchester United in recognition of Duncan Edwards, the footballer born in Dudley in 1936 and described by Bobby Charlton as "the best player I have ever seen". Edwards' life was cut short in the Munich air disaster of 1958, aged just 21, though as noted on the independent

Manchester United supporters' trust website, "he is still talked about and remembered, not only by the fans of the club for which he played and loved so much, but also by football fans throughout the British Isles, Europe, and indeed the world."

The game, which marked the opening of the Duncan Edwards Social Club, saw Dudley come out 3-1 winners. "Matt Busby brought along a United XI minus the first team squad who were away in Sweden," recalls Patrick Talbot on the Black Country society website, "although there were lesser mortals like Fitzpatrick, Rimmer and Aston playing." In 1999 a statue commemorating the player was unveiled by his mother, Mrs Sarah Edwards, and the aforementioned Bobby Charlton, in Dudley Market Place. There are also two stained glass windows at St. Francis' Church, Laurel Road, Dudley in celebration of his life. His grave in the Borough cemetery is constantly adorned with red and white flowers.

Although average league attendances hovered around the 400 mark towards the end of the 1970s, there was demonstrable evidence that success could, and indeed did, bring the crowds in. When the Southern League Midland Division was finally secured in 1984, with a 2-0 win against local rivals Stourbridge, Dudley were all set to play at Step 2 for the first time in their history and with ground improvements in place, including VIP section, press box and loud speaker system, as well as a partisan support, it should have marked the beginning of a golden age in the club's history. And then disaster struck.

During the summer of 1984 mine workings under the adjacent cricket ground collapsed. It wasn't the first time this had happened. Since the 1930s there had been twelve documented collapses and, given the warning signs outside, spectators often entered the ground at their own risk. Unfortunately, the collapse of 1984 was too significant for the authorities to ignore and the 40ft hole which appeared led to the club's stadium being closed down and condemned. It was cruel irony that the mines, so long a source of prosperity for the town, would prove to be the club's undoing. To compound matters, Dudley's sports ground was considered one of the finest stadiums outside of the professional game; its main 1,800 seat stand now preserved only in increasingly rare photo footage and supporters dwindling memories. There are probably only a handful of people left who can remember attending the game there. As Patrick Talbot recalls in his splendid reminisce on the long departed Cricket and Football ground, "part of my sporting heritage collapsed and crumbled away with the limestone (that day)."[1]

The ground has now been redeveloped by the council as 'Castlegate', a modern entertainment complex of cinemas and eating establishments. The name has the ring of a scandal and, from a historical perspective, rightly so. There is little to mark the site that was once home to thousands of fans and a half century of sporting endeavour. A generation of Dudleyites may grow up never knowing their proud football past and, mixed with the smog of traffic fumes and fast food outlets, there is more than a whiff of sadness that so many memories have been bulldozed into the ground.

There are times when a football fan's sense of proportion is blinded by their passion but given the recent tears in Dudley's socio-economic fabric, and the concurrent demise of its football team, I was interested in revisiting the themes in Anthony Cartwright's book. Given the ease with which unsubstantiated and at times patronising views can be formed, I was fortunate enough to speak to the award winning author and gain a first-hand view of the role football played in this part of the world, particular in reference to Dudley's now defunct ground.

"My enduring memory of the old Sports Stadium," he began, "was the game against the Wolves to celebrate the installation of the floodlights in 1981. I was eight years old and it was one of the first games of football I was taken to. I write about it in *Heartland* - it's a positive memory for all the characters in the book - although it obviously now seems very bittersweet given that it closed four years later. It was a big ground - I think it was the biggest in non league football at the time - and really atmospheric with the lights. I only went to a handful of other games although my uncle's family lived opposite and because of the position of the houses (they were raised above the main road) you could see half the pitch from upstairs, so I remember watching a few games from there. As a teenager I went to a couple of games when Dudley played at Round Oak - ironic in itself as this was the sports club of the once-mighty, long-closed steelworks."

---

[1] There are some excellent archive shots of Dudley's old Sports Stadium which can be found at www.blackcountrysociety.co.uk/articles/holeinground.htm, along with further reading

As someone who spent many years living in Sheffield, I had first-hand experience of the effect steel closures had on the local community and the ongoing efforts to recover from the decimation it had on both the local economy and the local people. Like the coalminers, the steelworkers lost not just a job but a way of life, a sense of identity. There are few more devitalising sights than seeing once proud men queuing for jobs in dole offices out of obligation rather than expectation and, for those disenfranchised by the closures, it was an emasculating experience which frankly I could never truly understand. Even with all the regeneration that has gone into pulling Sheffield out of the economic furnace, there are still huge expanses of derelict factories to the north of the city centre lying broken and vandalised like a macabre theme park. In a recent *Guardian* interview with Anthony, Chris Arnot argued that with the closure of the old Sports Stadium went a great source of local pride and identity. I asked for the author's views on this: was this merely a romantic notion or did it carry real substance?

"I tied in part of my book with the closure of the County Ground next door as well. In fact, we used to refer to it all - the football and cricket grounds - as the County Ground - which I realise was wrong but I think was done relatively widely, locally, unless it was just my family! Dudley is, or at least was, a great sports' town: in the 20th century it produced a Wimbledon champion (Dorothy Round) and one of the great footballers of all time (Duncan Edwards). Add to that a first class cricket ground graced by the likes of George and Ron Headley, Basil D'Olieveira, Tom Graveney and Glenn Turner (Worcestershire won the John Player League at home in Dudley in 1972) and I would say the grounds, and sport in general, offered a massive source of local pride. The timing of the closures, coinciding with the collapse of local industry, was a particularly hard blow."

Inevitably, this raises the question of the authority's response to such issues. Can (indeed should) sport be viewed in isolation from wider social events or are the two inextricably linked? It is easy to throw around highly polished rhetoric on such occasions and produce pop sociology theorem, but there is overwhelming evidence to suggest sport, particularly football, can be a force for good, especially when times are hard. Put in the context of recently localised race problems, the issue becomes even more salient.
"I don't think there's any doubt that football can be a great force for cohesion," Anthony continued, "When football people get together they're

just interested in the football, nothing else. We've got a great tradition in the area for football becoming a force for change and harmony almost by chance - look at the impact of the Black players in the pioneering West Brom side of the '70s and the wider social consequences of that (documented in the book *Samba in the Smethwick End* by Jas Bains and Dave Bowler). There is, of course, a risk of football being hijacked for all sorts of dodgy political reasons which hopefully it can resist. As for the local authority's response, I am of the opinion it would have been more of a shock if the council *had* done something to help the club. That isn't a party political point: Dudley has been Labour, Tory (albeit due to Stourbridge and Halesowen being part of the borough) and No Overall Control over the last thirty years but the council has always been pretty terrible. I can't see or think how they serve the people or the interests of the people at all, although I don't live there anymore, so I probably shouldn't criticise too much."

The morality of the issue, and the responsibilities thereafter, could be debated *ad infinitum*. Speak to a member of the council, either at the time of the ground closure, or as part of the modern incumbent, and you will no doubt get an eloquent counter. The simple facts of the matter are Dudley Town now play at the Dell Sports Stadium, a council owned athletics facility in Brierley Hill. How the club came to find themselves there is a little more complex.

After the Sports Stadium was condemned, Dudley Town moved to a new permanent home at the Round Oak Stadium in Brierley Hill. Unfortunately, by 1996 the costs of the ground were spiralling. The club officially moved out in 1996 and into a ground share with Halesowen Town. Plans were afoot to sell the Round Oak ground, but the sale became very protracted and, in 1997, facing increasing financial difficulties, the club was forced to resign its place in the Southern League and had to close down.

Later that year, the club reformed again and were accepted into the WMRL. After two years ground sharing with local rivals Gornal Athletic the decision was taken to leave the borough of Dudley and play at The Beeches, home of Tividale. However, after a four year exile, Town returned to the borough in 2003, having signed a deal to play for the next five years at The War Memorial Ground, Amblecote, Stourbridge. It was not until the 2007-08 season that Dudley found a place to call home at The Dell Stadium, which coincided with a return to the FA Cup after an absence of over 15 years.

Given the architectural splendour of the old Sports Stadium, their new, modern, purposeful yet characterless home holds a mirror up to the remorseless way in which heritage has been superseded and buried by the functional veneer of contemporary business practise.

Despite it being a month synonymous with showers, it was a hot day. There were a few hardened souls practising hurdles in the midday heat and the faint murmur of a hockey match in the distance. Occasionally the sound of crickets carried on the wind, breaking through the stifling air and evoking pleasant memories of schoolboy botany and the innocent joy of rolling around in long grass to the first throngs of sexual awakening. Although I was born and raised in the south, I have always considered the West Midlands my home. There was nothing spectacular about the running track and housing backdrop vista, and certainly nothing that should draw out my lyrical endorphins, but I felt a strange sense of kinship: I felt like I belonged here. The nearby Merry Hill shopping centre, for so many Dudley folk the scourge of lost trade and creator of Poundland empires, was more than a retail monolith, it was the place I used to travel to by bus as a child when I was alone and needed time to think. I still fondly recall the preamble through high rise Halesowen before the Midland Red pulled into the new shopping centre, its overhead monorail stuck in a visionary rut between innovative space age transport system and lazy ostentatious people carrier. I remember watching dusk gather from the vantage point that was McDonalds and, for a few joyous minutes, the trepidations and worries of a young teenage boy were magically lifted as the streetlights sparkled and carried my thoughts over the rooftops and away to a place where I was safe and no one knew me. Some people long for sunset over the Serengeti, but for me there was no more beautiful sight than night falling on the distant embers of Birmingham's skyline.

The first task of the day was to find Stephen Austin, the Vice Chairman of Dudley Town and, in keeping with the hands on role such title's carry in non league, I found him setting up the food kiosk in preparation for this afternoon's match. Stephen, like so many associated with the club, has been in it for the long haul. He first visited Dudley Town as a 15 year old supporter with his late father, after which his involvement graduated to programme seller, committee member and, eventually, Vice Chairman. As he set out the chocolate bars and homemade sandwiches, Stephen talked me through a lifelong devotion in soft Black Country tones.

"The initial attraction to Dudley town was that it was somewhere near my house and more importantly, somewhere safe. Crowds around this time (circa mid-1970s) were averaging 3-400, with big matches getting over 1,000. This helped to provide a very intimate atmosphere and as I became more hands on I realised that the active involvement, the opportunities and friendships with players and fans - who you know on first name terms - was something you may never get with a league club."

As we sat in what was ostensibly the dining area of the complex, it was about as far removed from a traditional football stadium as one could imagine. You half expected Gordon Brittas to walk in and ask nasally if we were enjoying the benefits of his latest soon-to-be doomed scheme. On the wall hung a pendant for Dudley & Stourbridge Harriers athletics club, their badge featuring a castle and what appeared to be a pig being winched to safety, possibly from the impending barbeque below. Although it isn't an environment for the football purist, it is nonetheless their home, something the club had desperately wanted after years of ground sharing in the local vicinity.

"We can never say never, and if the club or council became cash rich, a move would be considered, but right now we just can't afford it. There is a strong working relationship with the local authority and it should be remembered that the council agreed to spend a lot of money to get lights up to Step 5 standard (albeit as part of a generic site upgrade for all sports facilities there) which allowed continued participation in the FA Cup and FA Vase. What we have now is a foundation, something to work with as we attempt to climb the league. However, we need to be realistic. The aim of the club, barring a move to the single benefactor model, is to get into the Southern League Midland Division (Step 4). I am not sure how realistic this is right now given the current economic conditions, and as for a Dudley side ever playing in the Football League, well, I just can't see it in my lifetime."

On paper, this last sentence could be read with a tinge of sadness, but this assumes that anything less than league football, be it for Dudley or any other non league side, is somehow the golden fleece of achievement. In truth, Stephen is a man in love with his role and in love with his club, and for them still to be playing at all is a godsend in itself. As a manager at Citibank, a job that would be a drain on most people's time, Stephen admits there are three main streams to his life: work, family and the football club,

CHANGING ENDS Mike Bayly

of which the latter takes up a considerable amount of volunteer hours. It just seems a shame that this commitment isn't always recognised by a wider audience.

"Fans in the area are aware there is a Dudley Town, but there is a missing ingredient that we, and doubtless other non league clubs, just haven't found. It is cheap to get in here (£3.50 and £1.50 for OAPs) and we find that many people who visit us as newcomers really like what they find, especially when they can talk to the players and staff and really feel part of the match day experience. The club spend a lot of time talking to the *Dudley Chronicle* and *Dudley News* making sure we are kept in the limelight, but ultimately it boils down to personal preference. I'm still not sure why a family want to spend £100 rather than a £10 on a day at the football, when they could get a similar experience coming here, even if it meant just popping down once and seeing what we can offer. It's especially relevant for us, as an extra 10 or 15 paying members of the public each week would make a massive difference. We even send out free tickets to school and still can't get interest, so we rely heavily on people who want to help out with their local side. We have a strong team here who help out with press reports, website development, washing the kit, and other things which may seem minor but are hugely significant in our day to day running. You cannot put a value on the services these people do."

If the public have been slow on the uptake, there are positive noises coming from the business community. Focus DIY agreed a £1,000 sponsorship deal before the start of the season which helped to fund the new away kit and provide what the club hope will be a long and fruitful relationship. In a general attempt to promote themselves in the locality both on and off the pitch, Dudley have enlisted the services of local businessman Colin Richards, a committee member responsible for generating sponsorship, fundraising and awareness of the club.

"There are some people in Dudley who don't even know we have a football club," he began. "The town is dominated by West Brom and Wolves and it's important that people know we have a team, and a team to be proud of. Part of my role is maintaining the image of the club, and putting our name out there; the more people here about you, the more interest you will generate. It's also important that we adopt a professional approach, which includes things like keeping the website up to date and maintaining strong

relationships with the local press. There can be a danger of becoming complacent and if people see negative reports, a poor programme or look you up on the internet only to find your website is three months out of date, it makes people question your professionalism. Obviously we rely on a network of volunteers, and we couldn't survive without them, but these still need to be underpinned by good business sense and the correct attitude."
One of those volunteers was Chris Davies, who is responsible, amongst other things, for submitting the match report to the local newspapers and creating the match day programme. Chris is a non league club's dream. Whilst working in London he covered a similar role at Wingate & Finchley FC and, on his return to the West Midlands, offered his volunteer services to a host of clubs, of which Dudley had the foresight to take him up on.

"The one thing that has amazed me," Colin continued, "is how much work goes into running a club. It's not just a case of turning up, opening a food kiosk and selling a few tickets. The background work is phenomenal, but to be honest, I love it. In fact I couldn't imagine not doing it now."

Colin's route into Dudley Town is a story I shared huge empathy with. Originally a Wolves diehard, he stopped going to Molineux after finding the atmosphere at the ground unsuitable for his young children.

"There was swearing, jostling, shoving, it just wasn't very nice, especially for young kids. To be fair, I think I was also falling out of love with football full stop. The game was changing and I didn't really like it. Anyway, through contacts I was asked to come and watch a game down here and I've been hooked ever since. We like to promote a safe friendly family environment where you don't have people screaming abuse and this is a major factor for me. I think it's fair to say that my few years with Dudley Town has reignited my passion for the game as a whole. I even went out and bought a SKY Sports subscription so I could watch the odd Premiership game again. Dudley Town, it's fair to say, has given me more than I could have imagined. It's given me a love of football back."

Given the similarities with my own experiences, Colin could almost seem like a stooge in a beautifully executed script. But pop down to the Dell Stadium any Saturday when the Robins are at home and you will find him there with his dad cheering the lads on. If you go one further and purchase a replica shirt, you will even find his security company as the club's official sponsor. Meeting Colin offered more than another fan's take on the non league game. It also gave my own feelings some credibility and a reassurance that I was not simply being fickle about an increasingly changing sport. It didn't surprise me that Colin had found solace in the semi-professional game, but it did surprise me that his feelings were so aligned with mine.

Dudley's opponents today were local rivals Bloxwich United from Walsall, who went into the game challenging for the title, with the added incentive of a green light for promotion to Step 5. Although a Step 6 league, the WMRL has a wide geographical spread of teams, stretching from Ellesmere in north Shropshire to Ledbury in central Herefordshire; the fixture between the two sees the away team undertake a journey of over 100 miles.

My 'home town' team Ludlow Town (and I use that phrase loosely given my own nomadic background) also play in this division. Pedants may justifiably question therefore why I don't practise what I preach. If I had a home town team on my doorstep, was choosing Kidderminster Harriers simply a low level form of glory hunting? Well, in some ways, yes. But I should probably try and put this decision into context.

Ludlow Town used to play at the Riddings Park Ground next to the old MEB works in the notoriously tough Sandpits district of town.[1] When I first started watching them play in the late '80s (which in truth was only a handful of times) it was an incredibly basic setup, featuring a fenced off pitch and a small clubhouse with changing rooms. If memory serves correct, the club didn't install floodlights until the early 1990s and a few years later erected a small seated stand, presumably with one eye on promotion to the Midland Football Alliance, which was finally achieved in 2000, albeit for just four seasons. For a club the size of Ludlow this was a tremendous achievement, representing one level below the Southern League. The Ludlow Town I grew up knowing were light years away from such propositions and herein lay part of the problem. Ostensibly, they were just a park side. Our five a side team once played Ludlow Town reserves in a local competition, drawing 0-0, so the idea of supporting a team that we were almost on a par with

[1] In the late 1980s, a series of suspected arson attacks took place on the Sandpits Avenue Estae, leading to the rise of a schoolyard song which ran "we're gonna rock down to, Sandits Avenue, and set it on fire" sang to the tune of Eddy Grant's "Electric Avenue"

seemed slightly incredulous. Add to this the fact it was £3 to get in - half a weekly paper round income - and that I had already started watching Kidderminster regularly by this time, it was always going to be an uphill battle. This is not to say we weren't fond of them. I still have a picture of myself, my brother and friend Terry presenting a cheque to the club for £100 which we raised doing a sponsored swim at the local baths (although, history recalls that Terry sank after the first width like a corn fed Belgrano). It is fair to say I still keep an eye out for their results, and their squad and facilities (the club moved to a new purpose built state of the art stadium in 2002 on the outskirts of town after selling their ground for property development, and ironically shared with Bloxwich at their Red Lion ground while it was being built) are now more in keeping with what one would classify as a 'proper' football team (an arbitrary concept I grant you), even though they still play at the same level from all those years ago. Perhaps the other notable difference beyond the new ground is the changing demographics of the senior team. Certainly from memory, most of the players from my early visits were local lads but now the net is flung out as far as Telford and Birmingham, which either shows a marked change in ambition or a selectively parochial recollection on my part.

I managed to miss the match's first two goals as I was engaged in a fascinating conversation with one of Dudley's more senior fans called Frank. Frank has been following the Robins since the early 1950s when they were in the Birmingham League, at a time when they were commanding crowds of 4-5,000. As a dedicated fan, but also a realist, he had a more pragmatic take on the fate of smaller clubs such as Dudley.

"They were great times," he mused, "but as time went on, the crowds visibly dropped off. I used to go as it was close to where I lived but by the 1960s, as more people got cars, as football became available on TV, the numbers dwindled. As soon as you give people options, it is inevitable this would happen. The truth is money doesn't come into it; it costs me less for a season ticket here than it does for a single match at the Wolves. Once football drops below a perceived level, people just won't go and watch it - they think its park football. Because of this perception, non league football, especially at this level, just can't compete. Support is a generational thing, which is why you find so many older fans at non league games. I was brought up supporting Dudley because they were my local team. There was no other competition. Now, if you walk round Dudley town centre you will see

Wolves, Baggies, Liverpool and Spurs tops. Kids today are bought up on SKY and they simply don't want to know about this level of football. The only way, in my opinion, to get kids involved for the long term is to make them part of the junior set up, which also means their parents will get involved too."

Dudley Town have a strong junior presence with teams at Under 21, Under 18, Under 17, Under 15, Under 14 and Under 10 levels, of which they are rightly proud and it was noted that many graduates of these sides have gone on to play for the senior team. Whether this affinity has an effect on attendance is a little harder to establish. There was a modest crowd of 65 there today, decent by Step 6 standards but still well down on their Southern League heyday. Still, those who were there generated a lot of noise and when Jake Morgan scored Dudley's second goal of the game to make it 2-1 to the home side, the place came to life with rapturous cheers and fist pumping. Dudley still mattered. It reminded me of a poignant Blitz quote I once read: "you can break our homes, but not our hearts."

At half time I joined the club officials for light refreshments. The Chairman, John Langford, was pouring the tea and presiding over the Swiss roll and Jammy Dodgers, that sugary circle of serotonin inducing stickiness and sole preserve of non league shoestring catering. Gillian McKeith would have blenched. But then I find her disquieting scatological obsession of cataloguing other people's bodily movements equally unpalatable.

I took up a position in the main stand for the second half where Dudley regulars Margaret and Michael Turner sat. The couple have produced two books on the history of the club, including a complete season by season statistical guide, which features (increasingly rare) photographic coverage of the old Sports Stadium. As the sun shone down, and the game played out like a bruising welterweight contest, I felt the kind of contentment only a privileged man will ever know. From the fans on the other side of the pitch watching the match from an isolated park bench, Stephen living every pass and every tackle like his life depended on it, to the small contingent of Bloxwich followers wondering if their title dreams were being permanently derailed as Dudley knocked in a third and then a fourth, it was all about local people, local players, local passion. It was a throwback to a more bygone era, minus the flat caps.

Dudley won the match 4-1. In some ways it was a frustrating result for the home team given their capitulation against far lesser sides. The Bloxwich fans left with restrained umbrage: "we'll make sure you get the same warm welcome at our place" said one, in what sounded like a cross between an Edwardian gentleman's promise and a gangland threat. Stephen was ecstatic, in a Martin O'Neil sweatshirt-tucked-into-tracksuit-bottoms-punching-the-air kind of way.

By rights, Dudley Town shouldn't even be here anymore. When they had the geological rug pulled from beneath their feet, they could have easily gone the same way as their Steelworks, swallowed into the ground and replaced by an unmarked gravestone in another long forgotten corner of England. The ground may be gone and the team unrecognisable from previous heady incarnations but the club lives on; and for a town that has gone through so much upheaval, it is a symbol of perseverance, that some things are worth fighting for. Of course, the idea that a football club can combat all of society's problems is at best optimistic and worst plain foolish, but those I had spoken to today believe Dudley deserves a football team it can be proud of and this can only be an agent for good.

This sentiment is probably best summed up by the one man who embodies more about the club than anyone else, life President Nevil Jeynes. A well-spoken regimented gentleman who had been involved with the club since the 1960s, Nevil is in his late 80s now but still spoke with a passion for the game that is as bright and energetic as any I have encountered.

"It is important," he said, "for Dudley to have a successful team. Sometimes I think that there are those in power who really don't care one way or the other. We have sounded out the idea of a village scheme before, with facilities that go beyond just the football club but nothing seems to progress. It would be my wish to see Dudley in their own ground again one day, being a central part of the community to show what we could really do if we work together."

His eyes sparkled. "I think that would really be something."

Stansfeld Oxford & Bermondsey Club v Fleet Leisure

Kent County League – Step 7
Saturday 8th May 2010

Final Score: 4-0
Attendance: 100 (approximation)

In the grand scheme of things, there are probably better ways to spend one's free time than stood in a damp field, while horizontal rain and howling winds flash-rinse and spin dry your senses. But football is a curious beast, bereft of the usual sensibilities that imbue most leisurely pastimes. The cerebral cortex of fandom has no logic. There is a masochistic ritual to the sport, so emotionally obsequious that it will be our master and tormentor for the rest of eternity. To be a football fan is to journey down Dante's inferno. We are hard wired to be fools. As Nick Hornby once famously said, "I fell in love with football as I was later to fall in love with women: suddenly, inexplicably, uncritically, giving no thought to the pain or disruption it would bring with it."

With the end of the season rapidly approaching, I still hadn't seen a game at Step 7 of the National League System. Not that it was through lack of trying. Attempts to watch Milton Keynes Wanderers of the Spartan South Midland League had been buried under a blanket snow; a planned journey to Cromer Town in Norfolk was scuppered via a lack of working email addresses or phone numbers, as if modern communiqué was an ostensible cloak for a deeper enduring paganism. And despite protracted discussions, a trip to Sussex to watch Wisdom Sports in the Mid Sussex League, the team of my annoyingly handsome friend and star striker, Simon Sheeran, fizzled out owing to constant fixture rearrangements and demanding matriarchal ties. *Cherchez la femme*.

It would be untrue to say I am an optimist: whereas some see the doughnut, I invariably see the hole, but I do take comfort from Chinese philosophy that crisis is merely a form of opportunity. Although several regional leagues had finished the week before, some were also winding down, partly as a legacy of the winter which decimated week upon week of fixtures throughout December and January. After scouring various club websites, some of which were more outdated than Gerry Francis' haircut, I originally settled on Baldock Town Letchworth v Lemsford in the Hertfordshire County Senior League. Although not a direct reincarnation of the previously dissolved Baldock Town who once enjoyed Southern Premier League status, and famously sold Kevin Phillips to Watford, their website does make historical reference to the now fallen side. Baldock play at the Country Ground in Letchworth and, as home of the Hertfordshire FA, is a ground of considerable stature for such a low level of football. No doubt fuelled by a lust to fulfil stereotypes of park football, it just didn't seem to fit the bill. I wanted something more organic, more visceral, to the point where anything vaguely representing a 'stadium' would be anathema, in the same way a New Model Army fan might feverishly view soap.

Thankfully, I have not been alone when writing this book. At least not in the existential sense. If there is one thing the internet can provide, aside from unsolicited emails telling me I need a bigger penis or a financial allegiance with a usurped Nigerian despot, it's a constant stream of real time information about where fans are heading on any given match day. The Non League Matters forum[1], for so long my virtual companion and source of unrestricted field samples, was to prove my trump card once again, when one fan pointed out a potential title decider in the Kent County League between Stansfeld Oxford & Bermondsey FC and Fleet Leisure. The maths was simple: if Stansfeld won the title was theirs.

Stansfeld didn't have a website to speak of (at least not one that I could find) so it fell to the County FA website to confirm the match was being played at nearby Coney Hall FC as Stansfeld's Metrogas Ground was being used for Cricket. Coney Hall became tragically infamous in July of 2009 when their then Manager Ryan Musgrove was shot and killed by a masked gunman while the team were training at Sparrows Den playing fields. Coney's Tiepigs Lane ground is located in the middle class suburbs of Hayes in Kent, all mock Tudor and Volkswagen Passats, with the odd 4x4 thrown in to navigate those treacherous trips to Waitrose, lying approximately zero feet above sea level on easily accessible terrain. Frankly you almost wish someone would build a school or a supermarket half way up Scaffel Pike merely to justify these pointless gas guzzlers.

---

[1] www.nonleaguematters.co.uk/forum/gforum.cgi

CHANGING ENDS Mike Bayly

Stansfeld's club name has a decidedly incongruous ring to it. Oxford and Bermondsey are about as far apart on the social spectrum as one could wish for, Bullingdon Club on one side, hard drinking Dockers on the other. In this anomaly lies the source of creation though. The club's roots were formed in 1897 when Dr John Stansfeld, an Oxford graduate, visited Bermondsey and, on seeing the poverty, decided to form a club "to keep the waifs and strays off the streets." At one time, the organisation ran five clubs in the Docklands, Southwark and Bermondsey area. Today, its headquarters remain in Bermondsey, where over 200 members participate in a variety of sports such as football, golf, snooker, athletics and circuit training.

Coney Hall's ground is accessed through a pair of main gates with the Playboy logo on, which doubles as the club's badge. There is a large building which houses a bar, refreshment kiosk, changing rooms and a number of pitches for various sporting use. The ground itself has a small covered standing area for about 100 people (at a push and physiques pending) while the rest of the pitch is sectioned off by railings and advertising boards. Behind the far goal stood housing and, to the opposite side of the main stand, what looked like a large ditch or valley. There were no floodlights, but even by Step 7 standards this was still fairly impressive; other matches I had seen at this level over the years (albeit only a handful) were literally played on municipal parks with changing rooms a positive luxury if they happened to be near the pitch.

There was no one obvious to pay as I entered the complex, although a small crowd of middle aged men in drill coats were gathered outside the clubhouse talking in a scene reminiscent of a *Football Factory* casting couch. "The problem we have," said one in a guttural cockney accent, "is we aren't a football club: we're a social club with a football team. Step 5 football is another world. It was only a few years ago the lads used to warm up before the game with a fag and a cup of tea."

The Kent County League is unusual in that it sits below the Kent League at Step 5 with no bridging competition in between. Subsequently, promotion is made increasingly difficult given the huge leap in ground requirements between the two levels. According to the West Cheshire Association League website, Step 7 grounds do not require floodlights, a fixed capacity, a clubhouse or even recognised ground boundaries. Even the rules on pitch perimeter barriers are open to interpretation. This lies in contrast to Step

5 requirements which require all of the above, plus covered accommodation for 200, of which at least 100 must be seated.[1]

Given the investment required for such progression, and the amateur nature of many sides in this division, it is unsurprising that upward mobility is rare. On the flip side, the pyramid system remains aspirational. In 1997, VCD Athletic were promoted to the Kent League, albeit retaining their place by virtue of a ground share with Thamesmead until their Oakwood ground was bought up to league requirements. This season the club finished a creditable 8th in the Ryman League Division 1 South, after winning the Kent League in 2008-09.[2]

Whilst a ground share is a possibility for Stansfeld, it is a highly unlikely one. The mind-set still had its roots firmly in the amateur game, as no doubt did the level of football. "I hope you don't get neck ache," chipped in one observer, "you'll spend half the game filming the ball in the air." This was not a pejorative observation. The general impression I got was that being a good side in a good league was competition enough; any consideration of promotion to something as semi-professional as Step 5 seemed at best problematic and at worst completely abhorrent.

With kick off approaching, there was a healthy crowd of a hundred or so gathered in the fine drizzle. Large men with skinheads stood under umbrellas. Young mothers with prams balanced uncomfortably in high heels whilst passing their toddlers round. It was a mix of friends, family and the odd ground hopper. Plus one chap masquerading as a writer.

From the kick off, Stansfeld showed why they were on course for the Championship. Only ten minutes had passed when a neat one-two between Harry Draper and Charlie Howard resulted in Howard drifting into the area and then being clumsily tripped. There were a few half-hearted protests, but it was fairly clear cut. Diving doesn't really sit comfortably with park

---

[1] www.thefa.com/Leagues/NationalLeagueSystem/~/media/Files/PDF/Leagues/GradeF09.ash x/GradeF09.pdf

[2] After joining the Kent League in 1919, VCD visited Maidstone United on Boxing Day and played in front of the club's highest crowd of 13,500. The Vickers team that day contained seven Arsenal players who were finishing off their war service.

football. This is a level of the game where the only amateur dramatics come from kids on the sidelines being scolded by their parents. Anyone throwing themselves around on the pitch today was, as one of my friends once so eloquently put it, "likely to get a reyt shoein'."

Leading scorer Alfie Nunn stepped up and dispatched the penalty into the bottom corner and from then on it was almost a *fait accompli*. Stansfeld played some neat one touch football on a fairly unforgiving surface and the impressive Danny Tipple, who seemed to exhaust half the crowd just by watching him, continually put in a series of good balls via some spritely overlapping full back play.

When the game entered it's more soporific patches, there were other amusements to hold the interest: the Fleet manager with a rather splendid skullet; players having to navigate through long grass and stinging nettles when the ball went out - as it frequently did - on the far side of the pitch; the complete disregard for the "Respect" campaign from the assembled fans. The last time I heard this much profanity was during an episode of Keith Allen's *Tourette De France*. As well as the more earthy use of language were genuine moments of amusement. After a particularly deft touch in midfield by one of the Stansfeld players, an observer commented "he's got a bit of the Sheringham about him" to which a reply came "you mean he likes boozing and tarts?"

1-0 at half time. The clubhouse was showing *Soccer Saturday* so the vast majority headed in to see how Millwall were getting on against Swindon in their push for promotion. The Coney clubhouse is a testament to their youth team policies and pride in their club as every spare inch of wall space is taken up by photos of past and current teams at all levels and ages. The local WAGS (perhaps the most hateful neologism of recent times) took centre stage, whilst their respective children ran around, darting between legs in that exuberant way only kids can. I felt slightly uncomfortable stood alone in these unfamiliar surrounding with a long lens camera. It gives rise to the kind of sensationalist red top headlines that can damage a man's reputation for good: "Kiddy fan is kiddy fan" or something equally iniquitous.

The second half started in dynamic fashion, not before the Stansfeld officials issued a half serious warning about "losing too many balls over the fence." Two minutes in Stansfeld and Alfie Nunn got their second after a sublime pass from Terry Forsyth. The game had barely restarted before it was 3-0, with Harvey Gayle's twenty yard strike the pick of the afternoon's goals. It was no doubt demoralising on a Fleet side that were playing their fourth game in eight days. The Fleet manager had gone from manic to catatonic in a short space of time and with Stansfeld completely in control, no doubt thoughts were turning to warm showers and post-match drinks. At 3-0, and with the clock ticking down, there was a marked change in attitude from the home players as well. The title was now all but in the bag so thoughts turned to more pressing matters. "How are Millwall getting on?" came concerned shouts to the bench.

"They're winning, Leeds are losing."

"Get in. We're league champions and Millwall are going up. This is gonna be the best piss up ever."

As the game ran out, the Stansfeld no 9, a man so wide he almost needed planning permission, put himself about with a series of bruising challenges and direct attacking play. One industrious run culminated in a fierce clash that saw a Fleet player grabbed round the neck and thrown to the ground. The referee split up the ensuing rabble but it was all fairly good humoured. Pleasingly, no one was even cautioned. In the Premiership you'd expect a red card and a four day analysis by Andy Gray, not to mention a wide spectrum of pundits (and for pundits, increasingly read anyone who has been recently sacked by a Football League club or played the game in the '80s and rather needs the cash) throwing their hyperbolic two pennies worth around in high definition. Thankfully we were miles from the moral indignation of the TV studio or the theatre of the top flight. I struggled to take football seriously for a while after the embarrassing standoff between Lens Lehman and Didier Drogba which reduced what is euphemistically referred to as a 'man's game' to some form of homoerotic duel.[1] Many of us weaned on hairy arsed midfielders clattering into shinpadless opposition hadn't seen pantomime that bad since Frank Bruno appeared in Goldilocks. With ten minutes to go Jamie Turner netted from thirty yards to seal the victory and Stansfeld's first Championship title for fifteen years. The hardcore Millwall fans darted straight for the clubhouse but most lingered around to watch the Kent County League trophy being presented to club captain Neil Thurgood amid rapturous applause. Proud friends, partners

[1] The hideous episode involving Lehman and Drogba can be seen here www.youtube.com/watch?v=HyA_MB9l-b4&NR=1

and parents shared in the moment on what was a real family occasion. And this, above all, was the most endearing impression of the afternoon. It is easy to forget sometimes that footballers, at any level, are just working class lads who play a game they love. Somewhere along the line this notion was hijacked and, in some cases, the spectre of wealth and celebrity has transformed otherwise normal people into hardnosed mercenaries. It is astonishing that Wayne Rooney, the current saviour of English football, is heralded for "just going out there and playing like a kid in the park" as if those around him see football as a chore, a means to an end with handsome fiscal rewards. Lord Acton's famous observation that "Power tends to corrupt, and absolute power corrupts absolutely" has never been more salient in an age where players are becoming bigger than their clubs and making demands that are disenfranchising them from their original paymasters: the fans. Days like today really brought home what football is - or should - be about: The glory of winning and the joy of participation. It is unlikely anyone playing today will go on to make a full time career out of the game, but this is largely inconsequential, just as it is for the other 99% of people in this country who simply play the game out of sheer passion, dedication and camaraderie.

There are probably better ways to spend one's free time than stood in a damp field on a Saturday afternoon.

But not many.

Bath City v Woking

Conference South Play Off Final – Step 2
Sunday 9th May 2010

Final Score: 1-0
Attendance: 4,865

So, some seventeen games and several thousand miles later, I reach the finale of this wholly unique season. Of course, these travels need to be put into context. Compared to your average fan who follows his (or her) team around the country, there is nothing particular remarkable about my efforts. Compared to the almost obsessive ground hoping fraternity I am a mere whelk. At a personal level, it is by far the most games I have watched in an individual season, and without doubt the most varied. Granted, the choice of final game may be a little clichéd, but it nonetheless represents the finishing line of a season that seems to have endured *ab aeterno*. Accordingly, I am not sure if I am deliriously happy or intrinsically sad. My mood is often like the comedy tragedy masks, so perhaps somewhere in the middle: Britishly stoic.

As a location to finish my walkabout of non league football, I probably couldn't have chosen a more idyllic setting than Bath. As you pull into Bath Spa station, you can't help but be struck by the wondrous regality of its Georgian architecture and the warm mellow lusciousness of its honey stoned landscape. My ambition has always been to own a gentleman's townhouse, coupled with a wardrobe full of Paul Smith suits and a black book full of society women, though I fear it may be a stretch too far. As my brother cruelly noted, "you're living in a Hugh Grant fantasy world". I suspect he may be right, clandestine liaisons with street hookers notwithstanding. Bath is now a World Heritage Site and a hugely popular tourist destination, attracting nearly four million visitors a year. It is perhaps fitting that nestled amongst this celebrated built environment is another glorious example of period construction: Bath City's Twerton Park.

Described by David Bauckham as "a splendid example of... a 'traditional' football ground... a must see for any serious non league ground enthusiast"[1]

---

[1] www.pyramidpassion.co.uk/html/bath_city.html

it sits in the suburb of Twerton about two miles from the city centre. I would perhaps go one further than David's observations and suggest it is a ground that *any* football fan should see while they still have the chance. The first thing that strikes you on approach is the floodlights. I noted in the Ebbsfleet chapter how important I feel floodlights are to our national game and how increasingly rare they are, certainly in the professional ranks. These were monsters, Kraken like, looming over the rooftops and trees with ominous presence. Like an impatient child on sensory overload, I was desperate to see more but was halted by the enormous queue that was building up outside the ground. Football fans become expert mathematicians when kick off time is nearing and with thirty minutes to go the snake of fans trailing down the road were in no doubt the match would be delayed. "Half an hour from here" declared one confidently, hinting at a lifetime spent working at Alton Towers. Or queuing for football matches. I left the home supporters' melee and joined the away contingency which had reached as far as the local Blockbusters (a frankly obscure and pointless reference unless you know the area). Some of the Woking fans were slightly incredulous. "I've never seen any of these at home games" said one, with one eye on the turnstile gate, a mere speck on the horizon. A few Bath City fans cut across the queue into the car park, at which point songs about combine harvesters and carrot crunching broke out, ensuring regional stereotypes were firmly on the agenda. Quite where Woking fits into the grand scheme of things is anybody's guess. When they played up at Kidderminster the Harriers' fans sang "we hate fucking Cockneys" to which one protagonist replied "so do we" with barely concealed contempt. Moreover, agricultural accusations are a little rich given the Surrey heartlands are home to some of the most affluent farmers and land lovers this country has produced. A friend of mine who used to work in a pub in nearby Dorking commented "you can't move for mud splattered Range Rovers, cocked rifles and stag blood."

As more fans joined the queue, and the queue singularly failed to move, the atmosphere grew. Old and young mingled outside pubs, waving flags and blowing air horns (thankfully not the Vuvuzela, the trumpet so popular with South African fans which sounds like a herd of elephants being chased by a swarm killer bees, or, when played in isolation by one wheezy sports reporter on a pre world cup show, the teacher from *Charlie Brown*) adding to the huge sense of anticipation. Bath's participation in today's carnival owes everything to the revamped structure of non league football and the sport in general. In the timeline of football history, play offs are still a relatively new phenomenon. The Football League first adopted them in the 1986-87 season, amid controversy and violence: the Middlesbrough v Chelsea clash in particular was marred by major crowd disturbance. On a wider note, many commentators noted how unfair it was that a team finishing sixth or seventh in the league could usurp the team finishing third or fourth, which for decades was the promotional benchmark in Divisions Two, Three and Four. Similar debates still reign today, particularly amongst the non league fraternity, not least because the concept is still highly embryonic. The Conference National only introduced the play off system in 2002-03 and the Conference North and South as recent as 2004-05. Crucially, non league play offs are part of a wider plan to increase mobility between leagues. Traditionally, only the championship winners could ever progress to the tier above, which meant in a season where there was a runaway leader, the league would become meaningless very early on. Critics argue that if mobility is required then the top two from any respective division should be automatically promoted: fans of Hitchin Town will no doubt feel aggrieved that after amassing 100 points they still fell afoul of the play off system, allowing Chesham United, who finished some 20 points behind them, to gain promotion to the Southern League Premier. In truth this argument is slightly disingenuous. Unlike the Football League, non league play offs sought to introduce a second promotional place rather than change an existing method of progression. Prior to the play offs there was no "automatic" promotion for second place and arguments about morality and fairness from the runners up in a given league invariably dissipate when fortunes change the following season and the play offs become an outside chance of glory. Moreover, these games generate crucial revenue for clubs who often survive on a paucity of gate receipts. Wingate & Finchley, for example, who averaged 91 spectators in the 2009-10 season saw nearly five times that amount turn up for their play off derby against Enfield Town. Days like these can be the difference between some clubs going into the summer break on an even financial keel or not.

So, Bath City, mid-table in January of this year, and still outside the play offs as late as mid-April, found themselves entertaining a Woking side who had barely threatened the top five places all season until a run of eight wins in their final nine games saw them overhaul Braintree Town on the last day of the season. After fifteen minutes of queuing I decided to slip out, David Niven style, and try and find a quicker route into the ground. Inexplicably, there were no queues for the main stand and my fortune was amplified when a kindly gentleman in front of me offered a free ticket as his colleague couldn't attend.[1] As I passed through the turnstile and up the steep climb to the main stand, the panorama of the stadium came into full glorious view. It was beautiful. I can't remember the last time I had been so awestruck inside a football ground. The Emirates and Wembley may be architecturally impressive but they are designed for a newer, sleeker, corporate audience. This was like walking back through the passages of time: the large grandstand, the huge banks of terracing, the smell of cigar smoke and fried onions catching the wind. It was an oneiric never-never land, deliciously redolent of childhood memories.

The problem with dream states is the harsh reality of waking up. Unfortunately the seating at Bath is a little bit cramped (which is a bit like saying James Corden is a little annoying) to the point that anyone over five foot tall may struggle for leg room. Either way, I didn't sit down for long. The game had been delayed by fifteen minutes owing to crowd congestion which gave me plenty of time to wander round the ground and take some photos. I was hoping to do a bit of celebrity spotting given Ken Loach, the famous film director, is both a supporter and a shareholder in the club. Loach's recent work, *Looking for Eric*, starring Gaelic philosopher, actor and ex-professional football Eric Cantona, also raised the club's profile when he visited Twerton Park in 2009 to promote the new film.[2] Despite targeting every rotund spectator with a beard, I was unable to spot the seagull quoting genius. Although I did spy someone who bore a striking resemblance to Rowland Rivron, a man I only know of through watching multiple talking head programmes on Channel 4.

The main surprise for a game of this magnitude was the lack of segregation between home and away fans. There was obviously a section for away fans behind the goal, but this was by no means compulsory, as several Woking fans were sat in the main stand and mingling on the terracing below. Given the recent problems involving non league play off matches (most notably

---

[1] Given I spent hardly any of the game sat with the man who paid me in, I realise in retrospect this was exceedingly rude and, on the off chance he ever reads this chapter, would like to apologise unreservedly for my lack of manners.

[2] Details of Mr Cantona's trip to Twerton Park can be found here www.thisisbath.co.uk/news/court-King-Eric/article-1056810-detail/article.html

at Luton and then Boreham Wood, where a home fan reportedly ran on to the pitch and punched one of the Kingstonian players) it restored a degree of respectability to the notion of friendly rivalry that non league football is supposed to encourage. By the time the players were out on to the pitch, the ground had swelled and was a truly inspiring site. The official attendance of 4,865 (which took a long time to release owing to turnstile problems) must have surpassed just about everyone's expectations, given their average attendance for the season was only 633 and the semi-final against Chelmsford drew in less than 1,500. These were clearly Halcyon days. Two older gentlemen behind me commented it was the biggest crowd they had ever seen, though it paled in comparison to the club's official record attendance of 18,020 against Brighton in 1960.

The game's 'unofficial' attendance was no doubt boosted by the large congregation of flag waving supporters who were standing in someone's back garden which overlooked the ground to the far corner opposite the main stand. I counted about fifty in all. When the whistle blew for kick off the roar went up, the songs started and the tackles flew in. And here an attempt at a match report should start. But given the coverage and granular accounts in most of the national non league papers, as well as a plethora of other non league websites, I will fast forward until 75 minutes are on the clock. The truth is I was too absorbed in the match to even attempt making any notes on it and, in all honesty, the first half was pretty dire, which gave me a fairly decent caveat to opt out. When Kaid Mohamed's penalty shortly after the restart gave Bath the lead the tension began to rise. Now the empyrean of the Conference National was more than just a whimsy, it was within touching distance, and the nearer one comes to attaining something the greater the fear of losing it. At 0-0 there was still an atmosphere of calm but now it was turning deadly serious. Anguished shouts and cries came out every time Woking went on the attack and palatable relief seeped out when a wayward shot skewed over the bar or landed at the feet of a thankful home defender. With nine minutes left, Woking's Moses Ademola went clean through and somehow dragged his shot wide in a career defining moment. From now on, "doing a Moses" will mean buggering up your club's chances of getting promotion in this part of the world. No doubt that elusive 11th commandment made reference to "not sending 1,000 away fans home thoroughly pissed off".

Then, after the terraces had regained their composure, and pacemakers had regulated blood flow again, Woking scored. Or at least that's what the entire ground thought. The Woking fans certainly thought so, turning into a tide of red and yellow delirium, in stark contrast to the stunned faces around me who looked like they had just come home from holiday to find their house burnt down and a red gas bill on the doormat. Then, as is so often the case in football, the emotional pendulum swung the other way. A raised flag signalled a disallowed goal. The Woking fans went livid. The Bath fans cheered louder than when the earlier penalty went it. I often struggle to think of other scenarios in life that encompass the full spectrum of human emotion - despair, numbness, joy, elation - in such a fleeting moment of time. Sometimes I think only human tragedy can come close, but where the scars of loss or redemption can be long lasting, the football emotion is more acute, more transient, more ephemeral. Seeing grown men cry at the final whistle - some with joy, others with despair - makes you realise football has always been more than a game, it is a way of life, hard coded into our genetics. It may not be more important than life and death, but the two are often hard to separate. As hundreds of fans invaded the playing area (despite an earlier perfunctory announcement on the PA system asking supporters not to invade the pitch, which is a bit like the UN asking George Bush not to invade Iraq) the whole stadium erupted in an orgy of celebration, like a pressure ejaculation, to a backdrop of Woking fans applauding their players - and no doubt Bath City - on a hard fought and spectacular season. I didn't stay around for the presentations. I may be a football fan but I would have felt like an imposter. This was a personal celebration of a return to the non league top flight after a thirteen year absence, so I left the jubilant Bath fans to it and headed off for the not inconsiderable walk back to the station.

As I hurried back past the modern face of McDonalds and PC World and then onto the older Georgian squares of the town perimeters I slowed to an amble and watched the Sunday trading wind down for the day. Shutters were pulled down and market stalls packed away. It was reassuringly peaceful. The sun bathed the stone in a rich nectar of light and made the senses fuzzy, and as I lazily made my way to the train which would carry me back to London, the curtain fell on the most memorable season of my life.

Extra time - Final Positions

- Ebbsfleet United – Finished 22nd. Relegated to Conference South
- Enfield Town – Finished 4th. Lost in Play Off Final to Concord Rangers 3-1
- Colwyn Bay – Finished 4th. Promoted to Northern Premier League Premier Division after beating Lancaster City 1-0 in Play Off Final
- South Shields – Finished 11th
- Wealdstone – Finished 6th
- Truro City - finished 10th
- London APSA – Finished 13th
- Poole Town – Champions. Not eligible for promotion due to ground grading restrictions
- Stocksbridge Park Steels – Finished 11th
- Chelmsford City – Finished 3rd. Lost in Play Off Semi-finals to Bath City 3-0 on aggregate
- Biggleswade Town – Finished 12th
- Needham Market – Champions. Promoted to Isthmian League Division 1 North *
- Rainworth Miners' Welfare – Finished Runners up. Promoted to Northern Premier League Division One South by virtue of Bridlington Town not accepting promotion *
- AFC Liverpool – Finished 5th
- Dudley Town – Finished 5th
- Stansfeld Oxford & Bermondsey Club – Champions. Not seeking promotion
- Bath City – Finished 4th. Promoted to Conference National after beating Woking 1-0 in Play Off Final

*Note: Exact divisional placing for 2010/11 season still subject to FA approval at time of writing.

Conclusions

I am hesitant to use the word 'journey' as it is fast becoming the most bastardised word in the English language. Everyone, from all walks of life, seems to be undertaking one, be it plump teenage girls on reality shows masquerading as musicians, D-list celebrities pulling on ice skates or middle managers building rafts on corporate team bonding sessions in North Wales. But when you have spent the last nine months travelling around the country to far flung places that would otherwise remain just a quizzical entry on an Ordnance Survey map the term has a far more validated context. For me it was a very real journey, often into the complete unknown, without the need to resort to trite and unsubstantiated metaphors to qualify the experience. The question therefore is what, if anything, have I learnt?

Well firstly, I have only really scratched the surface. Seventeen games, a handful of clubs and a relatively small sample of leagues cannot fully represent the sheer vastness of the non league structure in this country. But then this was always going to be an improbable task. Instead, I have attempted to take an overview, a skimming, of what life is like below the Football League for various clubs at various levels around the country, whilst concentrating on issues that are relevant to the modern game as a whole. Perhaps the most revealing aspect of this *modus operandi* is the sheer scale of difference between Step 1 and Step 7 football, more so I would argue than any gap between the Premiership and League 2. The Conference National is now all but a professional league in name only, with crowds, stadia and, dare I say, ticket prices that are more akin to full time setups. As you filter down through the non league stratosphere, there becomes an almost marked difference at every level, not just in the standard of football, but in crowds, stadiums and, most importantly of all, match day experience. I can only go on the games I covered, but the smaller the club the more emotionally involved the staff seemed to be, both with the club itself and the paying fans. Of course, there is a degree of inevitability in this; it is considerably easier to be on first name terms with fifty fans week in week out than it is to be with five thousand, but for many fans I spoke to this was precisely why they found such a relative low level of football appealing.

Given my moderately small cross section, there were also a number of teams who I really wanted to include but simply ran out of time: Maidstone United and their quest to find a home back in the town; Dartford and their ecologically inspired council owned stadium; Sheffield FC, the oldest football club in the world; Milton Keynes Wanderers and their views on the MK Dons; the fall from grace of Bromsgrove Rovers and Scarborough Athletic. Additionally, there will be other fans who may pick this book up and say "we have a great story too", but a line has to be drawn somewhere. Moreover, one could argue that every club is unique in its own right and that even in the dullest and most prosaic corners of the country can be found a story that inspires the human spirit.

The sheer quantity of teams in this structure also means that there are an innumerable amount of views on the non league game, of which some have been expressed here and people will no doubt disagree with. The problem with non league football is there is no one size fits all solution, be it kick off times, regional structuring, revenue generating, season extension or any other contemporary issue you care to mention. What may apply to a team in the Conference South with four figure crowds is unlikely to apply - or even matter - to a county league village side watched by one man and his dog. Talking of 'non league' in homogenous terms is almost impossible to do.

Another by-product of the scale of the game in this country is unworkable economics. Of all the comments I have read attributed to football's finances perhaps the most pragmatic were Wealdstone Chairman's Howard Krais' that there are simply too many teams vying for the supporter pound, especially in concentrated areas like the South East. Several of the teams I reviewed live in the shadow of bigger more successful clubs, as well as a multitude of other non league sides on their doorstep. The problem even exists in more rural areas. Biggleswade Town, for example, a club with a seemingly remote and advantageous location, have Luton, Cambridge, Milton Keynes, Stevenage and Bedford all within simple commutable distance, which not only provides competition but means there has always been a historical support for other sides in the town. The reality, as Supporters Direct's Kevin Rye hinted at, is that clubs at all levels of the football pyramid need to allay fans' expectations with financial reality. England can support an unlimited number of football clubs in theory, providing they live within their means. Stansfeld, for example, very much saw their place in the grand scheme of things and many other clubs, especially those at Step 5, such as South Shields, realise that promotion just isn't a feasible option given the increased operational costs that go with it. The problem comes when fans no longer tolerate this perceived lack of ambition and either start making waves or stop watching the club altogether. This season has seen the sad demise of a number of non league sides - Kings Lynn and Farsley Celtic being two of the more high profile casualties, with Serie A giant killers Merthyr Tydfil teetering on the precipice - which begs the question do fans want a side they can watch week in week out at a sustainable level, or are they happy for their team to speculate with the caveat they could go bust? Many I have canvassed side with the former, but I still remain unconvinced if this would be so transparent in practice. Football supporters can be a fickle bunch and if clubs openly slash wage bills and budget with a view to consolidating a mid-table position, it won't be long before murmurs of discontent start circulating on internet message boards.

The demise of the aforementioned clubs also brings home a stark reminder that non league football is not the panacea to all of the sports ills. As has been highlighted during the course of the season, there is still a heavy reliance on unrealistic finances via unscrupulous borrowing or the single benefactor model. As the recent play offs have shown, crowd violence is still a problem at some of the higher profile games, particularly given the lax segregation, limited policing, and the opportunity for disorderly fans from more established clubs (or firms) to latch on to non league sides when a big game is on the horizon. The game is also imbued with many political and organisational problems, specifically relating to ground grading, regionalisation and administration, which has caused much umbrage amongst sections of the supporting public. One striking example was Gloucester City's inclusion in the Conference North following their promotion during the 2008-09 season, which for a club still without a home, represented a financial and logistical headache before a ball had even been kicked. Ask any official what they made of a trip to Blyth Spartans, Workington or Fleetwood and you may get a very short and terse response. Accordingly, it should be stressed that this book is not an anti-Premiership (or anti-Football League) rant. I am a SKY Sports subscriber: I occasionally watch Arsenal when there is a free ticket going spare at work. And I don't think that being a non league fan makes someone better or more 'real'. There are fans that have been watching clubs in the top flight for longer than I have been alive and to suggest anything derogatory would be a complete disservice.

Some might wonder why, in my attempt to look at alternatives to the Premiership, did I not simply look at other Football League clubs and there is a valid point in there. Several League 2 sides exist on far shorter shoestrings than some of their Conference counterparts and experience just as much hardship, and at clubs like Exeter and Brentford there is sterling work going on to ensure supporters retain a voice in their club at boardroom level. But the point about non league football is how encompassing it actually is. Yes, lower league professional sides are of course an option for the disgruntled top flight fan but nearly every town and village in the country has a non league team of some sort and, in terms of accessibility and local allegiance, this is the crucial factor.

If there is a failure of this book then it will invariably come from its loudest critic: me. The truth is I do not consider myself a particularly gifted writer. I do not have the prose of Harry Pearson, the range of David Bennie or the lyrical wit of Cameron Carter. I am, for analogous purposes, the Ian Marshall or Robert Rosario of wordsmiths; the odd moment of dynamism but ultimately very pedestrian. My English teacher once said my writing style was confusing, pretentious and verbose, "like a mouth with too many teeth" and I am the first to admit I will throw in the odd *bon mot* for superficial effect.

But in writing this book I have fulfilled an ambition. More than that, I have hopefully added something constructive to both the football debate and the role of non league football. When I first had the idea for writing a piece on the non league game, I had a lot of preconceived ideas, as well as many gaps in my knowledge. What I have discovered exceeded my wildest expectations.

Firstly, the hard facts. If you are someone who defines their enjoyment of football by a club's ability to win trophies, field the best players in the world, and to compete in the most prestigious global events, then non league football probably won't be for you. That said, I would still advocate giving it a go sometime should you get the chance. Many of the fans and even officials of clubs I spoke to up and down the country still had a 'big' side they followed, albeit some with more interest than others. There is absolutely no reason why fans of bigger clubs can't have a non league team as their 'second' side. Stepping down from the glitz and glamour of the all seater spectacle to something more modest doesn't mean you have to turn into Saint Francis of Assisi. As Dan, a Reading fan highlights, the two can happily coexist and at times may even surprise:

CHANGING ENDS Mike Bayly

"I've been a Reading FC season ticket holder for the majority of my adult life. It's fair to say I've become somewhat disillusioned with modern football and have been searching for something to reignite my love affair. As a proud resident of Reading, born and bred, I occasionally glance at the results of Reading's other football club, Reading Town FC. Town currently find themselves top of the Hellenic League and look very good for promotion to the Southern Football League. So whilst RFC play away out of town I endeavour to get myself down to the Lane to begin an affair with my new football mistress, Reading Town Football Club."[1]

Dan is not alone in his thoughts. There are many examples of fans turning to the non league game through disillusionment with League football. Granted, it is hard to quantify exactly how many and several will tell you that whilst top flight attendances have risen their own local club gates have fallen. Of course, this partly depends on how we view the demographic of those attending, as was demonstrated on my visit to AFC Liverpool. One also cannot underestimate the pulling power satellite TV has over lower league games, especially now pubs and clubs are increasingly finding ways to show televised matches at 3pm on a Saturday.

Ultimately it boils down to personal preference. One of the biggest criticisms of our modern game is the erosion of tradition and local identity, yet this only tells half the story. If you still long for games that kick off on a Saturday at 3pm, in grounds that still have terracing and floodlights, watching players who could still be the bloke next door and where you get change from a ten pound note on the gate, then you could do a lot worse than at least consider the option of watching your local non league side. Yes, the quality of football may not be brilliant - at times it might be downright awful - but there are just as many tedious encounters played out in the professional game to suggest parity is spread across the football spectrum. More than that, if you really want you voice to be heard, if you really want to feel that the club wants you there and that they value you as a fan rather than a turnstile statistic, there is so much opportunity to get actively involved, way beyond the obvious examples of supporter owned clubs. I can't comment on every club in the National League System but most of those I visited actively

---

[1]   Dan's personal blog of his time spent following Reading Town FC can be found here www.bandwagonintown.blogspot.com

212

encourage fan participation, not least because they are the lifeblood of the club. Players and officials are not just suited entities at these organisation, they are people just like you and I who are approachable and often transparent. Where else could you have a pint with the players after the game and discuss the club's chances with the chairman? If anyone ever questioned whether football had lost its soul, it's in these moments of amity they can be found.

There is also a world of heritage out there that any football fan would do well to research. Some of our non league clubs have been in existence since the late 1800s and their stadiums represent the last of the late, great architectural outposts of football history. It would be a crying shame if they were killed off by the cancer of progression before enough people had a chance to bask in their absolute splendour. My lasting hope is that those with power and authority recognise the importance of these institutions even if a wider fan base doesn't, as football clubs will always remain important foci for local communities, especially in times of hardship.

As for me, well, they always say you should practise what you preach. After spending the last nine months travelling round the country, I find myself firmly back home and have taken up the opportunity to work in a volunteer capacity for Wingate and Finchley FC who, at just over four miles away, are about as local a club as I could wish to have.

This is fantasy football non league style. And anyone can join in.

Featured club websites

Ebbsfleet United - www.ebbsfleetunited.co.uk
Enfield Town - www.etfc.co.uk
Colwyn Bay - www.colwynbayfc.co.uk
South Shields -
www.southshields-sandancers.co.uk/mariners/football_club.htm
Wealdstone - www.wealdstone-fc.com
Truro City - www.trurocityfc.co.uk
London APSA - www.londonapsa.co.uk
Poole Town - www.pooletownfc.co.uk
FC United of Manchester - www.fc-utd.co.uk
Chelmsford City - www.chelmsfordcityfootballclub.co.uk
Biggleswade Town - www.btfc.moonfruit.com
Needham Market - www.needhammarketfc.co.uk
Rainworth Miners' Welfare - www.wrenyoursmiling.intheteam.com
AFC Liverpool - www.afcliverpool.org.uk
Dudley Town - www.dudleytownfc.org.uk
Stansfeld Oxford & Bermondsey Club -
www.kentcountyfootballleague.co.uk/clubsdetail.asp?clubid=92
Bath City - www.bathcityfc.com

Further recommended reading

Mike Avery Non League Football Stats Site - www.mikeavery.co.uk
Non League Daily - www.nonleaguedaily.com
Non League Digest - www.nonleaguedigest.com
Non League News 24 - www.nln24.com
Pyramid Passion - www.pyramidpassion.co.uk
Tony's English Football Site - www.tonykempster .co.uk
Two Hundred Percent - www.twohundredpercent.net
When Saturday Comes - www.wsc.co.uk

Blogging sites
www.hoppysnaps.blogspot.com
www.leohoenig.co.uk

Acknowledgments

If this were an Oscar speech, it would be the part where I start breast-beating with Mediterranean emotion and thanking the most periphery of figures for helping me achieve my lifelong dream. Either that or I start heckling politicians over their decision to invade a Middle Eastern country. But this isn't an Oscar speech. And thank the Lord for it too.

Still, credit needs to be given where credit is due. Aside from all those who have featured in this book and offered their time and opinion, there remains a number of unsung heroes; the Dennis Irwins of literary support.

Firstly, I would like to thank my friends Danny Hannah, Danny Hatfield, Lee Weightman, Pete Atherton, Steve Spragg and Will Wears for their ongoing support and advice, as well as my brother Richard for bringing me back down to earth when required. A special mention must also go to Sabina Latif for her valuable and honest feedback on the layout of the book and Tom Wolfenden of Generic Multimedia for his thoughts on the book cover.

I am also eternally indebted to Kelly Nicholls, my copyeditor, for her professional, diligent approach throughout and the extra mile she has gone to ensure the work is as polished as it can be. And, finally, perhaps the biggest thanks go to Matt Smith of Blackline Press for not only publishing the book but providing invaluable advice over these last twelve months.

Disclaimer

Where possible, all articles were sent to club officials and/or fan groups for content approval and to ensure nothing was published of an inflammatory or litigious nature. The opinions expressed in the book are the author's and, unless otherwise stated or directly quoted, are not necessarily shared by the clubs and/or their supporters.

About the author

Mike lives in Finsbury Park, north London. He supports Kidderminster Harriers FC, is on the committee of a local club side and still regularly plays five-a-side football. His claim to fame is scoring an offside goal at Tranmere's Prenton Park. Although a previously unpublished author, he once won a year nine history essay competition at Ludlow School. In an attempt to impress the judges, he purchased Friedrich Engels' *The Condition of the Working Class in England in 1844* with the winning book token. It was fooling nobody.

Also available from Blackline Press

92 Pies

92 CLUBS. 92 GROUNDS. 92 GAMES. 1 SEASON. 1 HUGE ADVENTURE

Tom Dickinson likes football. A lot. In a slightly odd life-choice he decided to spend an entire year travelling all over England in his dodgy old Peugeot 206 watching a match at each of the 92 League grounds.

Tom got concussed at Morecambe, ate carrot cake at Exeter, witnessed a mass brawl at Stockport, saw a goalkeeper score at Reading, made a Chinese soul-mate at Everton, drank too much cider at Plymouth, invaded the pitch at Brentford and got confused by a man in a pineapple bikini at Cheltenham.

Oh, and he managed to eat 92 pies in the process.

Putting his relationship, health and sanity on the line, Tom watched 8,280 minutes of football and travelled 3,000 miles in a nail-biting race against time.

92 Pies is a hilarious, fascinating and often touching tale of what it means to be obsessed with the beautiful game.

FOREWORD BY BRIAN BLESSED

"A terrific book that gets straight to the heart of English football and captures the humour of the terraces perfectly." **LEE DIXON**

FOR MORE INFORMATION, PHOTOGRAPHS, FREE CHAPTER AND TO ORDER VISIT

www.92pies.co.uk

 Blackline|Press